CONVERSATIONS with US

Two Wheels – Fifty States – Hundreds of Voices

— One America —

CHRIS REGISTER

Thanks! Amanda! Lookin' forward to the next dance!

SPOKE & WORD BOOKS

Charlottesville, Virginia

Great Lakes States

July–September 2015
1,916 Miles

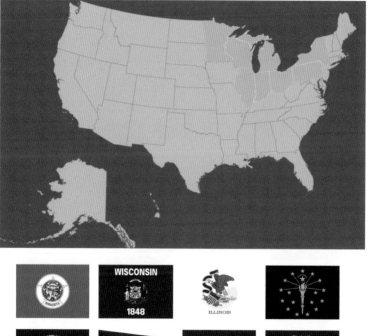

GREAT LAKES STATES

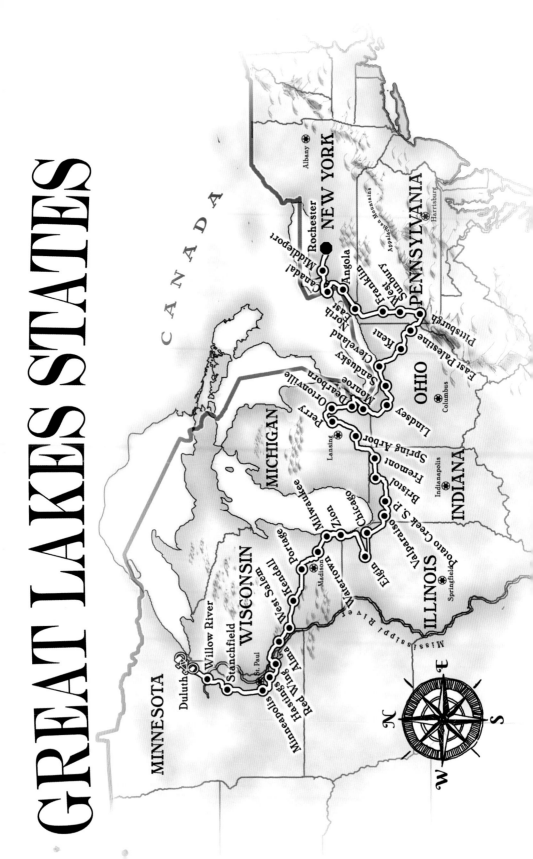

CONTENTS

"When I came along during the Depression we didn't have a thing.
I know what being poor is, and I know what it takes to lift yourself up."

"You hit that wall, *that wall hurt.*
Because I've done it a few times."

"I want her to finish school so that she can have a life,
have a career… so that we can live and not be failures."

"I have no issues about class or whatever. The issue here is about outside forces
who don't know anything about this neighborhood and don't care about any of it.
They're deciding what we're worth now."

"I don't even get high anymore. I just take it so I don't get sick."

"With some of the kids today, the grandmother's bringing them up,
the mother's on drugs, I don't know. It's just like there's
no sense of respect for yourself or your community anymore."

"When people say there's not jobs out there, I'll challenge them.
I've been trying to fill five positions for almost six months."

"My parents taught me that you have to give of yourself to others
to have real meaning in life. And also believe in God,
because he will help you get through all the situations that you face."

"May 4th, 1970. I was a freshman."

"I know, especially in the black community,
unions have really raised the standard of living for workers.
For blacks, there couldn't have been anything better
than a union membership."

"I think so many people rely too much on the government.
I think society as a whole has gotten too lenient with them, you know.
They don't have to do anything for their free money."

"When people get down on this country, I say: 'Listen. At the end of
the day, think of where you're at. Think of what you have.' "

PREFACE

America is a landscape shaped by journeys. The first North Americans likely walked here from Asia—whether hot on the trail of a woolly mammoth herd or merely enamored with the beauty of the rising sun, we will never know. Thousands of years later new faces arrived from across oceans. Many pursued dreams I think familiar to us all: opportunity, freedom, community, peace. Others mounted a desperate, last-ditch attempt to escape poverty, famine, war, the church or the sheriff. Some disembarked in chains, forced ashore by those driven here by greed. A few, pining for adventure, just rolled the dice.

From this foundation of human nature arose the United States of America, a nation shaped by ideals. I can scarce imagine an endeavor to equal the bold optimism so powerfully expressed on the eve of our birth. In truth, we have never perfectly honored the soaring faith in human potential and dignity enshrined in our founding documents. Nevertheless, I see the notion of America continuing to guide us while inspiring the world. Perhaps this is because we are still viewed as the place where ambition and ability matter more than pedigree. Or perhaps our formative values simply reflect the breadth of human yearning, set forth on parchment.

The ink has long since dried. Approaching two hundred fifty years old, what began as a framework of *ideals* has matured into a forum for *ideas* on how best to manifest those aspirations. We have emerged from a loose confederation of newcomers to become a people with a shared history and, most importantly, a shared future. Our collective journey continues.

America is, and always will be, a work in progress. Where we come from is instructive. Where we stand is unclear. Where we choose to go is paramount. *Conversations With US* is the story of my own journey into America to explore all of these, and my mission to share with you what I have learned.

I'm glad to have your company along the way.

—CR

"Stuff's always going to happen, but you gotta have bad to appreciate good. It's just keep on fighting, you know? That's it. With everything."

"The government took all of these young men and women into a war and we still don't know why. My own nephew died because of the war, even though he was back here at the time."

"Where do you think people would go if they got hungry?"

"I kept failing classes, didn't want to get out of bed, that sort of thing. I was trying to cope with the depression, not really understanding what was happening."

"You know, the East and I call it the Left Coast, them guys don't care about Midwest manufacturing. That's just the way it is."

"9/11 really hit me hard. When I was at work and saw everything happening it bothered me so much. I had this piece of white metal at home and, for some reason, I turned it into a flag."

"I think you have to have a family to have a perspective like ours, and maybe to have that drive to work."

"I think morale has gone down so much. With everything so standardized and technical you're losing that emotional person who's so into kids and who loves them."

"The bubble's gonna break one of these days and you're gonna see all hell break loose."

"The only thing that is going to keep American manufacturing going is that high-quality, 'buy one and you're done' attitude."

"There are so many good things happening but so often those things just become part of the fabric and we don't recognize them."

INTRODUCTION

Wondering often leads to wandering… though I suppose the opposite is equally true. On my best days, both of these nag at me with subtle tugs. More often, I have to fight them off, lest my semblance of a normal life unravel.

Though perhaps an eager participant, my innate restlessness was not the genesis of *Conversations With US*. The project began taking shape in my mind alongside concern about a different unraveling, one threatening the nation itself. I worried the headlines and social media posts were right— that the United States of America was coming undone. Cable news experts and internet trolls were tripping over themselves to portray us as little more than a corrosive amalgamation of distrust, tribalism, and misunderstanding, centered in a dysfunctional and disconnected Washington. I wondered if that dire narrative would stand up to an on-the-ground inquiry, out in the real America.

I wandered to find out.

An untested bike and its mild-mannered rider
after 0 states and less than 100 training miles
(Washington, DC 2010)

Seeking answers at a cyclist's pace seemed like the right rhythm to follow, one offering direct contact with the clues and details usually overlooked by the pundit class. I suspected a touring bike might also serve as a sort of terrestrial ice-breaker, a conversation piece on wheels, prompting folks to pause and ask: "Where are you headed? Need some water? Where have you been? *How much does that thing weigh, anyway*??"

Preparing for a solo journey through places I'd never seen felt easy compared to the final hurdle I had to clear: trusting myself to be an honest observer and reporter. I knew my blinders, biases, and prejudices would be deadweight I'd have to lug along with me. After a dedicated effort at procuring the most ultra-lightweight versions of these, I made peace with the space they would occupy alongside my other trekking gear. I would do my best to approach the project with an open mind.

That said, if an open mind is the same as a shapeless chunk of wet clay, I'm out of luck. I tend to prefer Fords over Chevys, NPR over cable, dogs over cats, jazz over country, ribeye over eggplant, and, on most days, the South over the North. I think we stumble sometimes over this tension between having preferences and values and personal history, on the one hand, and being "open minded," on the other—a struggle I hope doesn't erode objectivity so much as it serves to forge identity. Maybe reliable journalism doesn't have to be limited to robots, or people who pretend to be.

A weathered, proven bike and its borderline mad rider
after 49 states and over 15,000 miles
(Utah/Colorado state line 2017)

With this in mind, I toured the Deep South in 2010 and then put things on hold to litigate Texas-sized lawsuits in Houston. Finally getting back into the saddle in 2015 for my second tour, Great Lakes States, I committed to making my best effort at completing the 50-state, multi-year project. The book series begins there, with the American Southwest volume next in line. Deep South will be presented as a coda at the end of the series.

As Great Lakes States goes to press the touring bike and I have visited every state except Hawai'i. We will be saying *aloha* as soon as the first 5,000 cumulative *CWU* volumes have been sold. Because of you, that number is now, at most, 4,999 more books. Thank you.

I think it important to recognize *Conversations With US* may never have happened had I not lucked-out in the birth lottery. Fortune made me white and male in the USA, healthy, and financially secure enough to get a good education, have a safe place to live, and not be devastated by everyday mishaps or mistakes. My hard-working parents, who scrapped for every dollar they earned, deserve most of the credit for that. While the fulfillment of my dreams and potential has never been a forgone conclusion, it's fair to say circumstances having nothing to do with my ability or work ethic put the ball in my court. Of all the types of people making up America, I am among those with the least to worry about when traveling alone in unfamiliar places, knocking on strangers' doors, and generally being at the mercy of everything, and everyone.

From here on I'll try to get out of the way and let our nation speak for itself. The heart of *Conversations With US* beats with the words of nearly 400 Americans who shared their views and stories for the project. I hope other Americans might begin to feel a rekindled sense of unity and shared purpose upon hearing from and learning about these diverse folks, because their goals are our dreams; their worries are our fears; their problems are our concerns.

They are *US*.

🚲 🚲 🚲

PROJECT STRUCTURE

This nuts & bolts section is for readers wanting a peek into the structure of *CWU* before embarking on the journey that follows.

Equipment

Carrying me across the country was a black, steel-frame Long Haul Trucker 27-speed touring bicycle from a manufacturer called Surly Bikes. In fact, the rig *was* pretty cantankerous at times. Maybe that's understandable given how much weight he had to haul everywhere: my body's 170 pounds plus 100-125 pounds of gear and bike. My setup changed with every tour as I tweaked equipment here and there. Gearheads will find much more detail on the *Conversations With US* website and in the Appendixes to the third and fourth volumes of the series—Appalachia & Bluegrass Country and Prairie Heartland (more info on that below).

I begrudgingly admit here that, despite our occasional bickering, the touring rig did a great job getting us through many a tough spot.

Project Organization

The rig and I have tracked our stats so far: 355 aggregate days on the road covering nearly 16,000 miles, at the cost of some 700,000 calories and 6.3 million crankset revolutions. Even so, we weren't out to break any endurance records. Instead of exploring the entire country in one go I toured in regional blocks of around 1,900 miles and six weeks each. After each tour I would return home to rest, organize notes, fix or replace equipment, plan the next route, and unwind the general chaos that overtook other parts of my life while I was on the road. The regional blocks, each corresponding to a separate volume, are:

Deep South	New England & Eastern Seaboard
Great Lakes States	West Coast
American Southwest	Alaska
Appalachia & Bluegrass Country	Big Skies & Rocky Mountains
Prairie Heartland	Hawai'i

I planned routes by first choosing start and end points, adding a few must-see places, and then drawing a series of random 50-mile lines to connect everything together. I didn't seek established cycling routes, but was happy to be on those coinciding with my itinerary. This intentionally haphazard process helped ensure I met folks and visited areas that might sometimes be left out of the national dialogue, while also experiencing some of the towns, cities, and landmarks that have established their place in our story.

I spoke with people throughout the day, but for purposes of the project my goal was to conduct one on-the-record interview each day I was pedaling. In what some might consider a boring town in the middle of nowhere, I searched for a chat—just like I did in the center of a busy metropolis. I sought out both unique and everyday Americans, including those who might be living along the margins of society.

That said, I have no doubt I failed to capture the entire spectrum of the nation's diversity, even after speaking with hundreds of people. *Conversations With US* is not meant as a summary of the country; rather, it's a journal of my conversations with the people I was able to meet while exploring the country. I hope readers will trust I did my best to hear from the widest swath of America I could.

The Interviews

The thoughts, ideas, and concerns expressed to me by people from across the country form the core of this project. Although I usually refer to these as "interviews" I have never been entirely comfortable with that description. Most of the time when I sat down with folks it felt more like a friendly chat touching on the things important to that person, often intersecting with their views on America.

I'm regularly asked how I found people to interview. Many times I would meet someone in the street and ask if they might talk with me for the books. By "street" I mean: a café, the library, a bicycle shop, a bar, a motel lobby, a convenience store, the post office, a race track, a laundromat, or the street *(etc.)*. My overnight hosts were a great help in connecting me with locals. I sometimes contacted people directly whom I found while researching my route via the internet. Other times I called or emailed a town's Chamber of Commerce, Historical Society, Visitor's Center, Public Library, or any number of other organizations, and enlisted a helpful person there to put me in touch with a local. The ladies who topped-off my coffee mug with a "warmup" from behind a thousand diner counters were also an invaluable resource.

By and large I have dispensed with formal titles (Mr./Ms., Mayor, Admiral, etc.), instead referring to people by their first names for the sake of consistency. All of the interviews have been edited for brevity and clarity. I have tried to avoid overuse of what I call the "Mark Twain" style of transcribing dialogue (for example: *he kep' dat dawg unda de twee*), while also staying true to folks' actual grammar and words.

It constantly amazed me how open people were with a perfect stranger who probably looked and smelled a bit worse for wear. This trust is a privilege I respect, and I ask the reader to do the same. If I have done my job correctly, you will occasionally be shocked, offended, or troubled by things said by my interviewees. <u>Please be gracious.</u> Every one of the people you will hear from is real, and while they all agreed to be interviewed, most did not wake up on the day in question expecting to go on record discussing sometimes deeply personal matters. I imagine some would have said things differently with adequate time to prepare. Some may have changed their minds since the interview. As an interviewer I might have misunderstood someone or as an author failed to adequately capture and convey the meaning of what they said. Or, this person may simply have a view that differs from yours, or from the norm. I hope readers will consider these things before passing judgment. The goal of this project is to help us understand one another, and that can only happen when we are given leeway to be candid.

Chapters

Each chapter corresponds to a day on the road, beginning with a summary of tour stats and progress. People are often curious to know where I slept on tour, so under the day's mileage I reference the night's sleeping situation. These are the terms I use and what I mean by them:

Paid lodging
A (rare) nice hotel, a (sometimes seedy) motel, AirBNB, a youth hostel.

Campground
An official national, state, municipal, or private (like KOA) campground, with anything from a roofless pit latrine to a pool and bathroom with hot showers.

Urban camp
Camping, usually with permission, somewhere people normally do not camp, like behind a church or police station, or in a public park. I also include here the really neat quasi-campgrounds I sometimes came across in small towns, most common in the Midwest. These are basic spots set aside just so travelers have a place to stay the night, as opposed to the full "campground experience" with fire rings, trails, etc.

Stealth camp
Camping without permission somewhere people normally do not camp, like under a bridge, behind a shed, or on a paper-mill pine plantation. Also dysphemistically known as "trespassing." In urban settings like parks where I did not ask permission before setting up camp, the difference between urban and stealth camping rests on whether I slept in full view (the former) or strived to be invisible (the latter).

Wild camp
Generally legal camping on a random patch of National Forest or Bureau of Land Management public land, either beside the highway or in the middle of nowhere, with no bathroom or water services and usually completely alone.

Couchsurfing/Warmshowers
The good people of the internet-based Couchsurfing and Warmshowers traveler communities were a saving grace throughout my touring. Couchsurfing is geared towards travelers generally, while Warmshowers focuses exclusively on cyclotourists traveling by bicycle. Members register with the websites and host traveling strangers who themselves, when at home, likewise host traveling strangers (maybe even their former hosts). It's a great way to meet all kinds of people and help out those on the move. This lodging is arranged ahead of time via emails/texts/calls, be it 3 days or 3 hours.

<u>Arranged accommodation</u>
I have called ahead and know a couch or bed is waiting for me at the home of a friend, a friend of a friend, a friend of a friend of a… etc.

<u>Local hospitality</u>
I meet a random, kind person in a diner, or someone stops me in the street, and they say something like: "Hey, my daughter and her fiancé toured the country by bicycle last year and people were so nice to them. Do you need a place to stay tonight?" I smile and say: "Yes, thank you."

To maintain the privacy of my overnight hosts I usually refer to them simply as "my host."

Appendixes

I end each volume by discussing a certain aspect of cyclotouring, mostly based on what I learned through trial & error while on the road. I hope these sections serve to demystify cyclotouring and encourage more people to explore the country by bike. It's a great way to see America.

Multimedia

The rich landscapes and gritty details of the following chapters will feel more vivid with a visit to *CWU*'s content-rich website: *conversationswithus.com*. There you will find additional photos, actual GPS-logged maps of each route (wrong turns and all), audio recordings, and video ranging from grainy cellphone shots to epic drone panoramas. You can also keep up with the project via Facebook and Instagram.

I guess that's about it. Now turn the page, and enjoy the ride.

"It's really sad to me.
I don't understand why you guys do it that way."

"Small towns are starting to dry up
and we're trying not to do that."

"I think we missed out on a lot of the fun because of it. We tried to do
things now and then. We managed to take the kids to Disneyland once."

"I don't want more taxes just like the next person doesn't want more taxes, and I
don't even have children in the school. But we have to keep our school because we
need somewhere to grow our children. It's what holds a community together."

"What is great today is only good tomorrow. That's the market, pushing us.
So you have to constantly retool, educate yourself, read, know what's going
on in this world, because you're going to be left in the dust if you don't."

"You know, I've been called a cheater.
The way I look at it is: you do what you have to do."

"...wealth is no good if people don't stop to think.
There are empty buildings all throughout the city
that could be used to give people places to live, places to work."

"We're on our own. If somebody's coming at me
or after my kids or my animals and they have a gun,
it's not going to do me much good to have a baseball bat."

"Thousands and thousands lost their jobs.
And most of them were never going to find another job
that would pay as much as the steel industry did."

"Well, the way things are today if you say the word 'coal'
they're going to throw you right out on your ear."

"I believe the government's role is to try to create a structure that can
spread the good and help us look at the big picture a little bit more."

"I'd like to see people be friendly, help each other if their car breaks down or something like that—sort of like it used to be."

"I haven't bought a new pair of pants in, like, I couldn't even tell ya."

"Being American, we sort of shoulder the burden of knowing how aggressive America is. That doesn't feel good."

"We're only here for a little bit of time, right? So we can try to make it a little bit better, and show people how we do that."

"But you gotta understand that all these hydrocarbons like coal, oil, natural gas—all that decaying matter took from the time of dinosaurs to get down into the ground, and now we're pumping it out so fast and putting it all back into the atmosphere, so there's gotta be some consequences."

"Then they should try to live on our streets and see. They would understand if they could see how we're living."

"I just feel like colleges sometimes aren't preparing us for the real-life problem of finding and qualifying for a job. I sometimes think we put too much emphasis on liberal arts schools and not enough on technical schools."

"So here I am, working at City Hall, while my brothers are trying to burn the city down."

"We need people to have incomes to buy things.
So, yes, we can do all of the stuff we're doing with less and less people every day, and move toward that corporate model,
but what are those people going to do then?"

"I think the vast majority of people out there don't care about history. And they don't have a clue about things that have happened, or why they happened, or that they could happen again if we don't learn from our mistakes."

The Arc Of A Dream

What determines the arc of a dream? I pondered this as I boarded a flight, the arc of which would take me from Texas to Minnesota in search of a dream I had set in motion and then abandoned years before. Nearly a half-decade after the first *Conversations With US* tour through the Deep South I was older, less confident, less naïve, and more burdened by worry. Could my body endure five straight weeks of pedaling while exposed to the elements? Could my mind handle the long stretches of loneliness? Would America be open to me? If all else failed, would fears of seeing *I told you so* written in the eyes of my grownup peers be enough to keep me going? The jet engines droned in my ears as these doubts churned through my mind.

A dream needs time to mature, space to soar—but too much of either can exhaust its momentum. My touring gear had languished for years in a plastic storage bin while I hid behind button-up shirts, counting billable hours from a $950 ergonomic chair, getting soft around the waist, and lukewarm around the heart. The bike, long since a garage relic, had just donned its hundredth layer of dust when a synergy of life circumstances forced me to acknowledge the crossroads confronting *Conversations With US*. Unless I got behind it again, immediately and whole-heartedly, my rolling inquiry into America would plummet and crash before it had even really left the ground. I quit my law firm to start training, planning, and equipping. The reckoning that would determine the arc of my dream had arrived.

The captain's reassuring voice announced our initial descent. Scrolling through my phone's route-planning app one last time, I considered how the next few weeks would be the most important of all. I would either return home a failure, or finish the Great Lakes States tour and continue with the project until fulfilling my 50-state goal.

I had just stowed the tray table when the sunlight dancing on Lake Superior flashed through the cabin window to wash out my self-absorption. Below, Duluth hugged the southwestern tip of the massive lake, and when the airplane tires chirped on the tarmac I eased into a smile. Walking out of the airport, I made my first contact with Minnesota. I would be walking for a while longer, too, because my bike and gear were held up in transit somewhere to the south—leaving me little choice but to take a cab down a steep, green road and straight to a brewery in town.

At the top of my second pint I met Scott and Sally, friendly Cape Codders themselves touring around the country on vacation. Scott looked the part of the consummate old hippie with a long, gray ponytail, and round spectacles in the tradition of John Lennon. His stories of recurring run-ins with city officials who frowned on his self-sufficient living practices reminded me of a pair of right-wing survivalist brothers I had met in New Mexico a few months earlier. Scott and those libertarian guys probably watched different cable news channels and voted for different political candidates, but I felt certain they would have enjoyed taking a stool near each other to chat in a brotherly fashion for hours about all things rugged and independent.

The couple offered me a ride. An upside-down kayak capped their car, lashed with lines running through the doors' window openings. Scott and I discussed knots while Sally drove us along the lake's edge down a narrow spit of land called Park Point. A fellow bike enthusiast from the online cyclotourist community called Warmshowers was there with his wife waiting for me in a modest bungalow with an upstairs guest bedroom. Though total strangers, the couple greeted me warmly when I arrived. This was their way of giving back, they said, because of all the kindness shown by folks across the world to their recently-married daughter and son-in-law during the young couple's own long-distance honeymoon bike tour.

My wheels were in limbo and the tour wouldn't officially begin until the following day, but those first few hours in Duluth highlighted themes that would follow me for the next 1,900 miles: a plan that doesn't turn out as planned; passage through an unfamiliar but striking landscape; welcoming, kind, and helpful people; and seeing things that challenged what I might otherwise have assumed. Most importantly, I was already having *fun*.

Whether I would finish up a few weeks later in Rochester, New York I wasn't sure, but I was excited about hitting the road, and my dream was still aloft.

🚲 🚲 🚲

Day 1
Duluth, MN
23/23 miles
Couchsurfing/Warmshowers
Tom Mackay

READY TO GO

I marked the epic Day One launch of *CWU*'s Great Lakes States tour by straddling a girl's mountain bike that was three sizes too small, and purple. Rolling out of my host's garage, I thanked him for lending me his daughter's ride while the touring rig jostled around in a FedEx truck somewhere south of Duluth.

A few hundred yards west I turned onto a stubby street dead-ending in a big pile of sand. I had never before stood at the edge of one of the Great Lakes and, even with an idea of what to expect, cresting the dune I found it hard to accept the vast expanse of water spreading out before me was 'just a lake.' Small waves lapped at the driftwood-strewn, beach-perfect shore.

At Park Point
looking northeast across Lake Superior

Cruising through town I found an empty bench in the leafy Leif Erickson Park. Two castle-like turrets flanked a series of multicolored flags flapping half-heartedly in the breeze off Lake Superior, with the drifting clouds above spelling out 'lazy summer day.' No destination planned, no miles to make, plenty of food and water nearby, no interviews to get to, and a sure place to stay the night—I stretched out and promptly fell asleep.

After that guilt-free nap I rode to check out some of the 19th-century architecture I had glimpsed earlier. A few of the large, red-brick buildings looked well kept, but it took a deliberate imagination to see through the boarded-up windows and chipping detail work now hiding most structures' former grandeur. On the corner of First Street & 2nd Ave I pulled into a small plaza to admire a particularly striking example displaying along its façade, in snaggletoothed letters, "1896 -HRINE AUD-TORI--".

Turning around I realized I was at some sort of memorial. Embedded into a wall of light-colored concrete, three bronze statues helped tell the story of Elias Clayton, Elmer Jackson, and Isaac McGhie, black carnival workers probably falsely accused of raping a white woman in 1920. They were arrested, but before their trial a mob broke into the jail, dragged the three men uphill, and hanged them from a lamppost that had stood where my loaner bike now leaned on its kickstand. For a while after the lynching, local shops sold postcards boasting a photo of the men's dead, mangled bodies, two of them still hanging by the neck and surrounded by a semi-circle of young, smiling white men posing for the camera. Among the many words chiseled into the memorial's walls, a quote ascribed to a Native American elder considering his inner struggles struck me the most:

"INSIDE OF ME THERE ARE TWO DOGS.
ONE OF THE DOGS IS MEAN AND EVIL, THE OTHER DOG IS GOOD.
THE MEAN DOG FIGHTS THE GOOD DOG ALL THE TIME."

WHEN ASKED WHICH DOG WINS,
HE REFLECTED FOR A MOMENT AND REPLIED,
"THE ONE I FEED THE MOST."

A few minutes later I fed myself at an ancient hot dog shop down the street. The menu confused me. It offered a "pop & chip combo." Calling a hot dog a 'pop' seemed strange—even if it did sort of have the shape of a popsicle—but even stranger was that the combo cost more than buying the hot dog and the chips separately. When I asked the cashier about that she laughed and said a 'pop' was "what I think you call a soda." A man in line behind me asked me where I came from and what I had seen of Duluth so far. When I mentioned the memorial, he said:

"Yeah, sometimes I wish they hadn't put that thing up. There's a lot more to Duluth than those guys getting killed."

Grunting a response, I wondered if the man had ever taken a moment to read and consider the dog parable. To be sure, the memorial depicted an ugly moment in Duluth's past, one offering a concrete example of the country's history of cruelty towards black Americans. But, to me, the broader, more frightening point of the plaza—the point this guy may have missed—is that the people who dragged those men through the street before fitting nooses around their necks were not fundamentally different than anyone alive today, including me. The message etched into those walls had little to do with Duluth; the memorial wasn't erected just to dredge up sad and deplorable events from decades before. Instead, it suggests we are all Native American elders with inner struggles; we are all frenzied men shouting outside a jail cell. It reminded me that I must myself make a choice—and renew that choice—every day: which dog will I feed?

My phone rang. It was Brent Edstrom, owner of Galleria Bicycles, calling me with good news: the eagle had landed. I headed back towards my host's house where he was waiting to give me a lift to the bike shop. Near the bridge to Park Point I passed a swimming beach where a dozen or so kids were climbing and cannonballing off the half-submerged skeleton of a building. I was glad to see the lawyers and inspectors hadn't yet fenced-off summer vacation.

In the back of his shop Brent helped me turn a pile of parts into an outfitted touring bicycle. For my first time assembling the rig out of the box, we got everything together pretty quickly. The steep hills leading down towards town forced me to stop and make the brake adjustments I should have made before topping 33mph. Back at Park Point I found tons of people alongside the road cheering for runners in Duluth's "5-Miler" race. My host and his wife had a garden hose at the ready to spray anyone who requested a quick cool-off. I joined them with a beer and a lawn chair for one of those 'gotta love July' afternoons.

I had asked my host if he knew a local who worked on the water in some capacity. That's how I met 70-year-old Duluth native and enthusiast Captain Tom MacKay, whom I visited with after the race.

Captain Tom Mackay
at his home in Duluth's Park Point neighborhood

Tom grew up on Lake Superior, just a few blocks from where we sat in his backyard. Apart from his service in the Navy during Vietnam, he had rarely been more than a stone's throw from the waters lapping gently against the hulls of his small pleasure craft moored behind us.

"I'm third-generation American," Tom said. "My grandfather came here from Scotland and my grandmother from Southsea, England. But that's pretty much all I know about their background. Immigrants weren't very forthcoming back then. They just kept their mouths shut and became Americans, and that was it. So we've lost all that history. I wish I had learned more about them when I was young."

"How has the area changed since you were a kid?" I asked.

"Park Point used to be where all the poor people lived, but it was a beautiful place to grow up. Everybody pretty well knew everybody. Us kids couldn't do anything wrong because some parent would see us. My parents didn't have a car, but I had about 10 fathers around here that gave us rides when we needed them. This shallow area behind the house here is the first place to freeze every winter. We'd sled, play hockey, skate, everything."

Tom's voice dropped.

"You see, it was different back then. This used to be a place where people raised families. We had a school but they tore it all down because the people buying up houses here didn't have kids. It really changed the community around to lose that school. After that, we lost the fire hall over here. We just keep getting less kids and more rich people who are tearing down the original structures to build big, empty summer homes. I don't think anywhere will be as tight as this place used to be in the 40s and 50s, and probably into the 60s. This was just such a tight community."

"Have all the changes been bad?"

"Oh no, not by any means," Tom continued. "Years ago, that whole Canal Park area you crossed between here and downtown was nothing but junkyards, fish companies, and whorehouses. That was right up until the mid-60s when they built the Entertainment Center right on top of a huge old scrapyard. Then they started getting rid of the junkyards… there were a bunch of 'em, with those big magnetic cranes, cars falling into the lake, and all that. They changed all of those industrial buildings into bars, offices, and things like that. The change has been unbelievable.

"That's where I got my first job out of the Navy, at the Entertainment Center. I set up stages and things for events and concerts. That was fun but I decided I wanted to be outdoors and so went to work across the street for the company that runs the dinner boat cruises in the lake. Eventually, I worked my way to captaining one of the boats and did that for almost 20 years until I retired."

"When you think about the country generally, how do you feel about our current direction?"

"When people get down on this country, I say: 'Listen. At the end of the day, think of where you're at. Think of what you have.' I can't think of a better place to be than in the United States. I love where I live. I'm out here boating and stuff all the time. And as far as the country goes, you know, boy there's a lot of wacko people running it and all that stuff, and you can get kinda disgusted if you watch the news too much, but at the end of the day I want people to just live a good life and enjoy themselves, and enjoy this country. Most of what's on TV is bulls***."

"You think the media isn't doing its job very well?"

"They sensationalize things; they create fear. And our education system, too, needs some work, because it hides scary things sometimes. It makes me think of… my grandparents had a bench on their front porch, and the seat lifted up. And I'll never forget, I went in there one time and found a stack of magazines that I opened up and saw these pictures in there—pictures of Auschwitz, these bodies that were skin on skeletons being bulldozed into pits. And I remember asking my grandpa 'What is this? What happened?' and he told me. And I thought 'Wow, when I get to high school I'll get to learn about this.' When I got to high school there wasn't s*** about that. And there still isn't, because 'Oh we might scare the children,' you know? And at seventeen I was in the Navy; at nineteen I was over on an aircraft carrier blowing the s*** out of North Vietnam, and not having a real grasp of what we were doing, or why we were doing it. And I always thought about what a horse***t education I had. They were afraid to show me the truth. The truth might hurt me. They always say that thing about history will repeat itself if history isn't remembered. And, boy, there was a prime example in Vietnam. I've always been bitter about that, that I was never taught what war really meant."

"But overall you're optimistic?"

"I think so, yeah. For the most part, every generation has worried about what's going to happen, you know? I'm optimistic myself but, hey, you never know what the future holds. I quit smoking and drinking years ago, but back in my room on a little ledge I've got a package of Pall Mall cigarettes—never opened; I've got a Zippo lighter off of my ship, and I've got an unopened quart of scotch—Duggan's Dew O'Kirkintilloch."

Tom's eyes lit up with a flash. Smiling broadly, he said:

"So, just in case… I'm ready to go."

Back at my host's house I met two other cyclotourists he was hosting that night. We all sat down for a taco dinner and swapped harrowing biking stories until bedtime. The most unbelievable thing I heard, though, was when my host told us with nonchalance that he and a group of locals grew wild rice in the shallows of Lake Superior and harvested it from their canoes. It wouldn't be the last time—not by far—I found myself in some random corner of the country, surrounded by friendly strangers, hearing a story that made me wonder if someone was pulling my leg.

Day 2
Duluth, MN → Willow River, MN
60/83 miles
Campground
Ryan Schmidt

A Better Community—Seek It Or Build It?

Tom had inspired me. In the morning I, too, was ready to go.

After breakfast my host joined me for the ride to the edge of town. As we crossed the aerial lift bridge onto the mainland he described the day he had been windsurfing through the channel below us and had narrowly missed getting swamped by a huge passing "oar boat." I imagined him ducking just in time to avoid a knock in the head by a giant wooden oar from an ancient, rickety ship. We continued south into the heavily industrialized part of the city where trains lined up to unload massive piles of small, reddish-brown pellets into oceangoing barges my host called "salties."

"That's the taconite ore that comes down from the Iron Rage, 60 miles or so north of Duluth," he explained. "They process it into those small pellets for ease of shipping."

It then dawned on me: the windsurfing incident had involved an *ore* boat, not an *oar* boat. I kept that to myself.

We said goodbye at the Munger Inn, the starting point for the long Munger rail trail[1] I would navigate for the next day and a half. I pointed the bike into the forest and, since no one else was around, said a few inspiring things aloud before setting forth into the Upper Midwest.

Five minutes later my tour sendoff came to a halt at an orange TRAIL CLOSED sign and the impassable ravine behind it.

Backtracking to the trailhead would be like starting the tour over—a crushing anticlimax I might not survive. My map showed a parallel trail a few hundred feet up the steep slope beside me, so I began pushing the 100-lb bike through the trees and mud, hoping I wasn't making a big mistake. Twenty minutes and four rest-stops later I emerged onto an empty path that disappeared into a gaping dark hole in the mountainside to my right—the mouth of an abandoned railroad tunnel. A few timid steps inside enveloped me in a cool darkness, with only the sound of dripping water echoing off the damp walls. The tunnel's mystery held me for some indeterminate period of time until a loud group of fat-bike riders on their way through behind me broke the spell.

I turned around to continue in my original direction south, coming to a steep staircase built of railroad ties I would have to descend to get back on track. Four passing hikers must have seen the dismay on my face. They each graciously carried one of my panniers down the hill while I toted the bike.

From there the flat trail weaved through cornfields and swampy areas full of lily pads, and occasionally past someone's back yard. An old railroad bridge carried me over the rocky beauty of the St. Louis River, where a trio of shirtless boys had found the perfect diving rock in the gorge below. Gathering strength as the day warmed, the wind rustled the leaves of the yellow birch trees crowding the trailside. A shiny blue dragonfly fell in beside me to match my pace for a quarter-mile. Yellow warblers and black-winged orioles launched out of the brush as I passed.

No missed turns and no traffic—the cyclist's life was easy here—but anxiety gnawed at me nonetheless. The trail's solitude had offered few

---

1 Common in the Upper Midwest, rail trails are old railroad rights-of-way that have been converted to recreational paths. Municipalities and other government transportation agencies, local groups, and the Rails-to-Trails Conservancy are some of the entities involved in bringing these trails to life.

chances to interact with people. Worrying my first day out might be a failure in terms of finding someone to interview robbed some of the joy from the ride. When I saw a man and boy cutting brush, a knot formed in my stomach. *This guy doesn't want to be bothered*, I thought—but I brought the rig to a slow stop anyway. A minute later Ryan Schmidt and I were sitting in the shade for a chat.

Ryan Schmidt
taming brush along the Munger Trail

I first learned we were in Ryan's hometown of Carlton.

"I've lived here since I was three," he said. "My dad's side of the family has been here since the 50s and they all still live in town. I teach social studies and special education at the high school here. I also coach the varsity baseball team, and I'm the president of our local little league."

"Sounds like you're a big fan of Carlton," I said.

"It's a great place to live and raise a family," said Ryan, laughing. "I now have 5 kids of my own and they go to school here in Carlton. I'm really happy. I like where I'm at."

One of Ryan's sons leaned into the open hood of a nearby car while another continued trimming bushes a few yards from us.

"What are some of the issues you confront as a teacher with this generation of kids?" I asked.

"You know, when I was a little kid I walked this trail as a dead railroad track. Then somebody came along and put up the money and paved it and did all this hard work to make it a nice recreational trail, and I think kids today don't really realize that. They just assume it's always been this way. So that's one of the things we try to talk about in class, is that you have to go out and do some of this stuff so the next generation that comes through gets to benefit from all of your talents. We can't have a generation that just rests on its laurels and what's already here."

"Do you think that message gets through?"

Ryan smiled.

"I'd like to think so. I hope so. I wouldn't be teaching if I thought this generation was lost. We have days where the entire school goes out into the community to rake yards or clean up the parks, just to help the kids realize that if somebody doesn't do these things they don't get done. It doesn't always have to be you, but sometimes it will be."

"What changes in the area stand out in your mind?"

"Well, just after I graduated, Minnesota adopted open enrollment for schools. It used to be that your address determined your school, but now it doesn't matter where you live, you can go to any public school. So, for me, the change I've seen is kind of an erosion of loyalty from people to their town or their community. They're gonna go to whatever school has the best basketball team, you know. Instead of staying in Carlton, that's smaller, and working to form a choir—'cause we don't have a choir—we're just going to send our kid to the bigger school over in the next town that already has a choir. That school spirit is less common now. And, to me, that's where the loyalty to community starts. I think the kids might see it as a thing of the past."

Ryan's son walked over to show us where he had cut his finger while thinning the brush, but he was okay. Ryan continued.

"Yeah, so the idea that you just jump ship when things aren't going your way isn't a great lesson to be teaching our kids early in life."

"But we're all selfish to a degree, right?" I said. "It's hard to blame someone for not wanting to risk giving their kids a subpar education at an underperforming local school just so they can stay and try to maybe make it better."

"Right. Well, that's one of the roles of government, is to kinda squash that, because often times we will do what we can to help ourselves and not worry about other people unless we have to. I believe the government's role is to try to create a structure that can spread the good and help us look at the big picture a little bit more. What we're doing with open enrollment is just the opposite by creating an easy way to abandon schools that need more help. And those kids who can't make it to the better schools, either because of logistics or lack of money, they get stuck watching their local schools fall apart rather than grow and improve."

Ryan laughed again.

"It's obviously something I've thought about a bit," he said.

I asked whether he thought all Americans, regardless of location or background, have something in common.

"I think the things that make everybody similar are far more than the things that make us different. We all want what's good for our family, you know. We all want to live in a nice place. We all want a good job. The problem is that the focus tends to be on those couple of things that make us different. The media stirs it up for ratings, gets people excited about it, and then they post on Facebook and it goes downhill from there."

A train rumbled nearby, blasting its whistle. We paused for a few seconds because we couldn't hear each other.

"I lost my train of thought," Ryan said, with no trace of sarcasm I could detect.

"Things we have in common?"

"Right. I think the one thing we have in common as Americans—sitting here where we had a massive flood a few years ago makes me think about it—is how we pull together when something bad happens. If there's some form of tragedy, no matter if you're in New York or Houston or wherever, it seems to me like places pull together to help in these situations, even if it's hosting a spaghetti dinner to help someone who can't afford to pay for their kid's medical bills. We tend to save that mentality for when something bad happens, you know, instead of trying to find a way to work together and make things better before we get there. If we could keep that spirit, like, always [he laughed]—make that be the way we think of things as a country, we'd get along a whole lot better."

Ryan had weeds to battle so I got moving again, stopping about an hour later for a cold "pop" at a general store in Mahtowa. With the afternoon heat weighing on me I took a long break on the lopsided bench beneath the store's awning, watching a few kids play in the tiny park out front. Like with farming, I guess, weather and available daylight set the parameters of a cycling session. But my internal sunset alarm had already adjusted to the fact that summer days in the Upper Midwest go on forever, meaning I could be lazy for long stretches and still make it to my destination before dark. Sip. Yawn.

Pulling into small Willow River in the early evening I found a campsite near a reservoir of brown water. The shrieks from a group of young teenagers playing church games overpowered the scratchy songs of amorous cicadas scattered throughout the trees.

I had been still for all of five seconds when the assault began. Never in my in my life had I seen mosquitos that big. Slow and easy to kill, they were nevertheless unrelenting. I pitched the tent in a near-panic, shaking and kicking the whole time to avoid bites. Once inside I realized I couldn't change clothes or take a camp bath without entertaining my impressionable neighbors through the mesh walls. Stepping out into the swarm I attached the opaque rainfly, sacrificing fresh air for the sake of decency.

I was tired. My first long day of touring had been pleasant but my physical conditioning was not where it needed to be. Sleep came and went, with beads of sweat rolling along the folds of my stomach to tickle me awake throughout the hot, sticky night.

Day 3
Willow River, MN → Stanchfield, MN
59/142 miles
Local hospitality
Rosie Mielke

17F61 REMEMBERED

A warm droplet of water splashing onto my face stirred me in the early morning. I sat up to see the tent's rainfly soaked from the inside, which confused me since I had barely slept and knew it had not stormed overnight. Then I understood: the moisture was not rain but the dew, perspiration, and respiration the fly had extracted from the humid air over the past few hours. That left me to choose between stowing wet gear or delaying my departure while it dried in the coming sun. The latter offered an excuse for a hot breakfast in town instead of a bowl of instant oatmeal at a damp picnic table. I pedaled away without striking camp.

A Sunday morning silence hung over Willow River. I wondered if the café at the end of the street would be closed like all the other shops I rode past. As I approached the restaurant from behind, its stillness was so absolute that I slowed without checking in front and nearly turned around, and would have done so if not for the unmistakable, graceful sound I just barely caught through a screened rear window: the clinking of silverware against a porcelain plate. I virtually skipped through the entrance. The waitresses who served my omelet and coffee said they knew the perfect person for an interview, promising to contact her while I packed up back at the campground.

Rosie Mielke
at Peggy Sue's Café in Willow River

Fully loaded, I returned to the cafe to find Rosie Mielke waiting for me at a booth. We instantly recognized each other, probably because of our respective props: my bright red jersey and her thick blue album on the table. I ordered more coffee and sat back to absorb Rosie's encyclopedic knowledge of Willow River's history, including a list of all the schools and lumbermen's hotels that had been built and torn down over the past century. She noted some of the changes over her lifetime—mainly the closures of local businesses like the feed store, the creamery, the butcher shop, the florist, and the long-lived Willow River Mercantile.

"Why have things changed so much recently?" I asked.

"Well, since the 90s people have been driving out of town to K-Mart, Super One, Sam's Club. Stores here couldn't keep up with the prices. The farmers aren't milking cows here anymore. Now a lot of people are working at the drug addiction treatment center nearby, and the prison. Most locals work out of town. Really, there's nothing much here. We have two bars… towns always have bars."

She laughed at that universal truth.

"I was talking with a teacher yesterday," I said, "who felt like open enrollment had been bad for local spirit and pride, and the sense of community. Do you think so many people working out of town also hurts that sense of community?"

"I don't know if open enrollment was a good idea. The cost of gas for bussing those kids all around, you wouldn't believe. I was the business manager for our school here for 39 years, so I got to see all the numbers. I went to school there, and I started working there two weeks after I graduated. I was at that school my whole life until retirement!

"There's been talk about consolidation with other places like Moose Lake down the road. But we voted to keep our tax money here instead, and so we've built three additions to our school. People felt like diverting tax dollars from our school to the bigger one would make Willow fold. But we've kept going. So I think that's the mentality of the town, to have pride in the school. Small towns are starting to dry up, and we're trying not to do that."

After a moment's pause, she said:

"Oh, one business I forgot to tell you about was the telephone exchange."

I must have given her a blank stare.

"You know, with the cranker phones," she said.

"I've never seen one," I replied.

Rosie laughed.

"Oh, well anyway my folks owned that a long time ago. There was a switchboard in the corner of our house, and when it would ring we'd have to get up and answer and the person would tell us who they wanted to talk to, and then we'd have to connect them to that person using the code that each different phone had. Like the mercantile code was 17F61. The post office was right next door to our house, so if someone didn't answer, the caller would sometimes ask 'Well can you see if they are at the post office?' The creamery across the street didn't have a phone, and I remember as a kid if somebody there got a call I would run over and tell them, and then I would stand there and watch them make butter."

Rosie laughed again, a little deviously. I asked her to describe any changes to the town she'd like to see.

"I like living here. You can tell since I've been here forever. It's not too busy; kind of a quiet town. I can't really think of anything I'd like to see change, especially not the school, since I've put my life into that. It's also nice that we have young people moving here for a place to live, even if there isn't much work right here in town."

"What makes a school strong enough to last?" I asked.

"The teachers. The administration, too, of course, but the teachers are so important. We also have a lot of local organizations that give scholarships to kids. Of course, many of them aren't big, but everything counts when you're going off to school. You also have to have subjects that kids want, and of course nowadays you have to have all the up-to-date technology. Our music department was always really good. They raise money and go to Disneyworld or Washington, DC. Our Spanish class just got back from Belize. Things like that are good because many of those kids would never get the chance to go to those places otherwise."

"What do you think makes a good teacher want to come to a school in a small town like Willow River?"

"I think the best teachers we get are the ones who are young and starting a family. They like the small town atmosphere and they put energy into making the community strong since they're planning on raising their kids here. I think if small towns like this one want to survive, they have to do everything possible to appeal to those kinds of families. I hope we can keep doing that."

🚲 🚲 🚲

After a second cup of coffee Rosie and I said our goodbyes. I mounted up and got rolling again down the Munger Trail, where for 20 miles the active wildlife kept both hemispheres of my brain occupied. The right was enthralled with the bouncy flights and pretty orange-black wings of the ubiquitous Monarch butterflies moving among the flowers and milkweed. At the same time, the left was engaged in plotting and adjusting a trajectory to dodge around the black-and-yellow grasshoppers *all over* the path, sometimes flying right through the bike's wheel spokes or alighting on the panniers.

An anglewing butterfly joins us for a break

Leaving behind the perfectly-paved but lonely trail in Hinkley, I felt unexpected relief back in the company of drivers. I had missed the stimulation offered by highways. Accidentally running over a roadkill skunk and getting its stink under my wheel fenders brought me back to a sense of content normalcy.

The cornstalks seemed to stand taller as I moved south along Highways 107 and 36. Among a particularly robust set of fields I stopped to chat with a woman watering flowers in front of a small house. It surprised me when she said the crop had been planted in April. I had thought the Upper Midwestern winter more tenacious than that.

A few miles later I arrived in Stanchfield, where I decided to stay the night. The only people outdoors were two pre-teen girls walking a big dog near a nice-looking Baptist church. When I rolled up to ask how I could contact the church's pastor, a gut-check told me I was doing something wrong. I think it was my intuition warning me that if the girls' parents saw the scene they would presume I was up to no good and come rushing to save their daughters from the strange man on the bicycle. But the girls' smiles wiped away that ugly feeling. The pastor was their dad, and they went right then to get him. He came outside and said I could camp behind the church that night.

Town consisted of three or four buildings across the street. Rosie was right: one of them was a bar. I went in for dinner and struck up a conversation with Bryan and Kyla Rippey, a couple around my age who had recently bought a farm just up the road. When they invited me for breakfast the following morning I'm sure my instant "Yes, thank you" came out in a jumble.

Back at the church the friendly pastor let me shower inside his family's home, which sat behind the main building. Stealing a squirt of shampoo from the same bottle used by a man of the cloth made me uncomfortable— not the stealing part, but seeing the shampoo. It was like when you're a kid and you see your teacher in the grocery store and realize 'Oh, they're just a regular person, too.'

After washing away two days of dirt I visited with the family in their kitchen for a long time. They had traveled all over the country "in service of the Lord." The preacher's wife said people would probably think they were crazy letting a strange guy who just showed up on a bike into their house, "but this is what God sent us, and whatever he sends, we take."

Having that take-what-comes mindset meant the family was already 90% prepared for their own bike tour through America.

Day 4
Stanchfield, MN → Minneapolis, MN
70/212 miles
Couchsurfing/Warmshowers
Bryan & Kyla Rippey

HALFWAY HOME

Thoughts of a fresh and hearty Minnesota breakfast pulled me from my sleeping bag early and muted the pain of having to backtrack a couple of miles to get to Kyla and Bryan's farm. Rolling up their driveway I was instantly smitten with barn-envy for the big, red classic glowing in the morning sunshine. The sounds of bells and bleats rose from tidy little animal pens. I looked forward to learning how it all worked behind the scenes.

I found Kyla and Bryan waiting for me on their front porch. They invited me inside where Kyla stuffed me with eggs, sweet potatoes, hash browns, raspberry jam, and other tasty cycling fuel originating no more than 200 yards from the kitchen table. Only the bread and butter hadn't come from their farm.

Kyla & Bryan Rippey at their Stanchfield farm
with a few hens, a barn cat, and a favorite goat

I asked what a typical day of chores on the farm looked like. Bryan ran through the list.

"Well, the first thing I do after waking up is usually go straight out and open up the barn and feed the cats. We have them out there to keep the mice and rats and weasels away, so I try to be sure I don't feed them too much. Gotta keep 'em a little hungry, you know."

He chuckled.

"Next, I'll go let out all the chickens, make sure they got food and water, let everybody go do their thing. Then I'll go over to the guard dogs out in the pasture and move them over into the other pasture and feed them. We can't feed them in the goat pasture because the goats get curious and come over and try to get in their food and that usually doesn't work out too well."

I had seen the two dogs on the way in. They each looked big enough to eat an entire goat, and then some.

"Then I go to the goats and put out grain for those guys, make sure everybody's water is good. We don't have running water out in the pastures so we use big 60-gallon jugs out there and right now with the heat and the bugs I have to change it out every 3-4 days. That takes a while. Let's see... then I feed the ducks. And so like today we've got a sick kid out there; she had some pneumonia. I'll give her a shot and take her temperature and if she has a fever I'll give her some baby aspirin. That's always fun and takes a little bit of time, to get her to cram it down the gullet there."

By this time we were all outside walking towards the barn.

"After I get everybody fed and watered usually I'll sit out there with them in the morning for a little while and just watch everybody, you know? You can tell a lot from their eyes and their demeanor. They all got... personalities... almost like dogs. And once you kinda get to know 'em you can tell when something's not quite right. So I'm watching 'em poop, I'm watching 'em pee, looking at their eyes. Usually their eyes around the pupils are white, but if they start getting gray then they're getting a little wormy and then their stool will start getting a little soft. So part of it is just keeping an eye on all that kinda stuff."

"And then we shower and go to work for 8 hours at our real jobs before we come back home and do it all over again before bed," Kyla said. "But we love it. Last Christmas everyone in our family got baskets full of jams and jars of vegetables. Our root cellar is just about empty right now. We're trying to rotate out the last of last year's harvest to make room for everything that will be coming in soon."

The inside of the barn was all business. Thick wooden beams rose up at regular intervals from the hay-strewn floor, and a goat with a bell on its neck stood atop a pile of sacks of something. A small radio played slightly distorted classic rock. Bryan said he left it on all the time so the goats got accustomed to noises and wouldn't get spooked when he had to use the saw or drill to fix something.

From behind a hay bale emerged a fragile gray kitten. An angry, infected gash ran across the left side of its face and eye.

"That's Scarface," Bryan said. "We heard him meowing the other day from the ditch beside our mailbox. I guess people think that since this is a farm they can just drop off the animals they don't want anymore. I think he's gonna make it, poor little guy."

Bryan patted the flank of a small white and brown she-goat, one of the half-dozen milling around his legs. The slapping sound echoed around the barn.

"I love these guys. I was pretty bent outta shape when this little one got sick. They have a hard time regulating their body temperature and, especially in this heat, it can get serious pretty quick. I mean for the right price I'd sell 'em in a heartbeat, but in the meantime I really enjoy being around them and taking care of them."

We stepped outside through a pair of swinging wooden doors and walked towards a garden about the size of a football field end zone.

"How do your days differ in the winter versus the summer?" I asked Bryan, while Kyla shuffled something around in the barn behind us.

"There's a lot more work with the animals, I think, in the wintertime, just making sure they're okay and things like that, with the temperatures it gets down to around here. The year before last we had multiple weeks of 30 below zero with wind chills pushing 40, 50 below. So depending on the weather and what it does—MAYBELLE! GET OUT OF THE GARDEN!"

A black dog that had been loosely following us trotted out from between hanging rows of cucumbers. A goat or two, now behind us, bleated a response to Bryan's yell.

"Like right now, in the summertime with the animals out in the pasture, everything's kind of self-sufficient. I'm doing more stuff in the garden, weeding and gardening, mowing, trimming the apple trees. In winter it just depends on what the weather does. Sometimes it can be easy because the animals all stay close so I can check on them real easy, because they don't wander around the pastures like in the summer. Fall and spring are usually the busiest. In spring we're dealing with the pregnant animals and feeding, milking—MAYBELLE!! GET. OUT. OF. THE. GARDEN!!"

The goats bleated another response. Maybelle must have sensed Bryan getting serious because she darted out this time.

"Anyway, in the fall it's harvest time so we're outside every minute that we have daylight, and then it's the canning and processing. We do farmer's market stuff. And then just getting ready for the winter. Stockpiling straw and hay, and making sure the barn's set up and everybody's going to be comfortable for the winter. I would say the biggest difference is that I probably spend more time with the animals in the wintertime."

"Or that we just dread winter more," Kyla added, deadpan.

They showed me a row of sunflowers they planned to dry and feed to the goats, the cucumbers they give the animals as a natural de-wormer, and the growing pumpkins they sometimes smash on the ground in the animals' pens as a special treat. I asked what they did with all these goats.

"In Minneapolis there's a huge Somali population, lots of Muslims, and they like the goat meat," Bryan said. "We're one of the only countries that doesn't eat goat. We used to, but we got away from it for some reason. They're a great source of meat, real lean, easy to transport. It's a red meat but it's better for you than a skinless chicken breast. You gotta be careful with it, like a venison—slow and low with a lot of good marinades. I think there's a lot of people who just don't know how good goats are. Not just for eatin', but if you got land that needs to be debrushed, I mean they'll eat thistles, they'll eat everything. They're good for the environment, too, with their biowaste."

He grabbed a black goat by one of its 8-inch horns and gently shook its head around some—like you would tousle the hair of your little nephew.

"We got this big boy over here a while ago to sell, but everybody's always asking us what goat meat tastes like so we decided we're gonna slaughter him instead and invite the town over and let everyone try it out. That was part of our mission statement, was to try to help educate people. We always got kids out here."

"How do you think your lives have changed since you've moved out here?" I asked.

"Lots of community involvement," Kyla said, "much more than I expected. I've been teaching lessons at the school and 4-H on how to grow food. But that's good because sometimes it's hard to make friends being the new guys in a small community. That's why we talk to people at the bar, like you!"

"We have to spend a lot of time here, too, so I think it's brought our family together more," said Bryan. "And there's definitely more to worry about now with the animals, you know, but it's a different kind of stress. When I'm driving back from the cities, I hit a line about halfway home where I can just feel my shoulders drop."

"What made you want to turn this into something more than just a private farm?" I asked.

"We decided we wanted to do right by any land we purchased," Kyla said. "Use it for what it was meant for. And, I don't know, the idea of sharing with other people what we learn just sort of made sense. As a society we don't even think about where our food is coming from, you know? We're eating food from Chile in the middle of the winter... well, that's a whole lot of energy being expended just to get me some strawberries. We wanted to be good land stewards. We're only here for a little bit of time, right? So we can try to make it a little bit better, and show people how we do that. And then eventually pass it on to the next generation."

"And hopefully," Bryan said, "at the end when we get too old to be doing this we've improved it around here and we can make a couple of bucks go somewhere and relax."

I asked them if they had any final advice for other urban refugees. Bryan was quick with his response:

"Be prepared to spend more money than you ever thought you'd spend, for sure. Most of our extra income goes back into the farm now."

Maybelle walked over and Kyla gave her a pat on the head.

"We definitely have to budget now," Kyla said. "Before when we wanted something we could just go out and buy it. We gave up a lot—fancy clothes and shoes and vacations, new cars. Now we have to worry about whether we have feed for the month, feed for the next month, enough propane to heat the place in the winter, things like that. It does cause some tension sometimes."

Bryan summed it up: "I haven't bought a new pair of pants in, like, I couldn't even tell ya."

Leaving Stanchfield I headed south on Highway 65 but escaped to calmer backroads as soon as I was able. Roaring traffic shifted to dormant, affluent-looking school buildings and sports fields. In Isanti I stumbled upon a life-saving lemonade stand run by three enterprising girls on summer break. I purchased two 25¢ cups. The extra quarters still jingling in my change baggie made me think hard about a third round, but I feared being branded 'that crazy guy on a bike who drank all our lemonade.'

Great location, friendly service, and a high-quality product at a reasonable price
young entrepreneurs Aili, Mariah, and Breanna have it figured out
at their cyclotouring hydration station in Isanti

A long ride still separated me from my destination in Minneapolis. In a town called Bethel a man and woman on a Harley-Davidson thanked me for caring about "flyover country" and paid my lunch ticket. Twenty or so miles later I came to an industrial area that merged into parks and neighborhoods, including a boisterous place called Bunker Beach with a sign promising 1,000,001 GALLONS OF FUN. After crossing the derelict structure behind a BRIDGE CLOSED sign, I arrived.

The excellent cycling infrastructure downtown carried a steady stream of hip-looking Minneapolitans to-and-fro. It was getting late when I finally pulled into the Powderhorn neighborhood. A block from my final destination I passed four Hispanic teens sitting together on a street corner with their hands cuffed behind their backs. Three cops stood questioning a young white man and woman next to a bicycle. The woman was in tears.

Arriving at my host's address I found her and a group of young people having dinner behind their shared house. Inviting me to join the circle they explained how they lived communally, combining earnings and jointly deciding how to spend everything. After dinner my host and I sat up chatting for a while. She seemed happy with her unusual living arrangement. I was skeptical, but as I spread my sleeping bag over a sofa on their front porch I reminded myself that sharing pervades the cyclotourist's lifestyle, too. Because of strangers' kindness, my day's calories and comfortable place to sleep had come out to a grand total of 50¢.

Day 5
Minneapolis, MN → Hastings, MN
41/253 miles
Paid lodging
Shari Albers

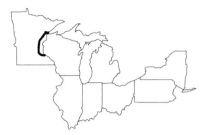

POWDERHORN PROUD

My host had posted a note about the *CWU* project on the Powderhorn Park community message board, where longtime resident Shari Albers found me. In the morning I headed over to Shari's house for a visit on her front porch.

Shari Albers in her backyard garden
with Powderhorn Park in the background

"I grew up on a farm about an hour from here," Shari began. "We were kind of poor farmers, but not poor like some of the people who live next door in these tiny one-bedroom apartments. We had resources: family nearby, always food to eat, animals, always a place to live. We had a safety net, you could say. But eventually my dad realized he couldn't make it anymore with just 150 acres and so he moved us to town where he could get a job in a factory. I got married and my husband and I bought this house here in Powderhorn—this edgy, mostly minority neighborhood where he had lived when he was growing up, before it had gotten a little dangerous. And we brought up our children here even though in the early years we heard gunshots and there was a lot of gang activity, and prostitution. We're still fighting that from time to time. It was edgy but affordable. Today it's a little less of both."

A visitor to Shari's front porch that morning might have been forgiven for finding her account of a rough Powderhorn hard to believe. A mild breeze blew towards us through the park across the street, carrying the sounds of children enjoying their summer vacation. Wind chimes jingled warmly from the eaves of the house. I doubt Minneapolis could have offered up a more peaceful place at that moment.

"When we first moved to Powderhorn, people would say 'You moved *there*? You bought a house *there*?' And I wasn't sure what kind of pride I had, you know. But we were putting so much effort into this house, I just decided I needed to defend it. I needed to love my neighborhood, and I didn't—I felt really ambivalent about it. I started meeting other people who had moved here for the cheaper housing, people who wanted to raise families, but we were all a little nervous about it. So we started working on building up the community and, you know what? We developed a lot of pride. It was amazing to find that.

"The first project I got involved in was getting new playground equipment. I mean, we had just *crap* out here on this beautiful 65-acre park. So we got together and one of the people who headed this new movement became park commissioner and eventually ran for city councilperson, and we supported her election. There was this... this kind of groundswell of pride in the neighborhood. Maybe that's why we decided to start calling the police rather than just letting the crime go."

A slightly disheveled cat hopped up on my lap. When Shari told me Bisby's age—18 years old—I was terrified that any sudden movement might cause him a heart attack, so I just let him sit there licking his feet and shedding on my bike shorts. I actually didn't mind all that much. Shari continued.

"We started taking matters into our own hands, too, for example with the prostitution. I mean there were Johns getting 'serviced' right in front of our houses! And you'd go out there and bang on the car and yell *get out of here*! Or we'd go out with a notepad and pencil and just stand in front of the car taking down the license plate number, and that would make them leave. I don't know whether we did that because we were proud, or if we became proud because we did things like that."

"It sounds like you guys were deliberate about trying to foster that local pride," I said. "It's not something that just happened out of the blue."

"We were very deliberate. People can get together with their neighbors, with their community, and talk about the things that aren't good and really… boost the things that are. Out of that kind of 'tot lot' activism—because it wasn't only fighting crime—we got better playgrounds, we brought back the soccer program, a theater program, just by banding together. Since there are so many artists here in the neighborhood we decided to start an art fair. We even decided to hold it on the same weekend as the major art fair in the wealthy part of town! We wanted people to know this neighborhood and this gorgeous park as more than just a crime story on the news. Our goal wasn't to make money on the fair—we only had a $300 loan that first year— but we made $3,000! It was a huge success; I think we're now going into our 23rd year. So we learned how community projects like that can bring money into the neighborhood for the arts, and for other programs."

"It's a trend, isn't it, that young white families are moving into low-income places like this and getting involved in the neighborhoods?" I said. "To what extent do you think that just pushes criminals and bad elements to another area as opposed to changing the area they live in so that they stop committing crimes and start enjoying the parks, start feeling that sense of pride you're talking about?"

"Wow, yeah. Sometimes it feels like we're just pushing out the bad elements, rather than fixing. I do understand the gentrification aspect of it. A lot of old white hippies live here, and I'm on the edge of that as well. A lot of the real hippies were angry at us because they felt like we were trying to gentrify the neighborhood… and I guess we are, you know?"

Shari paused in thought for a moment, before continuing.

"But, I guess gentrification brings diversity, too. I'm happy where that's happened. We have a lot of gay couples here, a lot of bi-racial couples, and it's more of a middle-class black family that lives here now. It does push out the poor people, no question, when rents and taxes go up. But kids come from all over to use the park still, a lot of them from poorer parts of the city."

Her face showed strain.

"I think it would be silly to criticize you or anyone else for working to improve the community where you live," I said. "What other opportunities has America given you?"

"I know living in America has given me access to education. I think most of us feel the country is big and bold enough, and that we're all a part of it, and that gives us a sense of security. I was able to get a good job; I wasn't stuck. I had opportunities.

"But I realize as I get older and travel more that many of those same opportunities are available in other countries, too. They're not unique to us. Sometimes I feel like we live in this bubble among many bubbles. And there are things I'm not proud of. Being American, we sort of shoulder the burden of knowing how aggressive America is. That doesn't feel good.

"When you ask about what America has given me, you know, I'm thinking of it all the time, because I'm seeing all of these young families moving into the neighborhood and I'm seeing what they go through because they don't have any money. And it makes me feel kind of funny, too, because since my husband died I now have this whole house to myself, with all of those families crammed into these small apartments, it feels kind of unfair. Now, I'm not ready to start bringing people into my house [she laughed], but I'm aware of what I have, and it makes the world more real to me, every day."

Leaving the city was a breeze along Minneapolis's superb bike paths. I pedaled down the Hiawatha Light-Rail Trail, the Minnesota Valley State Trail, the Big Rivers Regional Trail, and then miles of wide sidewalks running alongside moderately busy roads. The only real challenge came when I detoured for a glimpse of the massive, castle-like Fort Snelling and then had to push the 100-pound pack mule up a cruel hill to get back to the trail.

Crossing a tall bridge over the Mississippi River left me feeling invigorated, not so much for the view, but because this was the *Mississippi*. Making contact with its famously murky waters offered a sense of connection to the people and cities downriver, to Huck Finn and Jim, to our entire winding Story.

Minneapolis landmark Stone Arch Bridge also crosses the Mississippi
but I only saw it from afar, when arriving to the city on Day 4

Before long I arrived at the literal edge of the Twin Cities' suburbia: a brand-new development with HOMES STARTING IN THE $400's. Directly across the perfectly-paved street, fields of tall, green cornstalks stretched towards the sun with stoic, if futile, defiance. As I was taking in the metaphor a woman and her daughter pulled up to ask directions, for which I was useless. They gave me a bottle of water anyway. Further down the road I passed three or four little girls outside yelling and splashing around in a small inflatable backyard pool. I waved and rang my bell and it pretty much made my day when they all giggled and waved back.

After a few miles of countryside a detour up busy Highway 52 brought me past the brawny Flint Hills refinery before I rolled into Hastings. Seeing a SuperCuts, I decided on the spot to get my hot and sweaty hair completely buzzed off. When I then found a motel—a place with air conditioning, a shower, and a bed I could have all to myself for a few blissful hours—it felt like hitting the jackpot. Several nights of wandering and winging it had left me aware, and appreciative, of what I had.

Day 6
Hastings, MN → Red Wing, MN
31/284 miles
Couchsurfing/Warmshowers
Alan Childs

From Hunting Turtles To Splitting Atoms

The threat of being charged another night got me moving in the late morning, headed southeast along the straight and rural Red Wing Boulevard. At an intersection I chose the route promising to take me near the Mississippi again.

As it turned out I barely saw the water. After a dull ride through miles of fields and past a few small houses, the sign reading TIPSY TURTLE BAR & GRILL was like a magnet to a bored cyclist. That's where I met restaurant owner and lifelong area resident Alan Childs.

Alan Childs
at his restaurant the Tipsy Turtle near the Prairie Island Indian Community

Alan looked every bit the grandpa with his white hair, rosy cheeks, and soft build. His cheery demeanor brought it all together.

"I grew up about a mile away from where we're sitting right now, right on the banks of the Mississippi on the Prairie Island Reservation. It's a

Dakota Sioux tribe. Back then there was probably 50-75 people living here, so it was pretty secluded. We hunted, fished, caught turtles. The first time I had electricity I was nine years old, in the fourth grade."

All of that came as a total surprise. I hardly knew where to begin.

"Do you remember wanting for anything when you were a kid?" I asked.

"No, never. See, we didn't have TV, so we didn't know what was out there. We never went hungry. We had the best childhood I can think of. In the wintertime we'd spear or net fish, dig a hole in the riverbank or find a hole that a fox dug, fill it up with snow, pack the fish in there, let 'em freeze, and then in the summertime, probably all the way 'till about June you could get frozen fish out of there."

I half-wondered if Alan was kidding me.

"How deep would you have to dig that hole?"

"Not very deep—just keep it out of the sun, you know. And we had a deep well that we could throw turtles into in the summer and then take 'em out and eat 'em in the wintertime. So it was a good life. A very good life. We also always had gardens: tomatoes, corn, a lot of string beans, a lot of watermelons. We always had more watermelons than people when I was growing up."

"So... well, I grew up in the South and was never really around many Native American people, so, um... "

I fumbled with my words because of that gut-knot white people get when we want to mention race but are terrified someone will feel like we used the wrong word or tone.

"So, you're Native American, then?"

I hoped to Heaven I wasn't stepping into forbidden territory.

"Yep."

The quick bounce in Alan's response told me the topic was safe. I felt so relieved, and thankful. I couldn't recall having ever sat down for a conversation with a North American Indian.

"What language did you speak at home growing up?"

"English. My mother had been sent to boarding school where they wouldn't let 'em speak Native, you know, and all my aunts and everyone went, too. At that time if they spoke the Native they were punished. It was completely frowned on."

"But she grew up speaking... what is it, Sioux?"

"Yeah, Dakota Sioux. All my aunts, grandmas, when they were all visiting and talking among themselves, they would always speak Dakota."

"So you can understand it?"

"No. You know, the punishment my mother and family received must have been severe enough that they really frowned on it. They wanted us to adapt into the white society and, you know, we were taught we needed to get a good education. Out of the seven of us, I'm the only one of my brothers and sisters that didn't get a college degree. My mom singly raised us and she pushed education really... she stressed it. And after all of us kids were gone and out of the house she ended up going out and getting her GED."

"Wow, that's amazing. Raising seven kids on her own?"

"Well, you know, to survive we made souvenir drums to sell, just to have money. We'd take cans and cut the tops out of 'em and stretch leather over and lace 'em up. We did a lot of that. In the summertime we didn't wear shoes, and in the fall we got one new pair of shoes to go to school in, and we were sure not wear them out."

I wondered how many first-hand stories like this there were left in America.

"We lived by the tracks and a lot of times the road was flooded so the only way to get into town was on the train. You'd flag 'em down and they'd give you a ride into Red Wing for a quarter. Sometimes when it would stop for other people the engineer would tell us we could get up in the main engine and ride for free."

He laughed. In fact, Alan seemed to be on the brink of a laugh with about every sentence.

"Folks were just nice, you know? Anyway, after graduating high school I went to work at Sears and eventually made night foreman there, then went to work as a carpenter. I didn't like that because I had wanted to learn to build a house, but all they wanted was laborers. So then the nuclear power plant up the hill here opened and I went and applied there. I had to take a math test, and a couple of weeks later I got hired as an operator there, in 1973. I was one of the first non-nuclear people coming in there. Most everyone else was already licensed by the NRC or from the nuclear Navy. They flew me around to take the license courses and tests, and out of the 22 who started, three of us made it to get the license."

Now he was really blowing my mind.

"What does an operator do?" I asked.

"Well, I don't know if you've ever seen the inside of a control room—it's just thousands of gauges. You gotta start by learning all the designs, all the motors, every system that's there—electrical, all of your RAD[2] protection things, all your safety things. Fortunately I got there as it was being built, so I got to watch everything being put together, and that really helped."

"What kind of license are you talking about?"

"It's from the NRC, Nuclear Regulatory Commission. There are different levels of licenses, but the senior license is what you need if you're the one who interprets the federal rules and makes decisions about shutting down the reactor in the middle of the night because of an accident or something like that. I got that when I was 25 years old, I think. I was the youngest person to ever have a license and also the first Native American to ever have a license. And I retired when I was 40."

"Wow! And how many people got electricity from that plant while you were running it?"

"Oh gosh. Well, it was 1,000 megawatt… so I guess it could have been 300,000 or 400,000 people. And in the summertime I'd farm corn and soybeans, and also build houses once my sons were big enough."

"What!? All while running a nuclear power plant?"

"Yep."

"Ever have any serious problems?"

"No, not really. We had a generator tube leak one time. I mean, it was

---

2 Industry shorthand for "radiation."

serious but as far as being in control, we were. We followed the procedures that were in place and everything worked out fine."

"What about the locals here? Were they scared to have a nuclear power plant in their backyard? Was your family worried about you working in the plant?"

"Well, the locals never really worried about it. We knew the people working there and we knew they were responsible. When it was being built, truth is, I think nobody really understood what it was. Like, for me, I had never even heard of nuclear energy before I was hired."

This Alan, I'll tell ya. What a surprise.

"What do you think about nuclear power, generally? Do you think we should build more plants?"

"Oh, definitely. You know, there is the thing with global warming. I mean, in my lifetime I've seen it. We very seldom nowadays get those gentle rains that we were used to when we were kids, you know, nice and slow, getting everything soaked up. Now we may get three inches in one day but it's all within a half-hour. I've really noticed the change as a farmer. There are changes, whether it's man-made or not. But you gotta understand that all these hydrocarbons like coal, oil, natural gas—all that decaying matter took from the time of dinosaurs to get down into the ground, and now we're pumping it out so fast and putting it all back into the atmosphere, so there's gotta be some consequences. I mean, we're reversing what Mother Nature did for 600 million years, I guess."

Realizing that, like me, Alan was a details guy, I decided to indulge myself a bit.

"What do y'all do with all the spent fuel?" I asked. "Give me an idea, in terms of volume, of what kind of waste is produced in a year of electricity production."

"It's all stored on-site. So, let's see. The core is 12x12, and we used to replace a third of it in a year, so that's 48 square feet at 12 foot high. Now they enrich the uranium and so they can run it 18-24 months before generating the waste. So, you're looking at something like a block of waste 12 foot high and about 10x4 or 10x5 foot at the base every two years or so."

Using the restaurant as a guide, he showed me how big that would be: about a quarter the size of the dining room.

"We keep it all in a big concrete storage pit lined with a whole lot of water. Then they shift to dry cask storage which has thick concrete walls and an inert gas around it."

"How many years of storage does the field here have?"

"Well, I don't know exactly but the way they do it now I don't think they'll ever run out of space. The issue with the waste isn't space, it's that the U.S. government was supposed to take back the spent fuel and they never did that. So, the tribe is not too happy about that."

"And, knowing what you know about all of that, you think nuclear is a much better option than fossil fuels?"

"Right. I mean there is a risk here, but it's all contained in one area, and it doesn't have to ever cause any harm. With fossil fuels you've got health problems, problems with the environment, and that's being spread out all over the place."

"Then why aren't more nuclear plants being built?"

"These energy companies are in this to make money. They can't afford to build new plants under the current set of regulations—it's just not economical. Based on what I know the technology to do it is out there and affordable. We can also shift to hydrogen. What happens when you use hydrogen as fuel? You get water as your byproduct. Pure water. China is way ahead of us with solar panel technology but of course we're not allowed to import them here. None of this is going to change until we change our government to where they can't be bought-off by lobbyists from the big oil companies. Until that we're going to be stuck with fossil fuels."

I asked Alan to describe any changes in the area or the country that stood out in his mind.

"I remember when I was younger if someone needed help farming or fixing a tractor or something I would go and help them and not expect pay because I wanted to learn how to do that. I don't see that as much in kids today anymore. One of my best workers is from Peru and she grew up in the jungle and tells me stories like mine. I admire people like that. Now in

America we don't really have that kind of growing up anymore. I guess we all need to grow up poor."

He chuckled, then lowered his voice to a more solemn note.

"What I mean is that so many kids have everything these days that I think they're not learning what it is to work for things. Maybe on some of the reservations you have them real poor families like there used to be here, but any good values that can be learned from that are overwhelmed by the alcoholism there. I was lucky that my mom didn't drink but I have seen a lot of severe alcoholism in a lot of reservations. And I think probably that's what you see in a lot of poor communities and ghettos and places like that, is that drugs and alcohol are those people's way out. So, instead of saying 'Well, man, I should go try to help this guy out doing something so that I can learn and maybe next time I can get a job out of it and eventually earn some money,' they just get drunk or something. I don't know if they just can't see that far ahead or what. My mom would tell us 'If you don't like not having nothing, then *go to school*.' She told us that all the time."

"Is the tribal community here strong today?"

"I think it was stronger when it was smaller, back when we had to rely on each other for survival."

"Why is it growing?"

"Basically because of the casino. You've got people moving back here and anybody that can be enrolled gets enrolled. Back when I was a kid it was not popular being Native American. Now, with all the casinos everywhere, the popular flavor of people is, you know, Indians."

Another laugh. He continued.

"It's like going from not having no money to having all kinds of money. It's hard to say which is better, really. I mean there's nothing wrong with living poor and there's nothing wrong with living rich. I've done both. But I gotta believe that if you want somebody to be truly successful, the family has to sacrifice for that individual. I know what my mother sacrificed to get me to where I'm at. If you don't have that… then those values are not going to be there."

Alan's fairytale story at the Turtle was capped by a literary coincidence just down the road. Pedaling across a bridge I looked over the edge to see a massive snapping turtle floating just under the surface of the murky river below. Its beady eyes and monstrous head seemed 60 million years out of date.

After a two-mile climb my phone's map sent me along an unpaved road towards a pair of bridges that would supposedly get me over the Cannon River. Finding the first bridge a crumbling disaster behind a concrete barrier, I crossed anyway.

Instead of a road on the other side I came upon an open river bottom overgrown with tall grass. Using my front panniers to flatten a path I forced the bike through, hoping that sounding like an African water buffalo would frighten off stinging and biting things. After a few dozen yards I arrived at another fork of the river, this one very shallow but with no bridge at all. Turning back was out of the question at that point.

On the riverbank I had just started disassembling the bike for crossing when something under the shin-deep water made me double take. Two lines through the silt began at a tuft of grass, looped around in different directions, and ended at a pair of brown clams the size of softballs. When I waded into the river to get a closer look my legs sank almost to the knee in mud, making a sucking sound when I pulled free. I plucked one of the animals from the water and it immediately withdrew its gooey foot into a tightly-closed shell. It was heavy.

A Minnesota quahog

With three slow roundtrips across the river I got everything to the other side. After the delicate business of trying to put on socks without getting them muddy I followed a faint deer trail through the brush, finally reaching Red Wing's bike path. A family of four biking past were the first humans I had seen in over an hour. More cyclists rolled by on their clean rides as I slumped trailside in a mess, wiping muck off the rig and scratching a dozen bug bites.

Pulling into Red Wing I took a slow-roll down an active Main Street. It felt different than other surviving Main Streets I had seen... less boutiquey, I suppose. Across from a lively restaurant the sound of air ratchets whirring and clinking announced a working tire garage. I visited the Red Wing shoe store to see the namesake workers' boots popular with guys in construction and, as a bonus, stumbled upon 'The Biggest Boot in the World.' The town definitely seemed to have pulled itself up by those straps.

I was grateful to my hosts for offering a place to stay that evening but may have secretly cursed them a time or two during the long, steep climb towards their house. I forgot all about that, though, when they offered dinner and then took me down to the town's amphitheater for the Wednesday night concert series. It was about the best summer evening I could think of, with hundreds of Red Wingers relaxing to live music from speakers running on fusion.

Day 7
Red Wing, MN →Alma, WI
53/337 miles
Local hospitality

MIDNIGHT TRAINS

In the morning I crossed over the Mississippi into Wisconsin for my first visit to the Badger State. When a train lumbered by I decided to race it, and was neck and neck with car 4593 for a good half mile before diesel power won out. Catching up again twenty minutes later I passed the car and its locomotive stopped cold on the tracks. Further south I saw why: another train on the same railway had been on a collision course, and was now running backwards. This one stayed beside me a long time, hissing and scratching in slow reverse the whole way. I bet the conductor was cussing the whole way, too.

Cruising along Highway 35 was a delight, with stretches so long and straight the songs playing through open car windows morphed into slow tracks after the vehicles passed. At a widening of the river called Lake Pepin the geographical meaning of the word *bluff* became clear to me for the first time. The bank rose abruptly from the water—not narrow and steep enough to be a canyon, and not quite tall and jagged enough to be a cliff.

At Lake Pepin the rig threatened to jump in if I didn't give him a break
but we kept moving after I called his bluff

43

The east bank of the Mississippi blurred the distinction between land and river, with numerous bridges crossing over dark water choked with algae and marsh grass. Every few minutes a flurry of movement from the swamp materialized into startled birds: ducks, geese, small yellow songbirds with black wings. Once it was a pair of large crows suffering severe harassment by a smaller bird as they fled. So intently was I scanning the wetlands for wildlife that I nearly collided into a dead deer on the shoulder. Swerving at the very last moment, I clipped one of its rigor-mortis stiff legs with a front pannier. The carcass slid a little on the asphalt.

Other than meeting a few folks during breaks I had spent the day mostly alone. It was near dark when I reached the tidy little town of Alma, a thin strip of Main Street shops sandwiched between a towering bluff to the east and the railroad and river to the west. I stepped into a bar for a final shot at engaging someone in an interview. A woman I met there might have been a decent candidate except that she dropped F-bombs like personal pronouns, which would be awkward to transcribe, so I gave up and shifted focus to finding a place to sleep. When a guy named Mike said I could camp on the vacant land he owned at the south end of town, I put away my journalist's hat and followed him there through the dark.

Mike's parcel ran up a steep slope but the light shining through the windowpane of a nearby house helped me find a small flat area to pitch the tent. Moments after I finished setting up, someone opened the window. Although I wasn't breaking any law, my neighbors would almost certainly call the police if they heard me rustling through my bags out there in the night, so I left my clean clothes and bath cloths packed away and just lay down to sleep in my grimy, sweaty jersey.

I had just settled in when the trains started coming. My spot must have been at the edge of town where they were supposed to signal, because the long blasts seemed to explode right beside me every half hour or so. Besides jolting me to the core, the first horn also planted a vague idea in my head. After the second train, I was prepared. The third time the tracks began rumbling I got ready, and as soon as the blaring began I quickly undressed, wet-wipe bathed, and put on clean clothes, finishing before the noise had died away, and confident my neighbors hadn't heard a thing out of the ordinary. It was probably the most benign act ever committed under cover of a train whistle.

Sometime later a sloshing sound stirred me from my uneasy dozing. Sitting up with a start, I began preparing to cover the tent against the rain. But it didn't rain, even as the sloshing grew louder. I was wondering if the edge of the storm had stalled within earshot when a bright flash from the river below caught my eye. Stepping out to investigate, from my vantage point on the high bluff I could just make out a barge crawling south, sweeping its yellow spotlight beam back and forth across the Mississippi.

There in the middle of the night it struck me how, despite the language, skin color, and other things I shared with the bulk of Upper Midwesterners, this unique swath of America was different from anything I had ever known.

Day 8
Alma, WI → West Salem, WI
59/396 miles
Campground
Jack Spencer

MINDFUL

In the dark a.m. hours came the real rain. I leapt from the tent to attach the fly and then hunkered inside, sweating and awaiting daylight.

A dry breakfast at a downtown café helped reset the morning. I was arranging my gear outside when a woman approached to ask about my travels, introducing herself as Cate. When I told Cate about *CWU* she took me down the street to Alma's small theater to meet the man who had brought it to life.

I missed my chance to get a photo of Jack Spencer
but Alma's Big River Theatre is a product of his passion

The instant I finished explaining my cross-country mission to Jack Spencer, he launched into a fast-paced narrative.

"I grew up in Buffalo, New York, but I never visited New York City, out of complete fear that I would get mugged or who knows what. I went for the first time a few weeks ago, here I am 58 years old, and it was the best experience I've ever had. People were friendly; they were connected, mindful, and helpful. I felt like, you know, it isn't all what social media or Fox News is hyping to me about fear. We really are more alike and helpful to one another than those outlets would have you believe."

"What do you mean when you say mindful?" I asked.

"I grew up Irish Catholic and so things for me were always black and white, right and wrong. God says something, and that's it, you know? And I eventually found that belief structure to be a burden… a disappointment to me. It's like any doctrine; it can contradict itself, and then you start to lose faith in it. It's like the government. The government took all of these young men and women into a war and we still don't know why. My own nephew died because of the war, even though he was back here at the time. After being pushed into three tours in Afghanistan he came home and he couldn't adjust. He killed himself."

Jack caught me off guard. I felt at a loss for words.

"I'm sorry, Jack."

"He lost faith, like we lose our sense of faith in institutions. So, when I say mindfulness, it's kind of like we have to get back to a sense of self, a spirituality, a mindfulness of who and where we are. Now we're in a new world of technology, which gives us an opportunity to be of service to one another, to explore new ideas. I like the idea of what you're doing for that reason."

I hadn't thought of the project in that way before. I asked Jack if he was optimistic we would be able to shape the country into something in which folks could have and keep faith.

"I think things are coming around. The wheel has turned on the ship and it's going to take a while, but it's starting to come around. Young people are starting to see they can have some voice and they can make some small moves. They know they can't just sit around and wait for change to happen. They have to make it happen."

A repetitive beeping sound interrupted us. A few feet away a worker had started backing a small man-lift towards the theater. Jack quickly excused himself to attend to the construction underway on the side of the building, and I got rolling.

South of Alma I passed a line of old houses nestled between the Mississippi and the highway. The homes looked odd, and after a minute I realized it was because I was looking at their back doors. Fountain City's early residents had designed their buildings to face the highways of their day—the railroad and the river—and had never gotten around to rotating the structures to reflect the changing times.

Stopping at a bar in Bluff Siding taught me that, for about the cost of a newspaper, you could get almost as much information plus a chance to win cash if you chatted with folks while gambling on pull-tabs or rolling dice from a leather cup. Not much further south I took the Great River State Park Trail for several miles through solitary woods and swampland. My squeal echoed from the trees when a small snake half-heartedly struck at me an instant after I dodged to miss it. A minute later another tiny resident did its best to scare me away. If someone had told me I might cross paths with an angry *crawfish* on a bike trail in Wisconsin I never, ever would have believed them.

YOU   SHALL   NOT   PASS

Following signs showing a stylized tent, I kept my eyes peeled for a little backwoods camping place for people riding the trail. A long, sleek weasel shot in front of me; orioles and red-winged blackbirds fluttered overhead. Pulling up to the campground entrance I first thought I had stumbled into the middle of a raucous summer party instead of a state park. RVs with Christmas lights strung between them blasted music while old folks drank beers in lawn chairs and rowdy children darted everywhere. I stood outside the bathhouse for five minutes before finding someone with an extra quarter for the timer so I could take a 2-minute shower. A dollop of blue Dawn from my mess kit substituted for my lost bar of soap.

At 3:14 a.m. a truck towing a huge camper pulled into a spot two campsites from mine. For the next 25 minutes the driver cycled through a maddening pattern of hitting the brakes, pulling forward, and then backing in again, over and over. Each time the trailer moved its nose creaked on the truck's hitch in a way that would have shamed a banshee. Wanting *just one night of good sleep*, I erupted in a minor fit of cursing.

Deep breath. A week of pedaling had not inoculated me against everyday frustrations, but I knew the insights and stories of the people I was meeting could help put things in perspective, if I let them. Jack had suggested being mindful meant considering who and where I was, and what change I hoped to catalyze with my journey.

I took another deep breath—and searched for my foam earplugs.

Day 9
West Salem, WI → Kendall, WI
50/446 miles
Urban camp
Alice Sprain & Sue Strauss

CLOTHESLINES & NEIGHBORS

Another wet-tent morning. Mildew would ruin my equipment if this kept up much longer.

A West Salem historian had helped arrange an interview with the town's longest-term resident, 93-year-old Alice Sprain. When I pulled up to Alice's house she greeted me at the door and looked over the touring rig with a level of interest I hadn't seen from many folks a third her age. She invited me inside where I met her friend and also longtime local Sue Strauss, who sat and crocheted while the three of us chatted.

Sue Strauss and Alice Sprain
in Alice's West Salem living room

"I was born here in 1922," Alice said. "My aunt delivered me at my family's house because the doctor didn't make it in time! My dad had the garage in town and would fix and sell cars, and every time he sold a car to one of these farmers he would have to teach them how to drive it. My grandfather came from Germany at age 18 with just the clothes on his back. I remember he would always say *vayfel* instead of waffle."

Some quick math said Alice had probably been in the first grade, learning to read, at the time of the Great Depression. Jesus Christ—*the Great Depression*. And there she was in front of me smiling and bringing cookies and living on her own.

"After high school I went to WWTC, a technical college for women, just at the beginning of the War. I didn't want to be a teacher and I didn't want to be a nurse, at least not the bedpan stuff. I was interested in the lab type of work, the research. I'm interested in that even now. I love hearing stories about it on the TV."

"But I guess there wasn't much chance for you to do that as a woman," I said.

"Probably not. Anyway, my other option was office work. I worked in Washington, DC at the Pentagon for a while and then got married. My husband was the postmaster here in West Salem for years before he passed on. And now when I go down to the post office I see weeds all in the shrubbery and debris blowing around everywhere and I think 'Oh Leonard, if he saw that, he would just be miserable.' "

"Why do you think the people there today don't take pride in it the way your husband used to?"

"I'm not sure, but it might be because nowadays they are always just shifting around people and it's a mess all the time. I don't think all of the people who work there live here in town like they used to. I don't think they even see that it needs to be picked up and raked now and then."

"What are some of the other changes in the community or the country y'all have seen over the years?"

"Something that has really changed is having all the kids so involved in sports," Sue said. "And they don't have enough space and time for all of it during the week so they've taken over the weekends, too. In West Salem at least we're lucky they don't schedule things on Wednesday nights—that's church night. But even so, church attendance is way down. They don't have any family time together; they don't have an evening meal."

The ladies talked about how they used to walk places when they were children, but now parents drive their kids everywhere. Sue continued.

"One of the things I'm grateful for is to have grown up in the Midwest, because I think our values are a lot stronger than in a lot of other parts of the country, especially the East and West Coasts. I think we take more pride in what we have. I can't imagine growing up in one of those high rises in a city and having no room to play, nothing for yourself. You have to really admire those who have worked their way up out of it. I understand if someone makes a mistake once, and has a kid out of wedlock, but so many of these women are having 2, 3, 4 kids and they don't even know who the father is. Something isn't right. There are so many couples who want to adopt, and these mothers are just going to bring up these kids in all that poverty without a father. And because they are a product of that environment, that makes them not want to change. They don't know anything different."

Pausing for a moment, Sue then added:

"I think so many people rely too much on the government. I think society as a whole has gotten too lenient with them, you know. They don't have to do anything for their free money."

"I was thinking, too, that teachers aren't allowed to enforce discipline in the schools anymore," Alice said. "I have three grandchildren that are teachers, and they tell me kids can do anything these days. They can spit at teachers, just anything. Think of little kindergarteners just being awful, swearing. One of my granddaughters said you really just have to start from the bottom and try to help them. And you wonder why that is. When we were kids you would never have even thought of refuting the teacher. With some of the kids today, the grandmother's bringing them up, the mother's on drugs, I don't know. It's just like there's no sense of respect for yourself or your community anymore."

"What do you think we can do to get that sense of community back?" I asked.

"Put the clotheslines back out!" Sue said with a laugh. "Get the backyard neighborliness going. You know, there's a ban on them, I don't know if we can even put them up in West Salem anymore."

"Oh, I know it, yeah," said Alice. "Women could visit that way. And then you see these big fences across here. I almost cried when they put those up. It was all open and my husband and I just enjoyed watching those kids play in that pool, and slide down the slide, you know. But they have to put up fences for a swimming pool now. That way you don't even know the people anymore."

"Well, Alice, I have to ask you the question everyone asks you: how do you stay so healthy and sharp?"

"I think it's genes. My grandpa was 86 years old when his neighbors called me and said 'Do you realize your grandpa's out on top of his roof shingling his garage?' So I went over to talk to him and he said 'Well I'm almost done at this point so I'm going to go ahead and finish it.' He lived to be 96."

Sue offered another possible secret to longevity:

"We play a lot of bridge here, too."

Ninety minutes later the first flat of the tour happened beside a McDonald's in Sparta. I patched it under a tree before visiting the town's Chamber of Commerce in a repurposed train station, which I learned sits near the western terminus of the first rails-to-trails project in America. The 200-plus miles I had logged over the past few days along those crushed-gravel paths had all started in 1967 with the Elroy-Sparta State Trail.

I continued southeast in the direction of Elroy, with picturesque farms of big, well-kept barns and dome-topped silos visible through occasional breaks in the trailside leaves. A lanky doe crossed in front of me with a regal lope. Catching up I found her just inside the tree line staring back at me with black-glass eyes. I looked in the other direction for her spotted fawn, but if it was there hiding I never saw it. Further down, I was sure—almost sure—I saw an elongated mink scamper across the path with a rabbit dangling from its mouth.

But it was a working ride. Fiddling with my phone as I pedaled, I searched for a Wisconsin dairy farmer to interview. The first man I called hung up on me, and the two I spoke with after that seemed only marginally more enthusiastic. Compounding these disappointments was a problem I noticed with the bike: it moved slowly, as if dragging somehow. I checked the tires' air, which was fine, and the brakes didn't seem to be rubbing the wheels. Stopping again a short time later I checked the same things, cleaning and lubricating the chain, to boot. But nothing helped. I finally settled on the diagnosis of a failing rear-wheel hub bearing—something I could endure for a few days until finding a replacement.

At a shaded spot with water trickling through ditches on both sides of the trail the air temperature dropped suddenly and sharply—probably ten degrees. It intrigued me that evaporation from those thin streams could have such a noticeable cooling effect. But the dark truth of the chill's origin awaited me just up the trail. Rounding a bend I braked hard to avoid getting swallowed into the black maw of a tunnel yawning before me. A crisp wind blasted from inside, set free by the massive wooden doors swung open like an invitation to the underworld. I stood fast with skepticism until a couple walking hand-in-hand emerged to tell me how awesome it had been to go through.

Rolling inside I expected to immediately see the exit, but the only hint of it was a tiny dot I could cover with the tip of my thumb, hovering in the darkness ahead. My headlight offered just three feet of visibility because of a reflective mist shrouding everything beyond in white. Besides the bats and other creatures no doubt watching us grope around, the rig and I were alone for the length of the tunnel. Squinting in the sunlight at the opposite door, I checked my odometer. Our journey through the center of the Earth covered three-quarters of a mile.

Outside, the trail suddenly felt different. At first I thought the rig's easy 14-15mph pace came from his joy at escaping the inky lair and feeling the sunshine again, but I soon realized we were actually rolling slightly downhill… and that the uniform, smooth, and enclosed-by-trees railroad bed had played an enormously clever trick on my senses. With no visual cues to help my brain back on the other side of the tunnel, I hadn't understood the bike's lackluster cadence had simply been a case of *riding uphill.*

Arriving in Kendall about an hour before dusk I decided to stay the night there, somewhere. Once again, the only OPEN sign in town glowed from a bar window—but what was I supposed to do on a Saturday night, anyway? My cycling shoes clomped across the threshold and clinked against the barstool footrest. A man in his mid-40s, wearing a tucked-in orange polo with some industrial logo, said when he comes home on the weekend and is alone, he would rather just go back to work. When I asked if he had tried online dating he said: "I'm too old for that."

Sitting down beside me, a more informally-dressed man ordered a shot and a beer. I saw him have three rounds. I don't recall how we started discussing United States history but, after a few words on the subject, the man's face took on a look of utter surprise, his cheeks grew red, and his eyes watered over.

"Man, I can't believe I'm here in this bar having an intellectual conversation," he said. "It don't happen too often."

We sat taking drinks and comparing U.S. presidents for over half an hour. When he offered an apology for his lack of formal education I told him it didn't matter what kind of education he had—that he was smart and inquisitive and he should follow his passion and become the town or county historian. I wonder if he did.

Leaving the bar at a dark but respectable hour, I still had no place to sleep. In a small park next to a defunct locomotive turntable I spied a long, flat picnic table, and considered the following facts:

» clear sky
» favorable temperature
» tired (alright, fine, inebriated) cyclist
» so far, uniformly friendly Wisconsinites.

I unrolled my sleeping bag onto the wooden tabletop, leaned the bike against the bench, and passed out under the night sky.

Day 10
Kendall, WI → Portage, WI
60/506 miles
Paid lodging
Janet Fisher

Unexpected Kindness Along The 400 State Trail

A pink predawn light filled with frantic farm animal sounds forced me awake an hour too early. I think a sense of unease at sleeping without a flimsy mesh wall protecting me from the world had something to do with it, too. With Elroy just a few miles down the trail, I figured leaving right then would put me in town just as the local diners opened their doors. I got rolling on an empty stomach.

A chewed-up bridge along the 400 State Trail
shows use by snowmobiles, too

After breakfast the path changed its name to the 400 State Trail and continued carrying me southeast. Near Reedsburg I came across a silent little oasis under a tree offering water, snacks, and even hand cleaning wet-wipes. Flowers and assorted bits of Americana surrounded an inviting wooden bench. It felt strange, standing alone at a place where it seemed someone had known the bike and I were coming. I decided to go try and find whoever that was.

Seeing a row of homes through the trees, I continued down the trail until reaching the neighborhood entrance. I was standing on the sidewalk trying to guess which house might belong to the Good Samaritan when a blonde woman pulled to a stop and greeted me through her car's open window. Her name was Amy, and her young child stared wide-eyed at me from his seat while I explained myself. Amy declared she would help me find the trail angel, shifted her car into park, and walked me to the bungalow she thought might be the right one. There we found a woman hunched down at work in a small vegetable garden. Standing up to answer our greeting, she waved with a hand-shovel. It was her.

Reedsburg's own trail angel, Janet Fisher
at the rest station she maintains for folks on the 400 State Trail

Janet Fisher invited me into her beautifully-preserved home for a chat. A big, old cat named Milo came over to greet me while a few others kept their distance, lying atop original wooden window sills or slinking through the carved staircase banisters and newel.

"I'll just start by telling you why I do it," Janet said, after bringing me a glass of water. "9/11 really hit me hard. When I was at work and saw everything happening it bothered me so much. I had this piece of white metal at home and, for some reason, I turned it into a flag. I painted it with the stars and stripes and thought 'Now what am I going to do with this?' So, I decided to put it out on the bike trail behind my house. That started everything. The bike trail is so beautiful; it's a great opportunity for people to enjoy being outdoors, and I just wanted to make it nice. Then I added the painted kids' bikes, and I love dogs so I added the dog bowls and, anyway, it just went from there! And I love my country, absolutely."

"But that's a lot of work, isn't it? You have to maintain it, fill up the water, right?"

"It is. And, unfortunately, when I first started doing it I wasn't smart enough to lock things up, and things got stolen. Now you can see where I've had to lock things to trees, and the trees have grown around the locks! Last year during 4th of July someone yanked off the cooler lid and put fireworks in there. Silly things like that. I figured it was just kids being kids, not anyone being malicious."

"It doesn't seem like it gets you down that people have vandalized your work back there."

"It doesn't get me down, no. Because I've also seen people leave thank you notes, and one time someone left a brand new pack of paper cups for me as a way of saying thanks. That's why I leave that chalkboard out there, because I get to see notes from people from all over the place who are riding down the trail. It is so cool."

"What drives you to keep going, so long after 9/11?"

"I lost my sister and grandma at 8 years old when they were killed in a car-train accident. And I lost my mom at the age of 14. And recently I've lost two brothers. I respect that these things are part of life, but maybe that's made me who I am. I want people to enjoy life, and not just get mixed up in things like checking their phones every minute or how many Facebook friends they have or small things like that. I do it because I just love people. I love to encourage the connection with nature, the camaraderie, respect for others and for what this country means."

"Do you think those things are common in folks today?"

"Not as much as I wish they were."

"How do we encourage folks to take that extra step to help people out like you do?"

"I don't know. I'm older, and sometimes I feel like the younger generation doesn't respect what they have and what it took to get them there—the sacrifices and hard work of lots and lots of people before them. I just want them to respect what they have and what they might lose if they don't work themselves to maintain it and better it."

"How do you think we can help them realize that?"

"I struggle with that every day. I wish I had the answer. My whole life I've wanted to prove by example. This is what I do. It makes me happy. It's very rewarding. It's just in my heart. You don't have to get paid; you don't have to have… kudos all the time. You don't have to hear 'Good job!' But in your heart, you know you're doing the right thing."

"What has American given you?"

"It's made me feel safe. It's made me feel like I can do what I wanted to do, when I wanted to do it. Being able to make choices for myself. I can't imagine being in a country where I couldn't do that."

I thanked Janet and got rolling again, passing through a tidy downtown Reedsburg before coming to an area of rough urban sprawl. My supermarket lunch consisted of three bananas, a bag of Doritos, and a V-8, which I ate outside next to the rig and a garbage can. An elderly woman on her way in stopped to tell me she and a few girlfriends from college had spent an entire summer cycling through Europe in the 1950s. The Raleigh 10-speed she had toured with still hung in her garage. Really—you just never know who you'll run into.

Idyllic cornfields and farms graced my departure east along North Reedsburg Road. An INTERNATIONAL CRANE FOUNDATION sign brought to mind Aldo Leopold, one of my favorite authors. In the mid-20th century he wrote fondly about his Wisconsin 'sand farm' and his time in the out-of-doors, including his contact with the vanishing Sandhill crane. To me, Leopold personified a type of man that seems increasingly difficult to find in the modern world: one whose arm is equally comfortable toting an open-breach shotgun or setting down lines of prose, whose hand shows both ink-smudges and callouses, and who naturally blends rugged outdoorsmanship with stewardship of the Earth, public service with self-reliance, quiet contemplation with bold exploration. I wished he had been my third grandpa.

Few humans traveled the backroads that day, leaving me largely alone with the crops and the occasional animal, like the large German Shepherd lying in front of a farmhouse at the top of a low rise. During my slow uphill approach the dog and I kept staring at each other, wondering who would make the first move. It was him. Popping up, he trotted towards me and then stopped, watching me pass a few feet away. Up the road a hedge separating the asphalt from a field ended abruptly, allowing a full view of recently-harvested earth. At the same time I saw them, six brown, strikingly tall cranes picking through the soil saw me, too. With loud croaking sounds they flapped long wings and rose slowly into the air to escape. I wondered if the Foundation had something to do with that sighting.

A lonely road bordering a levy brought me through the Pine Island Wildlife Reserve and into Portage, a town with a sign announcing it was WHERE THE NORTH BEGINS. I wondered a lot of things when I read that sign: If the North begins there, doesn't it also mean Portage is where the *South* begins, too? Does the fact that I'm headed southeast mean that, for me, Portage is where the North *ends*? Rolling alongside the Wisconsin River, I pondered how the intractable two-sided nature of a line lays bare one's bias.

Four nights without a bed or decent shower meant I didn't hesitate to head directly to a motel my map showed on the south end of town. I found it with picnic tables, children's toys, and half-repaired vehicles scattered out front, signaling it catered not to tourists but to people who couldn't get a regular apartment because of bad credit or a criminal record. A sign in the office window had OWNER OUT BACK written in black marker.

Out back, two men stood looking over a restored 1964 Chevelle. Pulling up on the bike felt like I had just returned from a short bathroom break. The men didn't pause to look at me askance, say something about the rig, ask why I was there, nothing—I just joined the conversation. The car's owner said doctors in the U.S. were trying to get rid of old people by hooking them on pills and dehydrating their organs, citing as evidence that doctors in Canada prescribe fewer drugs. Then he told me locals had raided the nearby ponds for box turtles to sell for $1 apiece to the university, for experiments. But that was back in the 80s, he said, "when a dollar meant something."

The other man was the motel owner. He showed me to a room where, halfway after unpacking, I discovered a broken A/C. When I returned to report the problem I heard him muttering something about "crack." He changed the room and discounted it $5 for the trouble, and apologized that one of his residents wouldn't pull up his shorts.

"I'm going to start calling him butt crack because he's always showing his butt crack," he said.

I thought he was exaggerating, but on my way back across the courtyard I passed a shirtless fat man with his shorts drooping down to expose a good four inches of his rear end. From out back, the Chevelle owner greeted another resident, asking the man how he was doing. The man responded, with a straight face:

"I'm surprised I feel so good today. My laxatives ran out this morning."

I very seriously considered halting the tour altogether to stay for a while and write an entire book about just this motel. I had never encountered such a wellspring of vignettes.

Day 11
Portage, WI → Watertown, WI
60/566 miles
Paid lodging
James Baerwolf

SMALL & SASSY

Leaving Portage I dodged trucks along a nerve-wracking highway to a town called Rio, which I learned was pronounced not like the Brazilian city but instead like *RYE-o*. A supermarket owner who looked exactly like Chris Farley told me his building had been around forever—first as a concert hall, then a post office, then a dozen other things, then a supermarket. It even predated the fiery Great Train Wreck that rocked the town several decades before, he said. Unmarked graves filled the local cemetery where locals had buried the unrecognizable bodies.

Following-up on an earlier recommendation I called Farmers Equipment, Inc. to see if someone there could help connect me with a local dairy farmer. The man who answered the phone suggested a creamery not too far from Rio. After a quick call with that dairy's marketing person, I headed that way.

Several miles of pedaling under a blazing sun brought me to a sloped gravel drive with a red barn at the top—the retail front of the Sassy Cow Creamery. The rush of cool air greeting me when I opened the door answered half the secular prayer I had repeated a dozen times before arriving. The other half was fulfilled a moment later when the young woman who had taken my call met me at the counter and offered an ice-cream cone of *any flavor I wanted* (cookie dough, obviously). Being already sweaty, gritty, and (presumably) smelly, I fought extra hard to keep the treat from running down my fingers while waiting to speak with Sassy Cow's owner. My foothold on a professional presentation was tenuous enough.

Arriving a few minutes later, James Baerwolf looked first at me and then his employee with eyes that could not have more clearly said 'What the hell am I doing here and how long will this take?' He wore sneakers instead of boots, a polo instead of plaid, and had a fit, compact frame and soft-spoken demeanor that didn't match my notion of a rugged Wisconsin dairy farmer. That's because my notion was wrong. Like most farmers, I would learn, James was a businessman—not a cowboy.

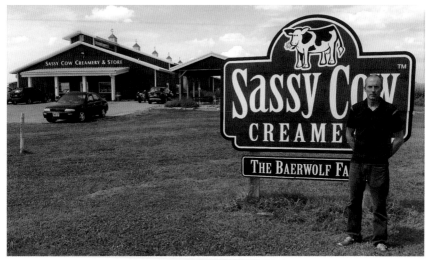

James Baerwolf
at his family's Sassy Cow Creamery

I invited James outside to see the touring rig, hoping that might soften him up some before we sat down in the shade on a nearby bench. A couple of kids braved the heat in a small playground in front of the shop while their moms chatted. I asked how he got into dairy farming.

"My dad was a farmer. We grew up working on the farm. I guess a lot of it came from seeing what he started and built, and knowing that lifestyle. Generations pass things on to the next, so I'm sure that's a big part of why we got into it."

"It seems like farming can have a lot of ups and downs, so it might not be an automatic decision to stay with it," I said.

"Yes, obviously there's a lot of variables: your weather, your growing season, your animals. But it still takes on a certain routineness. I mean, spring comes and crops go in, then you have summer, and then they come out through fall. I guess when you've been doing it so long it doesn't seem so complicated. A lot of it is out of your control, but that's not so unique to farming. Anyone can lose a job or have a setback."

"What are some of the impediments to the development and success of small to medium-sized businesses or farms like yours?"

"Well, for farming it's the land cost that's so prohibitive. But operating on a smaller scale is more costly for any type of business, so whatever you produce is probably going to cost more than the same type of item from a large-scale producer. Capital outlays on machinery and equipment have to be financed. I sometimes look at someone who starts up an internet company or some type of business like that who doesn't really need any capital, and I think 'genius!' I mean, there's no replacement cost, there's no depreciation, nothing breaks down. Your income is more actual income. For a business that makes or builds something, there's an endless list of things you need just to stay operational. And by the time you get your loans paid off, well now your building is 30 years old and might need work or replacement. That part of it is difficult to overcome compared to those businesses that just pop up and there's no expense."

"I wonder, though," I said, "if there is some advantage to a community having businesses that make things as opposed to a more transient service business that can just start up and wind down with very little investment."

"I think so. Just taking us as an example, we're always adding, building, repairing things. We put on an addition last year, added almost half-on again to the building here. Out on the farm we have a project going where we have to add housing for cattle and then more storage for feed. That kind of thing keeps concrete people going, builders, electricians going. The money that businesses like ours receive goes back out—by necessity. And so it kind of has that compounding effect or whatever they call it where your dollar is doing more because it is cycling around more. So that part of it is a very real advantage to a local community."

"Our economy—farming included—seems to increasingly favor larger corporations and businesses," I said.

"It does. And, you know, efficiency is good and all, but at some point it starts to take away from other things. Like the amount of milk we produce here in relation to our payroll and to the number of employees we have…

it's pretty darn inefficient. If done by a larger bottler, it would take way less time with less people. And it's that way with a lot of businesses. But, a big difference is that everybody who works here is getting a decent wage, I mean relative to their position at the company. And if everybody gets all efficient, and nobody has a place to work, who's going to buy your stuff?"

James laughed, in an exasperated sort of way, before continuing.

"We need people to have incomes to buy things. So, yes, we can do all of the stuff we're doing with less and less people every day, and move toward that corporate model, but what are those people going to do then? They've already stopped farming, by and large. Pretty much the same with manufacturing. Pretty soon you gotta ask, well what the heck are we going to do? We were talking about the service industry, but long-term you can't make an economy out of just taking care of each other. What are we actually... producing? So that's troubling."

I let a few moments pass in silence while thinking about what James had said, betting he was getting ready to continue on his own. I was glad to see his shift from skeptical to fully engaged. My bet paid off.

"You know, I'm directly affected by minimum wage laws, because I'm a small business. But I also know that if people aren't making enough money they aren't going to buy stuff. Farmers are a good example because they aren't good savers. They reinvest, spend, you know? In a good year when prices are high, that profit doesn't get squirreled away. That gets a new tractor, or a new machine, or this bigger grain bin, or this barn addition. So then you need to have a construction crew out there, and that's jobs."

"What opportunities has America given to you?"

"That's kind of a tough question. Part of it is the idea that you have the freedom to do what you want. You know, this country didn't just come out of the middle of nowhere. It took a lot of work from a lot of people, farmers, to get us to the point where by and large people aren't worried about where they're going to get their next meal. I realize that is a problem for certain groups in the country but in this area we usually don't see that so much. So, for me, America has allowed us the freedom to start up a new business in farming, and being able to do that long-term, without having to worry about many of the things people in other countries do have to worry about.

"And generally people have been pretty receptive to what we're trying to do here, too. When you're thinking about buying something, and the only factor in making the choice is price, then you'd always buy the cheapest there is. But fortunately today a lot more goes into people's buying decisions, especially with food. And that's good because it allows for more diversity, more businesses, and more people to participate in a given industry. If it all came down to price, then you would have just one or two big businesses doing everything, with no competition. But with those other factors involved you can get a Sassy Cow Creamery, or a small brewery, or whatever it may be. So that's been a real blessing to businesses like ours. A lot of people are out here working in the food industry and in agriculture who simply wouldn't be if that change in eating choices wasn't taking place."

A man wearing a button-up shirt tucked into his jeans and a very clean green cap approached our bench with a glossy folder in his hand.

"Here's the guy," James said while looking at him. "We were just talking about having to buy half-million dollar machines."

The man let out a quick laugh.

"Where do you find one for a half-million?"

Just down the road I pulled into a bar/grill that should have charged a cover, because it was full of comedians. The gray-haired, pot-bellied bartender wore his dark sunglasses indoors and yelled pretty much everything he said. He was one of those jolly fellows who always repeats the punchline of everyone else's jokes before belting out a laugh. When I told the other retirees on the stools there about my rule to shower at least once every three days, one of them said: "Whether you need it or not." As I exited the door, another man reminded me not to leave without the bike.

Across the street, trucks filled the parking lot of a nondescript white building with no sign. The barstool jokers had said the place was a strip club, which of course I didn't believe. But when I realized they were serious it forced me to examine my perceptions and rethink my expectations. I dedicated a full three miles to pondering how proud red barns could coexist alongside an adult entertainment venue at full capacity at 1pm on a Monday. The best I could come up with without shattering my narrative: the club's patrons had labored all morning until it got too hot to be outdoors, then went to the only place around where they could catch up with other farmers in the air conditioning and relax for a few hours before getting back to it in the late afternoon. Either that, or the local fellows preferred beginning the week with booze and women over work.

A typical Wisconsin farm, near East Bristol

Near dusk I arrived in Watertown along streets prowled by shifty-eyed people who looked up to no good. The tidy town center contrasted with the shady outskirts, making me wonder at the chasm between the two groups of residents: those who identified with and took pride enough in the city to clean it up and plant flowers, and those who viewed it just as something in the background where they could drop their trash. How to bridge that divide seemed like the most important puzzle a municipality, or even a country, could solve.

I checked into a motel owned by a friendly and talkative Serbian lady whose daughter had married a local. After a solid shower I had dinner at a restaurant where I saw my waitress get fired halfway through my meal. Off the clock, she sat down with me to chat—I guess I had become her confidant by speaking to her in Spanish. The boss was angry with her, she said, because she had refused to go along when he would invite over his friends and instruct the waitresses to flirt with the men and ignore their wandering hands, in exchange for tips. It was the latest in a regular stream of personal confessions and stories finding their outlet in a traveler just rolling through.

Day 12
Watertown, WI → Milwaukee, WI
56/622 miles
Couchsurfing/Warmshowers

I Pedaled From Watertown To Milwaukee

To be blunt, Day 12 was not noteworthy, except:

» At an out-of-service bridge across the Ashippun River workers said I could add eight miles to my route by taking the long way around, or push the rig through some mud and across a board stretched between the banks. We walked/rolled the plank.

» The men at a small-engine repair shop were too busy to chat but directed me to the Harley-Davidson headquarters on the outskirts of Milwaukee. The young man working the visitor desk there phoned a long-time local and Harley enthusiast who expressed interest in the project but never showed up for an interview.

» I entered the city via the Miller beer brewing headquarters, then crossed a bridge over a wide tangle of a dozen or more train tracks.

Wandering around for a while led me to my host's house, a communal living space similar to the one I encountered in Minneapolis. I washed clothes and called it a day.

Day 13
Milwaukee, WI → Illinois Beach
State Park, IL
51/673 miles
Campground
Mark Gill

You Can't Get Too Much Family

In the morning I got the chance to talk with Milwaukee native Mark Gill, a founding member of the Bayview Ecovillage where I had spent the night.

Mark Gill
holding some beans plucked from the Bayview Ecovillage garden

"I think right here in Bayview is the best neighborhood in Milwaukee," Mark said. "I've lived in the city my whole life, 60 years now. We have a fabulous sense of community here."

"What changes have you seen in Milwaukee during your lifetime?"

"Well, for one it's safer than it used to be. Sure, we still have crime but focusing on isolated events belies the fact that we are living overall in a very peaceful period in history. The truth is that the golden era of yesteryear was a far more violent and dangerous and scary time for the vast majority of people. So, I think there are lots of positive changes and, in some ways, I would say we're living in a golden era now. I mean we have food today that kings would never have had the opportunity to eat. Our access to knowledge—you got a question and you get an answer like that [he snapped his fingers] within seconds via your telephone! There are so many good things happening but so often those things just become part of the fabric and we don't recognize them. At my Unitarian church we're working to address racial injustice in the community right now. That's the side of change I want to be on."

"You have a pretty unique living situation here that I think most folks, including me, might not be familiar with. Do you want to talk some about that?"

"Sure. Our intentional community is called the Bayview Ecovillage. We are a group of 16 at this point and we live in two duplexes here next to each other, divided into five units each. We live by the cohousing model where you have your own unit but we share common areas, have lots of community dinners, a community garden. We have one washer/dryer that takes care of the whole place. We have a car share, a family cell phone plan, and just one internet connection, so my internet costs are like five bucks a month or something ridiculously low like that. So, in a lot of ways, this is a model that gives you an economic advantage. In fact, because of that, I was able to quit my job. Now I do jobs I find more interesting and that don't require me to work all the time. I drive for people, I work at Summerfest, I bartend, I work on a CSA farm. I feel good about the jobs I'm doing now whereas before, as a quality assurance professional, I felt like I was a cog in something that was destroying the planet or whatever."

He laughed at that.

"Our community has enabled me to take that leap," he continued. "I haven't owned a car since 2007 and I feel really good about that."

"How do you guys decide who does what work, what expenditures are needed to fix the houses, things like that?"

Mark's slight sigh before answering told me a lot.

"That's a great question. We're kind of in a transition period. Right now we meet once a week and talk about issues, and projects, and what-not. As we've grown we've run into the need to have more structure, more understandings, and have them written down so that everybody's on the same page and feels that it's an equitable arrangement."

"You mentioned this is an intentional community. What's the intentional part?"

"The intentional part is that we are not here by accident. This is something we've created, something we've planned and worked at. The glue, or the thing that brings us together, is the environmental aspect; that we want to live in a more healthy way, organic, less consumerism, less energy usage with our solar setup. And I think we've done that—not that we're entirely sustainable but we're moving that way."

A boy who looked to be about 7 years old had been playing in the small yard in front of us while we spoke. He came up on the porch to show Mark a small beetle he discovered under a bush.

"Do you guys ever share the responsibility of watching the kids?" I asked.

"Sure," Mark said, putting his hand on the boy's head. "I've got this guy right here for the week, and one of our members babysits the other kids once a month I think so their parents can have a date night. I think we've all helped out at some point."

A woman bringing groceries into the house stopped for a moment.

"Most of the time it's pretty informal," she said. "Like when one of the parents has to run out to the store or something like that, they might ask one of us to watch their kid for a few minutes."

I turned back to Mark.

"How do you guys deal with conflicts when they come up, like somebody leaving dirty dishes in the sink or something like that?"

Another sigh.

"Yeah, that's a great question, too. I think we've been successful in creating kind of a low-drama environment. We participated in a nonviolent communication workshop and got some training there. We knew when we came into this there would be conflict. But that's just a normal part of people living in close proximity that is just, you know, inevitable. I can say that we haven't had much conflict here."

"I bet a lot of people would look at this and say you all are a bunch of communists or socialists," I said.

Mark laughed.

"To me, that's kind of a narrow-minded view. Sure, there are aspects of socialism—I think lots of people don't really know what communism or socialism is, or the difference. In Milwaukee we've had a series of socialist mayors who have been fantastic for the community. So, I'd say there are a lot of good attributes to socialism; that instead of it being a swear word people should look to see what it actually means. Social Security is socialism, so is our military, basically.

"We don't think about it in terms of socialism; we think about it in terms of sharing. And I think everybody knows sharing is a good thing, a healthy thing. If we share as much as we can then we're not constantly consuming more and more of the raw materials our planet is giving up, and then turning it into landfill. I don't think socialism necessarily works as a sort of national unit of governance, but I think there are absolutely healthy aspects to it. We're looking at healthy living approaches. We don't care what you call it."

"You said you attend church. Maybe I'm wrong, but I feel like many people who hear about this type of living arrangement would think everyone here would be very non-mainstream, or even radical in some way."

"Yeah, we're aware of that. Or they think it's some sort of commune, or all sex, drugs, and rock n' roll, or whatever. This is a serious living arrangement for serious people. As for the religious aspect of it, we've had very devout people who have lived here, so that's not an issue at all. Everybody is encouraged and free to participate in whatever faith group they choose. People can think what they think but we do what we do."

"Sounds pretty American to me," I said, "equality, democracy, freedom to live like you want to. Is that how you see it?"

"It's a balance. There's a balance between freedom and responsibility, and I think when you honor that balance it's the best of both worlds. Yeah, it's freedom to do what you want but if we just had anybody doing anything, that would not be a good living arrangement for anyone. So we have understandings—some are formal, others are implicit. You know, I think of us as friends, neighbors, and partners. We're partners in something that is more than just being roommates."

"On a personal level, how has America enabled you to fulfill your potential?"

"Wow, that's a big question. I guess I start with the framework, the structure, our history, you know, and all of the work that's gone into—before I even got here—making this a safe and equitable spot to live. I feel grateful for so much that I've been given and had handed down to me. I think at times so many of us don't recognize that we've been given this great gift. We think that we've somehow earned it, you know? But it's just like starting on third base or something. I'm so lucky to be alive in this incredible, amazing time. So, I want to make sure I'm able to hand-off to the next generation what I was given. And I'm having trouble doing that, honestly. I feel like it's getting harder and harder."

"What do you mean?"

"I think our world is challenged. I think climate change is a huge, huge issue. There's more and more antagonism, and taking sides, and not thinking critically about what's going on. Thinking about who said it instead of what they said. I feel that oftentimes we're divided and it's in somebody's financial interests to keep it that way. I feel like it's gotten worse over my lifetime.

"But I also see a lot of gains in things like civil rights, marriage equality lately. So, in many ways, the continuum is moving towards the good. So often we focus on our differences, even while our commonalities are huge. To me, it's like a fly in the bottle of chardonnay. I mean, we've got this gallon of fabulous wine and all we can focus on is that there's a fly in there. So many times our problems are small and yet we magnify them and amplify them and make them so big and terrible. That's why it's so nice living in this type of communal situation. I really feel like we've become a family. You know, you can't get too much family in this world as far as I'm concerned. It's great to have so many people with diverse skills and resources and attitudes. It's great to share your life with a great group of people."

After our chat Mark showed me around the Ecovillage gardens, which boasted much more produce than I thought could grow in such a small backyard space. I thanked him and began heading south towards Illinois through the middle of Milwaukee's airport, and eventually along a paved bike path flanked by marsh grass and high-tension wire towers. In a town called Racine I got my first good view of my second Great Lake. Like Superior back in Duluth, Lake Michigan was nothing short of a freshwater ocean. Stopping for a closer look at a park in Kenosha I found lots of people out wading in the light-blue water among small waves, or sunbathing on the sandy shore. The lake even had a lighthouse perched on a distant spit of rocks. Had I suddenly woken up there without knowing better, I would have sworn with full confidence I was at a salty seaside beach.

Simmons Island Park in Kenosha
with a red lighthouse (on a lake!) in the background

My rear tire tread had detached from the inner liner, flapping around and begging for a puncture if I didn't address it immediately. I pulled into the first bike shop I came to after crossing the state line at Zion, IL. Seeing my long-distance setup the Croatian shop owner waived the labor fee to mount the new rubber. As I stripped down the rig so it would fit into the repair area a man named Chris Pritchett walked in, accompanying a boy who was about to get a new bike someone had donated. Chris agreed to meet me the following morning for a chat.

With the bike road-worthy again I had dinner at a Chinese restaurant across the street where I struck up a conversation with the owner's niece, a Taiwanese college student spending the summer in the U.S. to earn cash and practice English. She was at my booth with a pen and napkin trying to explain how written Chinese characters work until a stern glare from her aunt/boss got her moving again.

Under a dimming sky I took a lonely dirt road into Illinois Beach State Park. A hazy orange glow just north of the campground marked a nuclear power plant in operation. I wondered if my ankles glowed that way to the dozens of mosquitos keeping me company at the picnic table where I called my mom to check-in. I didn't have a big family like Mark, but his words had reminded me that you can't appreciate the family you *do* have, too much.

Day 14
Illinois Beach State Park, IL → Elgin, IL
64/737 miles
Couchsurfing/Warmshowers
Chris Pritchett
Ernie Broadnax

The Barber & The Witness

In the morning I took my time through the park on the way back to downtown Zion. Low dunes and a calm Lake Michigan reflected a palate of orange hues in the early sunlight. A row of abandoned bathhouses along the beach beckoned a second look. Repeating concrete arches and playful waved roofs suggested an art deco style from the mid-twentieth century, with formerly lively pastels barely noticeable after decades of neglect. Dry weeds erupting through cracks in the walls served as a reminder that everything I was undertaking, too, would one day be a quaint relic people glanced at with passing interest before moving on.

Chris Pritchett
at his barbershop in Zion

Chris Pritchett arrived to our meeting on his own black Surly to show we were name brothers *and* bike brothers, and did not rub it in that his was an upgraded version with disc brakes and leather-wrapped handlebars.

I asked him to describe the changes he had seen in the area.

"You know, a whole lot of things have changed, but they come from… you. You're the person that changes, you know what I'm saying? So, your outlook on stuff is different. I think things… like, this is a constant."

Chris picked up his empty paper coffee cup and tapped it back down on the table.

"It's always going to be a cup. It's always going to be what it's going to be. But it's your perception that changes. Like, when I was a kid, I looked at the road from my house into Zion and I said 'This thing is huge! I can't get to Zion on my bike from here!' But as I got older I realized it wasn't so bad. My concept of the same thing changed."

"Do you think our concepts evolve into something better over time?"

"Sometimes you evolve and sometimes you go back. You regress; you know what I'm saying? So, it depends on what type of environment you put yourself into. I mean—the World Trade Center bombing. Man, that was screwed up. All this terrorism and stuff going on. We're over in other people's countries. We're the police of the universe. It gets kind of sickening, you know? We can't take care of ourselves at home! We got veterans out here, people out here living under bridges that are homeless, you know what I'm saying? I mean, there's a plethora of things going on out here, even though we're supposed to be the most advanced country. We can't stop the teen birthrate from going up. We can't stop suicide. Then we got these people… people are starting to see things in transverse now. I have friends who are homosexual but it's my opinion that is not what God ordained us to be. If you really do believe in God and what he ordained, he didn't ordain a man and a man to be together. It wasn't by design and it's not by nature."

"What do you mean by people seeing things in transverse?"

"People are starting to accept things, the falsity of things, you know what I'm saying? They're starting to look at things that were wrong before, and they're coming around and saying 'You know, I guess that can be right.' And if they can accept that, they can accept anything. It's like 'My kids can say what they want to, they can do what they want to because now it's become the norm.' So, then we get kids having kids. You know you got 12 and 13-year-old kids getting pregnant."

"And you're worried people might eventually say 'Yeah, that's fine' ?"

"They doing it now."

Chris went on to tell me about his barbershop in town. I asked how business was going.

"Uneasy is the head that wears the crown," he said.

He paused to let that sink in before continuing.

"With my shop, I get all kinds of people. I don't care who it is that comes in that door. One of my best friends is a Muslim; I'm a Baptist. But we gel so good, not because of our religions, it's just because we're people with the same kinds of relationships, going through the same kinds of things in life. We have things in common that bridge that gap.

"I think like people attract each other. I think everyone gravitates towards the aura that's in my shop. We crack jokes. If you have something on your mind I can hear it; if we disagree on something we can bring it up and talk about it. I got preachers, drug dealers, black, white, Hispanic, you know what I'm saying? It's not about a black barbershop; it's a barbershop, period. That's the aura I have—it's like family."

Chris then told me about the kid he had been helping in the bike shop the day before, and how he brings the boy to the barbershop sometimes to sweep the floor, take out the trash, and clean up outside.

"I'm trying to give him the skills, to show him that he can do something. But he has to listen to me, to pay attention."

"Why is that important?"

"It gives him a sense that he has to follow directions. You have to be able to take orders and follow them sometimes. Because in life you going to be given a lot of directions and people aren't going to sit back and wait and be kind all the time, you know what I'm saying to you? They going to just pass you over. You going to miss out on a lot because you can't follow no directions. Directions are how you get to and through places. You don't just walk through life, you know; you got to learn these things. It takes time, because we do go through life like bullies at times. You know, saying 'Well, I don't want to do this.' You can't be like that. You hit that wall, *that wall hurt.* Because I've done it a few times. And I think letting him see that somebody love him, you know, somebody that he don't belong to, that right there means a lot to me. You know, sometimes I tell him 'I appreciate you.' When he's wrong, I tell him he's wrong. I smack him in the head. But when he's right, I pat him on the back. That teaches you to be a part of society. How to take compliments and, you know what I'm saying, how to take criticism constructively and understand that. Whereas, if somebody just cracking on me and talking crazy to me, and not showing me what I'm doing right and doing wrong, how am I going to know the difference?"

"How has America treated you? How has it helped you be successful or how has it held you back?"

"America hasn't treated me. I don't let anything disallow me or prevent me from doing what I want to do. I'm just a part of this country. I was born here, raised here; this is just where I happened to be put on Earth. I choose to do what I want to do."

"What opportunities have you had here?"

"I haven't had opportunities; I've made my opportunities. I've been behind on my child support—had to go to court. I raised my kids myself, so how do I still owe child support money? And if I don't pay them, they take my license. Then I can't work. How do I justify that? Kids were living with me but I still owe their mother money—how is that? The court don't see that. That was a burden I had years ago but I let it go, so I'm good now. So, America was trying to put a cinderblock on me but I wouldn't allow it. Because you do walk around like that… feeling unjustified. Know what? Two years ago I paid my taxes for the first time in years, because before that they were taking money from me. Know what? It felt good. It felt relieving to be able to say I'm above ground, I'm doing what I'm supposed to do as a citizen now, I'm going to follow the rules, I'm going to get ahead. I'm going to see if it works. And I'm going to see if it allows me to do anything else."

"Be part of the system rather than trying to dodge around it."

"Yeah, because it's easy to dodge it. Now I'm going to see if playing by the rules enables me to do something. You can get back to me in a couple of years and see."

I told him I would.

Pedaling side-by-side, Chris and I rolled towards his barbershop in the west part of town. A passing driver slowed to a stop, lowering his window. Chris leaned inside for a chat while I kept my distance to give him privacy. After the vehicle pulled away, Chris turned back to me.

"You gotta know what's going on; gotta treat everybody with respect."

We said our goodbyes in front of the shop and I headed south down the easy Robert McClory Bike Path. In a small village called Lake Bluff, white women wearing three-quarter-length yoga pants and sunglasses up on their heads sat in groups at the three or four cafes on the town's two blocks. I stopped to sip a gourmet coffee beverage and scroll through my phone. From there I pointed towards Elgin, where the director of the city's history museum had helped arrange an interview with a longtime local.

Though he excelled at scenic highway touring, the rig clearly resented the rote miles through Chicago's stop-and-go suburbs. No matter how hard I pushed the heavy ox he moved at his own stubborn pace, probably irked at being employed to just get me from point A to B—and on time, at that. I could hardly blame him. He wasn't lugging around camping gear and trail mix for mere commutes.

At a 7-Eleven near my destination two boys had just spent their grandmother's gift of $5 on an armful of outrageously junky food that, frankly, looked very appealing. I told one of them if he ran home to fetch some full-size tools I could probably fix his bike's damaged rear wheel. I tinkered with the thing for a few minutes before realizing I was running short on time, and left the disappointed kid there on the sidewalk with his pliers and broken ride.

After a wrong turn and some backtracking I slipped into a grocery store bathroom on the edge of the city to wipe my face and neck with damp paper towels. Then I went to the wrong museum. When I finally arrived at the correct place an hour late I found Ernie Broadnax and his daughter Robyn waiting for me. If my tardiness bothered them they were gracious enough not to show it.

Ernie Broadnax at the Elgin History Museum
with a sign describing the Project 2-3-1 exhibit he helped bring to life

Ernie began by apologizing for his weak voice.

"I'm dealing with my third bout of cancer," he said, with a slight rasp. "But my daughter helps me eat right. I used to be a big sweet eater, you know, cobblers and pies."

"*Used* to be?" Robyn asked, raising an eyebrow.

"Well, I guess I still am when I can sneak some. I got a pretty tough sheriff there."

I liked Ernie, instantly and very much. I asked him to tell me about his background. Robyn, sitting next to her dad, listened silently.

"We've been here for seven generations. My great-great-grandmother was a slave before she arrived in 1862. A contingent of Union soldiers from Elgin went down South with the army, down in Tennessee near the Alabama and Mississippi state lines at the battle of Shiloh. And because the Union army had taken over all of the plantations there they felt like they were responsible for the thousands of black slaves they found. A lot of them had no clothes, no shoes, nothing. A colonel from Elgin saw this and wrote back to the First Baptist Church here—the white First Baptist Church—

and asked 'Can we bring some of this contraband property back home? Will we educate them? Will we feed them, clothe them? Will we help them find jobs that pay? Will we help them build a church; will we help them build a school?' And the church back here in Elgin said 'Yes.' So the colonel loaded two railroad boxcars with people they called 'contraband'—mostly children—and brought them here. They got off right downtown. And that's how the first 110 black people came to Elgin."

I just sat there with my mouth closed while Ernie continued.

"The white people here then took them into their homes, let them stay in their barns, helped them build shacks, and got them paid jobs. And one of the freed slaves who came a few months later worked at a lumberyard and was able to buy property, which turned into the three blocks that became the heart of the black community in Elgin. Folks in town called it 'the Settlement.' Freemont Street was the center of things there."

Ernie went on to describe a number of people who came from the Settlement: a young woman who was the first black valedictorian of the integrated high school; a postmaster who built a house that became an important black recreation center (that Ernie later directed); a Harlem Globetrotter; a professional NBA player; the first black taxidermist in the state of Illinois; and a brilliant man with over 100 patents.

"Blacks couldn't get patents until the 1900s," Ernie said, "so there were lots of things invented by blacks that white people got the credit for, and made the money. So many firsts came out of those three blocks. I was the first black to have an office at Elgin's City Hall. And that was during the times of the racial problems in the 60s and early 70s. My three brothers got involved in that. So here I am, working at City Hall, while my brothers are trying to burn the city down."

He laughed. I could only imagine what trials and hardships that laugh covered up.

"My dad was a shoe rebuilder. He had a shop for 45 years on Dundee Avenue down in the basement—they wouldn't let him come up on the ground floor. He raised 14 of us with that shop. We had such a large family we had to eat in shifts."

I laughed out loud, but then realized it might not be a joke.

"Wait, are you serious about that?"

"I'm serious about that. We didn't have a table long enough! The older ones ate first. But, you know, it worked out somehow. I don't know how my dad managed to feed all of us. We did get food stamps and that helped. It was amazing.

"It was a really interesting area to grow up in, them three blocks, because it was the only integrated area in Elgin. We had blacks, some Italian Americans, three white families. We had Swedish, some Germans, and one Jewish family, all in them three blocks. And us growing up with those different people, and them growing up with us, I think it helped all the families because all the families looked out for one another, like during the War when we shared a lot of things.

"I went to Elgin High School and then Elgin Community College where I was the first black basketball player and the first black on ECC's speech team. I won a lot of trophies there. And of course I remember going to basketball games and speech tournaments, and afterwards the team would go out to eat at a restaurant, you know. And I would have to sit in the bus and my teammates would bring me out something to eat. You couldn't go inside lots of restaurants back then."

Sitting in front of a man who *himself* had been forced to wait outside a restaurant because he was black stirred feelings of shame and anger inside of me that even the best PBS specials had never tapped into.

"Even with Elgin's history of inviting all those freed slaves here and helping them out, it was segregated here?" I asked.

"Yeah, the segregation and all that stuff, it was here in Elgin. My mom and sisters and aunts always had problems buying clothes because they didn't dare go into the white dressing rooms. They could buy the clothes, but then they'd have to come back home to see if they fit. And a couple of the largest businesses in the city wouldn't hire blacks. The Elgin National Watch Factory was one of the largest watch factories in the world, with 3,000 employees, and they wouldn't hire us. The second largest employer that wouldn't hire blacks was the City of Elgin. No black policemen, no black politicians, no black nothing. Boards, committees, commissions—no blacks. All that changed over time. I worked for the Parks & Recreation Department as the president of that Freemont Recreation Center I was telling you about. And that later became the Boys & Girls Club of Elgin. See, we couldn't belong to the YMCA or the YWCA. We had to go 22 miles to Aurora to swim. Well, one day two black boys crossed the river to the west side of town—you didn't cross that river back then if you were black—well they went over there and jumped in that swimming pool. And *aaaaallll* the whites got out. And when that happened the city swooped in and gouged out part of the riverbank just north of our library here, and brought in sand and made a black beach, so that we could swim in the polluted Fox River. It was nasty; it was worse than nasty. You went in with your sneakers on because of all the broken glass on the bottom. There were two junkyards and the foundry right there."

"It took some guts for those boys to jump into that pool, didn't it?"

"Oh yeah, it did. But it helped change things. People started working together more in Elgin, and then the civil rights laws came. Before then the banks wouldn't lend you money, the real estate agents would only show you places in the Freemont area. Today, blacks of course live anywhere in the city that they can afford."

"Did you find that white people were resentful when those changes started happening?"

"Oh yeah."

Ernie pointed to a photograph on the wall showing people wearing white tunics and pointed hoods.

"See the Ku Klux Klan? A lot of people didn't know it but Elgin was the center of the local Klan for years—over 600 members. One of my friends was accused of fathering a child with a white woman and the Klan got him and took him down to the park and tarred and feathered him. When my mother and his grandmother went to the police station to get him the police said they could take him home to clean him up but he had to be out of town within an hour. Well, that didn't happen. The black families gathered around his house to protect him, and instead of him leaving they found 17 of the Klan members who were responsible, prosecuted nine of them, and three did go to jail. That was kind of unheard of back then."

I glanced at Robyn, who looked to be not far from my age, and shook my head in disbelief. I assumed that she, like me, had never seen anything like that. Ernie continued.

"I can remember when I was young the other kids coming to our house and talking about a big parade they saw with clean white sheets and nice pretty horses with braided tails and silver saddles and a big drum—*toom, toom, toom*. My dad walked up the stairs and stood for a second on the porch staring at us, and told us to stay away from those people because they didn't like blacks. He knew who most of them were because he could tell from their boots.

"He told us three things, my dad did. We had to go to church until age 13. After that we could decide what we wanted to do on our own. He said learn some patience. And he said have a sense of humor, because if you're black and don't have a sense of humor, you're going to be in trouble!"

We all laughed at that.

"And so I remembered those three things when I left home at 21 years old to go the Marines' "A" school in Florida. I had never seen mountains; I had never seen the ocean. My dad said 'Son, you're getting ready to cross the Mason-Dixon Line now. If you read your signs and watch what you're doing, you'll be okay.'

"It went in one ear and out the other. In my head I was going to see palm trees, take my first airplane ride—I was excited about it. So I got that airplane ride, got off and picked up my sea bag and threw it over my shoulder and walked towards the terminal. I was looking at the big fountains, the sunshine. Took two or three steps into the terminal and I almost got knocked right onto my butt. Somebody yanked my sea bag off me, knocked off my Marine Corps hat, and I almost went down too, but there was a cop at both of my elbows and they kept me up. They had me up on my tiptoes and then I saw my sea bag slide across the floor to the other side of the terminal and I asked what was wrong, what did I do? And one of the cops looked at me and said 'Boy, you must be from up North. I don't care where you're from, but while you're down here with us, you better read your signs.' I had walked into the white people side of the terminal."

"I'm so sorry you had to go through all that, Ernie," I said. "Did your time in the military change or shape your perspective on things?"

"I think one of the things that can wake somebody up is to travel," he said, "to see the bigger picture, to see how people in other places live. I remember the second time I went overseas with the Marine Corps we were in the Far East and I would see those kids standing around the mess halls waiting to dig through the dumpsters when we were done. After that was when I first noticed how much food was being dumped over our ship's fantail into the water every day. So much wasted food.

"And you know the V.F.W.?[3] For the veterans coming back home? We couldn't join, and we couldn't join the American Legion here, either. We couldn't join the Kiwanians Club and all those things either. Well, my brother-in-law wrote a letter to Washington to complain about that and some folks came down here to Elgin and straightened that out, so he wound up becoming the first black Commander of our V.F.W."

Ernie was one of the few people I had ever met whom I could hear outline the systemic injustices inflicted on blacks over the course of American history, without feeling like I was myself being accused of a million sins that happened before I was born. His candid, buoyant, friendly demeanor almost entirely diluted the thick sludge of our discussion, leaving me feeling comfortable enough to ask real questions, as opposed to devoting my energy to trying not to sound smug or ignorant. In short, he made it easy to talk about race.

"Ernie, can I ask you something kind of broad? You mentioned integration and the civil rights movement and how you saw the rights of blacks, or the ability of blacks to participate in society, improve during that period. Do you think we're still making progress on that? Do you think our progress has sort of plateaued and we still have things holding back black people? Or do you think things are pretty much equal now? I mean, how do you feel about where we stand today?"

"Well… "

He hesitated just a moment.

3 Veterans of Foreign Wars—a nonprofit veterans service organization with "posts" serving as gathering places in towns throughout the country.

"I've witnessed a lot in my 80 years. I'd say there's been, you know, an improvement. But, I think we still have a long ways to go. We've got some new problems we're dealing with, in terms of black communities and the relationships with police, for example. There's also still some hidden racism. It's undercover. You can't put up the signs anymore. But there are still several ways blacks can be segregated, still be dealt with unfairly. Income is one of them. They can still play games with hiring. There's nepotism in some places, where blacks haven't been hired but a whole white family is working here or there. Same thing with promotions in places, including in the Armed Services.

"But there have been some great things that have happened, too. I can speak for Elgin. For instance, our community college has a program that starts in the 7th grade where if a student stays with the program from then until graduation then he or she can get a scholarship to go to college. There's a problem now with a lot of young black girls getting pregnant and quitting school. Well, there are special schools now that provide babysitting so those girls can stay in school. Those programs are for everybody but a lot of it is focused on blacks. They aren't trying to make everybody into doctors and lawyers but there are ways kids can learn a trade where they can make a decent and honest living.

"There's also a group of people—I'm one of them—going around to places like black churches and trying to talk to young people. We tell them if they don't want to go to college and instead just hang around here on the streets that there's a real good chance they're going to wind up with problems. They're going to want to do something but not have the money to do it and so they'll end up getting involved in dope and all that mess, and eventually will end up in jail."

"How do you get young people to listen to that message?"

"Well, it's difficult. One of the things I used to do when I found a kid who showed an interest in something was to try and take them to visit successful people who are doing that very thing in the community. If we can get that kind of thing integrated into the school system I know that would help a lot."

"Is it important for young black people to see other black people who have been successful?"

"It's very important for them to see that. What's taught in black homes is a lot different than what's taught in white homes, especially when it comes to black males. These kids need to know that they can be successful, too, but there are some things you have to do first. You're going to have to get educated and learn various things, and work at it."

The museum director came over to tell us the building was closing. I was ready to beg for more time when Ernie and Robyn suggested we just go over to the Elgin Public Library to continue our chat. After a short ride through the dark and a quick tour of the superb new facility I sat down with them again, in a small meeting room. I asked Ernie if he had finished answering the question I had asked back at the museum—where he saw America today on the issue of race.

"When I grew up it was kind of bad," he said. "We had segregation and a lot of those types of problems. But it was kind of good, too. I made lots of white friends, got to see some of their rich homes; they learned about me; I learned about them. Most of those kids weren't cruel; they were just uninformed about black people. I knew kids who didn't realize blacks had to get haircuts! But those good experiences, and then traveling the world, helped me realize that the United States is probably the best place in the world to live a life, even with all of its shortcomings. Because if everybody works together these shortcomings can be overcome; a lot of them already have been. But we still got some things to do, some changes to make."

"What are some things black people can do in their communities to improve the prospects of young people there?"

"They can start stepping up. A big reason we have a lot of single mothers and grandmothers raising kids and things like that in the black community is because of our history. A lot of it stems from the days of slavery, where you were bought and sold, and your sister went to this plantation, your brother went to that plantation, your ma and dad were ripped apart and went to different places. In a sense, blacks are still dealing with that. We don't have that sense of community sometimes that you see in the Jewish population, and now in the Hispanic population, where people are looking out for one another. Our black communities still aren't as cohesive as they need to be. I think if we were more cohesive, more progress could be made. But I do see today how some blacks are stepping up. Single mothers are marching in the streets of Chicago at night, staying out there and watching their kids because so many are getting shot and killed right in the street."

Robyn agreed, offering a couple of stories about both obstacles and positive change she had seen in black communities. The library lights flashed to tell us closing time was near.

"Is it a choice?" I asked. "Does it simply start with one of these single mothers, or whoever, one day just saying 'That's it. I am going to make this community better. I may not know how to do it, but I am going to start figuring it out today. And I'm going to do it again tomorrow, and the next day, and the next'?"

"Yes."

Robyn and Ernie said it at the same time.

"That is what *has* to happen," Ernie added.

I so wanted to hear more but the library lights flashed again. It was time to say goodbye.

My host family for the night lived a few miles west of town, giving me time to think, think, along the dark half-hour ride. An overloaded brain reduced my surroundings to a blur, leaving me with only the blue line on my phone's GPS screen, and my thoughts:

For those of us less burdened by its weight, history might sometimes feel like just a series of old stories… like a movie we watch and say 'Well, that was sad/interesting/terrible/awesome' as we exit the theater back into a world having little to do with the events that unfolded on the screen. But when we have a chance to visit with someone who has lived that history—someone who can hold out their hand and show us the lines history has etched—it serves as a reminder that the past is not something time has just packaged up and stashed away. Stories from people like Ernie help us remember that history is not abstract—it is both the paper onto which, and the ink with which, today's story is being written.

During the past two weeks through the mostly white Upper Midwest I had found few opportunities to speak with black folks, which had made this day all the more special. Although none of them seemed to dwell on it, I had little doubt Chris, Robyn, and Ernie experienced even a modern America with more obstacles than mine. I also knew Ernie was right: America was making progress, and held great promise.

I checked my GPS again. The blue line had grown shorter, but I still had a ways to go.

Day 15
Elgin, IL → Chicago, IL
22/759 miles
Couchsurfing/Warmshowers
Nick Tipre

The Raising, Then Razing
Of A Chicago Neighborhood

I pedaled back into downtown Elgin for breakfast with a reporter from the Chicago Tribune. We were in front of the restaurant checking out the touring rig when two women stopped to ask about my travels. One of them handed me a $20 bill and said to spend it on anything I wanted, so I ordered the large orange juice for a change, and added the reporter's pancakes to my check.

Skipping 40 miles of suburbia with a train ride straight into Chicago seemed like another acceptable splurge. The station's ticket salesman told me I would need permission to load the bike into the car. When the train arrived a young man with tattoos on his arms, neatly cropped hair, and diamond studs in both earlobes stepped down onto the platform to check tickets. I ran up to ask if the rig and I could board.

"The train is leaving *right now*, man," was his answer.

I sprinted to grab the hundred-pounder and then struggled to get it up the car's stairs while the ticket guy watched with his arms crossed, close enough that I could smell his overdone cologne. Here I had cycled hundreds of miles and fended for myself in all kinds of gnarly situations, but this bejeweled, perfumed punk, standing there doing nothing to help, still pulled-off 'tough' better than I did. I wanted to yank out his fancy earrings and fling them onto the tracks. A boarding passenger finally took hold of the bike's rear rack and helped lift.

Sitting down to passively watch Illinois fly by was an unfamiliar guilty pleasure. The suburban view from the window soon shifted to nondescript concrete walls as we pulled underground into Union Station. After fighting the bike onto the busy platform I weaved through the undulating crowd into an elevator. A ding later I backed out onto the sidewalk. Turning towards the bustling sounds behind me, I got my first view of Chicago.

Chicago's Cloud Gate (often called the Bean)
reflecting the downtown skyline, a hot sun, and the squatting photographer/author

I almost hyperventilated. The rig and I had experienced a few large cities together, but never a fast-paced metropolis like this one. Fleeing to a shady spot I put my back against a wall and just watched, absorbing the rhythm of the city, hoping to eventually jump-in on beat. After five minutes of silent pep-talks I clipped into the pedals, exhaled, and bounced off the sidewalk into the flowing streets.

Within seconds I learned that city cycling goes smoother if you clench your jaw and look sternly ahead. One minute more and I had become part of Chicago, moving confidently down the well-designed bike lanes when available, staking-out territory in the vehicle lanes when necessary. I realized drivers and pedestrians alike were entirely used to cyclists and would give me just enough space if I was ready to take it. Shooting through intersections and darting around stopped buses, I blended seamlessly into traffic. Not a single horn blew my way. Zooming down the Magnificent Mile was one of the most invigorating experiences of my life. The closest I came to an accident was when another cyclist nearly clipped my elbow while passing with no warning. If I could have reached out and knocked him off his bike I probably would have. I was getting cocky.

The accounts of sticky Chicago summers turned out to be true, but I never saw a hot dog stand. Instead I lunched on a deep-dish pie at a pizzeria while my eyes burned a hole through the window separating me from the bike, locked but by itself outside.

On my way to sightsee around Wrigley Field I stopped by a hardware store to replace a few assorted bolts that had vanished along the route. When I asked an employee if he had any suggestions for a longtime resident who might chat with me, he didn't hesitate.

"Go to Tipre Hardware on North Avenue and ask for Nick or his mom. They've been here forever."

With those golden words I scrapped Wrigley and headed back the way I came.

Minutes later I found Tipre Hardware on the south side of the street. Pulling up to the storefront I saw a stocky man, about my age, smoking a cigarette and reading a book in a small nook on the sidewalk next to the front door. Something told me this was the guy I had come to see.

"Are you Nick?"

"Yeah," he said. "What's up."

His statement had no inflection to suggest a question mark.

I described the project and asked if he had a few minutes to chat. Looking at me sideways, he finally said I could come back when the shop closed and "we'll see if I can answer a couple of your questions." I rode through nearby Old Town hoping to meet someone else to interview as a hedge against Nick's skepticism.

Fortunately, I didn't have any luck.

Nick Tipre
and the original 1850's-era storefront hidden below Tipre Hardware

The first thing Nick said to me when I returned made me a little giddy:

"Want to see what Chicago used to look like 160 years ago?"

The place was empty except for the two of us. Nick let me bring the rig inside and then led me down a raw lumber stairway into the basement, saying that I had arrived just in time. Their new landlord had refused to renew the store's lease. Tipre Hardware would relocate within a few months.

"There's a lot of history here," Nick said, "aside from my own history here. I'm not happy to be walking away from it."

A final step down brought us into the 19th century. Stout wooden beams spanned the basement ceiling, supporting the shop's main floor above.

"These are original 6x6 and 10x10 joists," Nick said, "from back when they were actually six and ten inches wide."

Augmenting the sesquicentenarian timbers were several steel I-beams, themselves functional antiques. Even more support came from a series of worker jacks Nick's father and uncle had installed in the 70s. Grasping an old pipe, Nick bent it slightly with his hand to demonstrate its age—it was made entirely of soft lead. The hulking iron boiler that used to heat the building sat at the rear like a fat, stubborn old bull. The ceiling above it showed a black char.

"Did the boiler get too hot there?" I asked.

"Oh, no. That happened when the top part of the building was destroyed in the fire."

He said *the* fire, not *a* fire. I searched my thin cache of knowledge about Chicago history.

"You mean the Great Chicago Fire?"

"Yeah. It basically leveled the whole city back in 1871."

Jesus. The fire damage itself was an antique.

"What got you interested in the history of the city?" I asked.

"I was lucky in that I just grew up around it. My father was into it; he was involved in everything in the neighborhood. He grew up in the neighborhood, his father grew up in the neighborhood, his grandfather came to this neighborhood from Hungary, so this has always been where we've been. My grandfather bought a house that I was told was the oldest on the block. It was right around the corner. They tore it down and built a unit condo."

The tone of Nick's voice when he spoke that last sentence bordered on disdain.

"So this is where you want to stay?" I asked.

"This is my life. I couldn't leave. I mean as a person I could go anywhere. Things change, I get that. But sentimentally speaking, this is the only neighborhood I'll ever have. My dad's name is on the corner. This is our place. This is what I do; this is what I've always done; it's what my dad did. This is what I *want* to do with my life. I could not run a store somewhere else. I could not exist and thrive somewhere else and just pretend everything was okay because I'm just selling paint or just selling tools. No. The whole point of this store and what we try to do is that we're providing a service to the people of the neighborhood that we're a part of. And even though the neighborhood itself has changed fundamentally—and it's never coming back—I still want to continue with it. See, my dad was willing to provide that service for people without really making the buck that today's idea of

America has come to be about. Now it's all about money, and that creates a whole different set of issues and a stress level that, unfortunately, he didn't survive."

Pointing out the forgotten storefront door that used to open onto the sidewalk, Nick explained the whole of central Chicago was raised with hydraulic jacks in the 1850s and 1860s to fix flooding and drainage issues. An empty, rusted sign bracket still hung over the old entryway. I wondered whether the pedestrians I could hear walking along the sidewalk above us were aware of the rich history under their busy feet.

"Why has the neighborhood changed?" I asked. "What's been the catalyst?"

Nick sighed.

"This neighborhood used to be almost entirely working class, regular people. My dad's customers were homeowners. They had a stake in the neighborhood. But they were behind the curve. They owned property that people with a lot more money and connections wanted. So, as the investments started coming in, their taxes skyrocketed and they couldn't afford the yearly increases. They got pushed out. Money came in and ruined everything.

"It's like what's happening to us. When my dad opened the place we were a real hardware store. We had drywall, concrete, lumber—enough lumber to build a house from scratch. We held onto that for as long as we could, but that's gone now. At our new shop, we'll focus mainly on paint and some other things. But the truth is we can never be the type of hardware store I grew up in."

"Why not?"

"Because 15 years ago a huge home improvement store moved in just up the street. They sell building materials basically at cost because they make their money on other things. And as soon as they started selling things at what *we* pay for them, that was it. The man responsible for that development did what all rich people do: you go into places and you ingratiate yourself to the people who matter. He provided vacations to powerful families, and they would have all these great times together, and so the mayor happily gave him *carte blanche* to build. That store sits there and does business on city property—f***ing city property—that shouldn't have been given to them."

To say Nick spoke in paragraphs would be an understatement. He was delivering a *manifesto*.

"I have no issues about class or whatever. The issue here is about outside forces who don't know anything about this neighborhood and don't care about any of it. *They're* deciding what we're worth now. But for people who have something, and who worked for it and earned it, and had a real something, a real piece of property in a part of the city that nobody gave a f*** about before, but they knew each other, and they had a neighborhood… how do you value, or how do you devalue that they want to be *where they know*? That they want to have their children grow up *where they did*?"

"What are the benefits of growing up in a place where you know everyone?" I asked.

"Well, in a world that has nothing but change and insecurity, it gives you identity. These weren't people who were just scraping by; these were people who did all the right things, and were still intact, and were living under the idea of a real America, where entrepreneurs could run a small shop in a small neighborhood, and live."

We started back upstairs. Lightly, to avoid splinters, I ran my hand along an ancient creosote-coated beam next to the open staircase. It smelled like an old railroad track tie.

"Before our neighborhood was destroyed, the people here had a place in life," Nick said. "A lack of place in life makes it harder to have a purpose in life. And what happens when you wind up in a place where you don't know anyone and nobody knows you? When you have no emotional connection to where you are? How much damage does it do to a person's psyche, to not be part of anything?"

Nick's question hung in the space between the basement joists as we stepped back into the Chicago of today.

Checking my phone, I saw my efforts to find a place to crash had finally paid off. A young couple from one of the online traveler communities accepted my request at the last minute, and I had a pleasant ride north through the city to their apartment. We went for dinner at a trendy restaurant a short walk away, where a thin young man with a high-pitched and sort of annoying voice took our order. His tight-fitting plaid shirt, dark-rimmed glasses, and incongruent mustache painted the textbook portrait of a hipster. If I had to guess, I would say this guy enjoyed living in Chicago but had most likely moved from somewhere else, had virtually no roots in the city, didn't know much about the history of the place, and did not plan on growing old there. The same could probably have been said for nearly all the boisterous patrons crowded around nearby tables.

As usual, my mind drifted. Poking a fork into my dish of fusion something-or-other, I didn't know whether to laugh at my hosts' light jokes and offer smiling commentary on the food, or to look down at the floor and ponder what might lie in ruins underneath.

Day 16
Chicago, IL → Valparaiso, IN
68/827 miles
Couchsurfing/Warmshowers
Mary & Ryan Kopka

EDUCATION + HARD WORK = ??

Leaving downtown Chicago felt more like a farewell than an escape. A stress-free ride via marked bike lanes brought me from my hosts' place to the shore of a gleaming and sailboat-dotted Lake Michigan. The perfect Saturday had the spandex crowd out running, biking, walking dogs, or striking elegant poses along the lakeside park paths. Though framed by an urban setting, the ubiquitous color green softened edges of concrete and steel. Behind the Shedd Aquarium I had to drop my head and plow through clouds of hovering dragonflies, hearing the sound of cellophane when one snuck by and hit me in the mouth. The Windy City skyline across the water could have been a postcard.

Despite the *living is easy* flavor of the summertime morning, anxiety squeezed at my gut as I neared Chicago's South Side. Having heard things like everyone else, I threw up my guard once the bike path gave way to nail salons and plain, marginally-kept apartment buildings. An older black man standing idly on the sidewalk watched me coming up the road. When I was close enough he yelled: " 'Sup, Old School?!" My brain almost short-circuited with simultaneously considering whether to request an interview, trying to figure out how the rig and I looked old school, and struggling to come up with a likewise cool-sounding response. A dullard's "Hey man" was all I managed to utter before pedaling on.

Other than Old School, the only person to acknowledge my presence was another older black fellow, wearing a cowboy hat, who approached while I lunched.

"Hey buddy, you know you need to be careful around here, right? This is South Chicago. People see you and know you're not from around here and know you're not going to recognize them or stick around and press charges, and they'll knock you down and take that bike. So be careful."

Right there, I removed my dog mace from my blue pannier and stuck it in my pocket.

The man's warning lingered in my mind as I continued south along a bike path and promptly got lost in a vacant field under a highway bridge. It was the kind of place one dumps a dead body. Trash and skeletal appliances lay scattered around dirt roads and paths; bulbous-lettered graffiti tags covered every surface that made for a decent urban easel. I was entirely alone (I hoped) and an actual, rare sense of alarm ushered me to quickly find the way back to the proper trail. Later, a sign noted the area used to host a Nike anti-aircraft missile silo that protected Chicago during the Cold War.

Dozens of miles of bike trails and paths carried me virtually the entire way to Valparaiso, the Indiana city named after a Chilean one. I parked next to a Mexican restaurant and ordered a margarita to celebrate my first time in the state, but also to drown my sorrow for a little while. Somewhere along the day's ride the bike's beautiful flagpole had vanished. I had been so proud of that flagpole.

After ordering replacement flags online I set out to scour Valpo for an interview. Passing through the tidy grounds of a courthouse I came across newlyweds Ryan and Mary Kopka relaxing on a bench.

Mary & Ryan Kopka
outside the Porter County Courthouse in Valparaiso

Mary had recently graduated with a teaching degree from Purdue. I asked what had made her want to work in education.

"I really think it comes from having a kindergarten teacher who liked to write little notes on frog-shaped paper. I just loved that. I can honestly say I've never wanted to be anything else. But I've had a lot of trouble finding work."

"What are you doing now while you're looking?"

"I've been working as a substitute teacher lately. I've been thinking of selling my crochet work, too. I need to do something to supplement my teaching income because it's so low, and then on top of that we have to buy so much stuff for our classrooms. I feel like to be a good teacher I have to spend a fourth of my paycheck on supplies for the students."

"What about you, Ryan?"

"I was born and raised in the country, south of here," Ryan said. "I lived my entire life at the same house until I married her. My dad has worked at the same company my entire life, and I just went to work there, too. I'm welding like he used to do. Right now we're building trailers for hauling dumpsters. We build them from the ground up."

"Have you seen products arriving from overseas that compete with yours?"

"Oh yes, lots of it. For example, I know of a local company that ordered a Chinese cylinder for their vehicle fleet. It was cheaper and lighter, and it failed. The company had to refit 200 trucks with that same part, but built in America. Another example is Chinese steel we see sometimes. It's cheap and works for most things but every now and then you'll come across a quality issue like a slug of nickel in the middle of a sheet. You can't cut that with the torch. You can blow the whole chunk out if you're not careful."

"Do you find those kinds of problems with American steel?"

"Not generally. Usually it's mixed better than that."

"He talks about quality all the time," Mary said. "He's told me how they go over everything he makes and if they find an issue they make him redo it. I'm not sure that's something they do in places like China."

"Yep," Ryan said. "Our area in the shop is pretty small, so we all kind of see what everyone else is doing. If somebody goofs something up it gets noticed and corrected real fast."

"Do you feel confident your company will be around for a while?" I asked.

"Oh yeah, it's not going anywhere. What worries me is when we have a quality slip-up. We can beat Chinese competition only because people are willing to pay more for a higher-quality product. We're already beat on price, so if we fail on quality then we're done. The only thing that is going to keep American manufacturing going is that high-quality, 'buy one and you're done' attitude."

"You guys aren't very old, but are there any changes you've seen in your lifetimes that stick out to you?"

Mary answered.

"It's not a change *I've* seen but my mom told me that in her day it was pretty easy to go out and get a job and get trained at the job. Today it seems like everyone only wants teachers with prior experience. How do I get experience if I can't get a job?! I think there's a huge misconception about going to college. You see those big signs: 'Get Your Degree Now! There Are Jobs Out There!' Well, that's not always the case."

"How would you turn that into advice for young people who might read this?"

"Well, it wouldn't be to *not* go to college! Education is a good thing. I just feel like colleges sometimes aren't preparing us for the real-life problem of finding and qualifying for a job. I sometimes think we put too much emphasis on liberal arts schools and not enough on technical schools. When I went to school I had to take a lot of classes that focused on teaching problem-solving skills. How do 'problem-solving skills' get you a job!?"

"What are some things y'all think we're doing right in the country, and some things we need to improve on?"

Mary answered again.

"Well… someone I know told me one day: 'Welfare is just the best thing ever. I can't wait to have another baby. All you have to do is feed them, change them, and you get paid a bunch of money!' She eventually had her kids taken away from her, thank God. But we're supporting people who just say 'Why should I work if I get paid by the government?' When we support those kinds of people we take money away from education and old people who served in the military and who now are not doing so well."

"Yeah," Ryan said. "Instead of fixing roads, fixing the VA, we're paying for people to be lazy?"

"Look, I'm not saying that nobody deserves help," continued Mary. "There may be a time when you're doing your best, you're working three jobs and you still can't make it work. I completely support helping people who are trying to help themselves. But I have a really hard time justifying helping people who don't want to help themselves."

"I'm sick of seeing handouts," Ryan said.

"How do you guys feel the system has treated you?" I asked.

"I've generally avoided it," Ryan said. "Family, friends—that's my system. If I need something, I call them. I don't go crying to the government saying, 'Hey I'm out of a job today, can you give me some money?' There are a lot of able bodies out there who say, 'Oh, I'm mentally handicapped, physically handicapped, I can't move my thumb, so I can't work.' There's guys out there missing legs that go to work every day! The system is played by too many people."

He was pretty hot with disgust. I asked Mary if she felt the same way.

"Yeah, pretty much. They say money is out there to help you with college. Well… I don't want to offend anybody but this is how it was for me… I'm a middle-class white person who did not get help from my parents to pay tuition. Try to find a scholarship if you're in my shoes. If I was left-handed, if I was really short, if I was Latino, if I was black, if you're anything other than an average white person, you're going to be okay! Unless you're white and on welfare—then you'll be okay, too. The woman I told you about got pregnant with her fourth kid and said 'I got enough money to get a new laptop!' Well, I didn't even get enough money to pay for my books! I used the money I earned working at the water park—all of it—to pay for my books. And I had straight A's! But she gets a check because she doesn't work, and everyone else gets a scholarship. It just seems sometimes like people who know how to play the system do better than people who work really, really hard."

With daylight fading, I said goodbye to Ryan and Mary and tapped my hosts' address into my phone. Three miles later I realized the GPS had sent me on a wild goose chase in the wrong direction. Since I would now be pedaling in the dark and arriving late to my hosts' house anyway, I decided to stop for dinner at a 7-Eleven.

It was the best decision I made all day. A gray-haired man wearing a kilt stumbled out the door and bumped into a garbage can the moment I pulled up. I bought a donut and milk and was eating outside when the man returned from his vehicle to explain his kilt and intoxication were due to a family reunion, but now he was lost and needed directions to a town called Hammond—"but don't worry because the wife is driving." I helped him find it with my phone. Back inside, the Indian store owner behind the counter had his shirt unbuttoned down to his belly, exposing an exotic-looking gold necklace that glinted from a bed of dark chest hair. I listened to him talk-up

the new $5 pizzas 7-Eleven had started offering—how HUGE they were—
and was soon joined by two other young men likewise considering dinner
options. We must have looked skeptical.

"You know what, I'm just going to show you guys," the owner said, and
was away just a moment before returning with an admittedly large frozen pizza.

"I told you. You know, 7-Eleven isn't making any money on this. None
at all. They're just all about pleasing the customer, pleasing the customer."

"You're going to put Domino's out of business!" I said. I would have
said anything to keep him going.

"Yeah, and we sell *chicken wings*, too," he replied.

Leaning towards me, he then raised his hands into the air, waving them
in circles before saying, in a very low voice:

"And they're BIG chicken wings, too. BIG."

Why that had been a secret for my ears only, I wasn't sure, but I bought
some of those wings and then bolted from the store before the man
convinced me to buy a few gallons of gas, too.

Day 17
Valparaiso, IN → Potato Creek
State Park, IN
53/880 miles
Campground
Gail Horein

Don't Forget The Y

My Valpo hosts joined me for a 15-mile morning ride to Union Mills, and then I was alone, passing through seas of soy swaying in a nearly imperceptible breeze. Only while biking across the Upper Midwest had I witnessed actual waves coursing through crops as if they *really were* the sea—a phenomenon particularly striking in bean fields. Like ocean froth, an olive-drab line moving through a mat of dark green marked the advancing crest of the wave, as the passing wind briefly flipped over the plants' leaves to expose the lighter-colored underside. Elsewhere, small birds darted above a recently cut field, feasting on stirred-up bugs. A big irrigation sprinkler overshot its target by a few feet, throwing a cool spray across the asphalt to mist a hot cross-country cyclist. Coming upon a swath of forest in the middle of many dozens of square miles of agriculture roused my curiosity. How had this patch of nature survived? The numerous tall cottonwood trees meant it had been left alone for a long time.

At a ballfield near Walkerton the rig shows-off his new flagpole
lovingly fashioned from a stick-flag glued to a modified driveway reflector
but still awaiting the state flag adornments

108

Souring weather greeted me in Walkerton. I caught up on internet things at a McDonald's while trying to figure out the urban-talking, tattooed young people coming and going in what I had assumed to be a small farming town. A rainstorm whipped up the instant I got rolling again, forcing me to duck into a nearby bar for shelter. Inside the dim place a group of thin white women with sunken eyes and bad teeth killed time alongside me. I kept to the periphery of their banal conversations about so-and-so who had been in a fight, another guy who had gotten drunk and made a fool of himself, and similar uninspiring topics. Contributing only when politeness required it, I mostly sat in silence, perplexed at the women's unhealthy appearance and rough language. Virtually none of what I encountered in that supposedly bucolic hamlet seemed to fit into the narrative I had been expecting. I couldn't understand what these people were doing there.

A break in the rain allowed me to make a run for Potato Creek State Park. At the campground entrance I met a chipper and friendly woman named Gail Horein.

Gail Horein
outside her registration station at Potato Creek State Park

"Both of my parents moved here to work factory jobs," Gail said. "They worked their whole lives just trying to earn a decent wage so that I could be the first in my family to go to college and go on to get a job that I loved. I have always been thankful to them for that."

We squeezed-in our sentences between camper registrations and crackling two-way radio chatter at Gail's kiosk.

"Tell me about that job you loved," I said.

"I taught kindergarten for 33 years! Most people think of kindergarten as little kids running all over the place, swinging on the rafters, you know. But we didn't do that! We laughed together and had fun together, but we learned, and that's what I wanted education to be."

Gail's spunky voice dropped an octave.

"But it's changed so much. Now they have mandatory reading groups instead of unstructured time. You're going to have this group of little readers but they're not going to know how to socialize and interact with each other... play with each other!"

"What made you want to become an educator, to begin with?"

"I've always loved people. I just liked being in school; I loved reading, things like that. And I love kids, of course. I've taught so many of them. Let's see... I taught about 25 kids per year for 33 years, so you do the math![4] Everywhere I go I see either someone I taught or a parent of someone I taught. One time I was in the mall and I said to my daughter 'Hey look! There's the father of one of my kids!' And she said 'Mom, do you realize how that sounds?' "

"I still remember my kindergarten teacher," I said, after a laugh. "Her name was Shirley. I can hear her voice right now."

I thought about how fond I had been of Shirley, and how these now grown folks must feel when they see Gail around town, the woman who helped them learn songs and picked them up when they fell down on the playground.

"I still remember my teacher, too!" Gail said. "I thought she was just about to die at the time but she was probably no older than I am now."

She let out a big laugh. I asked her what she believed kids were supposed to get out of kindergarten.

"You know, I want them to learn letters and sounds and things like that, but I think they should also have time for play. Kids learn so much through

4 My phone's calculator put that at 825 kids.

play. Years ago, Piaget[5] said 'They have to learn X to learn Y to learn Z, and you build on blocks.' Well, so much of the time now they just want to jump from X straight to Z. You get these parents and even higher-ups who are working so hard on the reading that they're forgetting these little kids need to know how to hold a pencil.

"And I want normal kids to be able to work with those kids who are not so fortunate. I want it to be more of a family situation. In my classroom we had all kinds of kids. Six years ago my class had a little guy with Batten disease,[6] and everybody knew him. I would always talk to him and one of my little kids told me one time 'Miss Horein, he can't talk back. Why are you talking to him?' And I explained that he could understand more than he could speak. I want my kids to learn empathy. I taught them more than just books. You do, you teach kids more than just books."

"It sounds like you don't like standardized testing very much."

"Just by observing those kids I can tell you how they're going to do before they even take the test. I can tell you what each one of them needs to work on, where they might be stronger, what they like. But we have to do these strict standardized tests, and you're giving these tests to these little kids at five years old and they don't know how to do it. They're five! It's just too much right now."

"I've talked with a lot of teachers who don't really like standardized tests," I said. "Do you know of any teachers who do like them?"

"You need to know how your kids are doing. You need to have some type of testing. But most of the time teachers can make their own tests that tell you more of what you want to know and how you can work on that. The state says you have to teach this, and this, and this under their guidelines. Well, my kids learned those things but had no idea they were learning under the proficiency requirements. I tried to make it fun. I want kids to love to grow."

A man named Ralph drove by in a golf cart and eyed me leaning into Gail's booth window. When he stopped to check on her she waved him on before continuing.

---

5 A Swiss clinical psychologist who worked with child development theory in the mid-20th century.
6 A rare neurodegenerative disorder that begins in childhood and progressively impairs a person's motor function.

"You hear people talk about wanting to run a school like a business. You can't run kids like a business. In a business, if you have a faulty part, you're going to get rid of that. In teaching, when we have kids who don't understand something we don't get rid of those kids, we work with them harder! And so if I have a kid who's gone from *here* to *here* (she put her hand at her waist and raised it to her shoulder) and then another kid who's gone from *here* to *here* (shoulder to eye-level) with *here* (eye-level again) being where the tests say the kids need to be, well then the test says that the first kid has failed. I don't look at it that way. For me, that first kid has learned and improved way more than the second kid, even if he's not quite where he needs to be yet."

Gail's tone dropped again.

"You know, it seems to me like they're trying to get rid of the public school system altogether," she said.

"You really think so?"

"Yep, I do. And they say they're being fair by giving a voucher to everyone, but if a family is poor they can't get the gas to take their kid to this far-away school. They're still staying at the local school. So, it's not fair to everybody. It's not."

A man and woman, both with bandanas on their heads and deeply suntanned skin, pulled up on their Harley-Davidsons. They were road-worn but happy French Canadians on a dream motorcycle tour of the USA. After Gail had registered them I asked what had made her want to switch jobs from teaching to working at the park.

"Well, they were getting ready to change our retirement program and so I thought it was time to go. I decided to apply here just because I knew it would be fun. I make a lot less than I was making as a teacher and that doesn't matter at all. I just really enjoy it, meeting and helping people, being outdoors. It's like a new family now. I've gone from working winters and having summers off to working summers and having winters off!"

She brought me inside the booth to show how she had organized the registration cards and reservations with binder clips on the wall. She had a very neat and legible list attached to one of those ubiquitous brown clipboards with the chrome metal clip. For my last question, I asked her to describe any changes in the area or the country that stood out in her mind.

"For me, it's the teaching, and what they expect of teachers. I think lots of teachers are sad because we can't reach out to our kids like we used to and teach them in the way we know works for them. I think morale has gone down so much. With everything so standardized and technical you're losing that emotional person who's so into kids and who loves them. And we're losing creativity. I really hope we can get all of that back."

My weather app beeped a warning about another big thunderstorm headed my way. I thanked Gail and hurried to set up the tent, attaching the rainfly and anchoring the guylines with extra stakes. As I was doing so bits of a white, waxy substance fell into my hands. After two weeks of baking in the sun while rolled up on the bike's rear rack, the fly was shedding its waterproof coating.

Arriving minutes later, the heavy rain soon began dripping through the damaged sections of nylon. I gathered what I would need to take refuge in the dry bathhouse, but before making a run for it decided to first check the radar function in my app to see what I might ascertain about the storm. The screen showed a thin green band of precipitation moving away from Potato Creek, so I stayed put to see what would happen.

Sure enough, the rain began to slacken. The slowing rhythm of pings above my head combined sweet notes of relief with a more ambiguous melody—almost like a dirge. The long reign of Uncertainty in the kingdom of weather and other aspects of everyday life was drawing to a close. After the last drop fell, my smartphone glowed on through the darkness while I pondered which traditional mainstays of the world I had known would be replaced by technology. Shopping, banking, finding romance, and even medical care were increasingly taking place via the digital screen. But a teacher's warm hug?

There's no app for that.

Day 18
Potato Creek State Park, IN → Bristol, IN
49/929 miles
Campground
Vic & Connie Kegley

Concerned About Their Turf

Sleep finally came in the early morning after the dry thunder calmed, but by 8:30 the sun had turned my tent into an oven. I broke camp and chanced a closed dirt road as a possible shortcut out of the park. The locked gate at the end would have blocked a motor vehicle, but I happily passed my gear piece-by-piece over the barrier in exchange for shaving six miles off the route. Once back on the pavement I pedaled towards South Bend, first through a cool forested area and then back in the familiar company of corn and soy. I rode up on a raccoon walking around in the middle of the road, seemingly unaware of me as I rolled within a few feet of it. Whether it was a grief-stricken mother searching for her kits or out of its mind with rabies, it felt a little sad knowing I would almost certainly be the next-to-last person to see the oblivious creature alive.

Arriving in the city I pulled up to St. Joseph's Sanctuary, where my Valpo hosts had scheduled my meeting with lifelong South Bend residents Victor and Connie Kegley. The retired couple greeted me out front and invited me to the facility's dining room for lunch.

Vic & Connie Kegley of South Bend

114

"How do I explain it?" Vic began. "Our capitalism is going to *pot.*"

It was the first thing he said after we sat down.

"The government wants to dictate everyone's salaries, even businesses, tell 'em what to pay. Well, how the hell can they know what to pay those employees when they're not operating the businesses? In other words, they want equal income. Equal income for everybody. Well, that's a socialistic state. That's socialism and I'm against socialism. You can't just give everybody something; you have to help them to help themselves. Look at all these people who are on welfare now. It's getting to be more and more and more."

Vic's wrinkles and feeble voice could hardly hide his fiery character.

"You only get out what you put in," Connie added. "If you don't put anything in yourself then you should not be getting anything out."

Vic continued.

"I was a farm boy, brought up on the farm. Right out of high school I went into World War II where I worked as a medic in England, France, and then Germany. I took care of the Quartermaster Battalion that was hauling the stuff up to the front lines and doing all of the trucking. And when I got out in '45 I went to Michigan State and graduated from there and then went to work. I met these guys in… Chicago… "

Vic paused to get his words together.

"I wish my mind was working better," he said after a few moments.

I felt a jolt of sadness for him, and then anger, that he was forced to fight through the injustice of old age. Connie and I both reassured him, her gently and me awkwardly. He continued.

"Anyway these guys in Chicago had this big sod business and said they had huge fields of it. Well, South Bend didn't know what sod was. So, I kept thinking about sod and that's how I got started, with seven acres. Then I grew to 200 acres, and that wasn't enough, so I bought some more and we ended up with 600 acres. We sold it in giant rolls to builders and those types."

"That's a lot of grass to mow," I said.

"It's a headache, I'll tell ya, being in business for yourself. But when you get up in the morning you have something to do, and you love to go to work because it's yours. And our boys put themselves through college. You know how they did it? After school they would go to the sod farm and work. I paid them $0.20 a yard to lay sod. And they would organize their own help and get it done themselves. Kids today aren't being taught how to work. The government is furnishing them free money. Another thing is these kids have only mothers, no fathers. They're not getting married—you know that. That's the trouble: nobody teaching their kids."

"Have you seen any changes over your lifetime that you like?" I asked.

"No."

I waited for a moment, expecting him to qualify that, or say something like 'Well, maybe X.' But Vic remained silent, ready for the next question. The "no" was it.

"So, you think the country has gotten worse over your lifetime?"

"Well, we're in debt!" Connie said. "That doesn't help us at all."

"Yeah," said Vic. "Trillions of dollars in debt. The bubble's gonna break one of these days and you're gonna see all hell break loose. That's my point."

"You have to understand, he grew up in the middle of the Depression," Connie said, "so we've seen how bad things can get. But during those times families seemed to stick together more, to work harder. And then his generation went and fought the War. They did what had to be done."

Returning to check on us, our server commented on my empty plate, making me realize how fast I had inhaled the senior-citizen sized portions. Connie magnanimously gave me leave to order a second lunch if I wanted it. A little embarrassed, but still hungry, I did.

"Vic, why did so many Americans in your generation risk their lives for a war that was so far away?"

"Hitler was a monster," Vic said, his tone making it clear he thought it a silly question. "He would have taken us over if we hadn't stopped him. He almost did."

"Why didn't you want Hitler to take over? What were you protecting here?"

"Freedom," Connie answered. "The ability to live your life the way you want to live it. We still have that freedom, but they're encroaching on a lot of those freedoms now."

I asked her if *she* saw anything going right.

"Well, first of all, I'm happy to see my children grown up and with families of their own. We've had our glitches like everyone but on the whole, we've enjoyed life and been very happy. We've got great-grandchildren now. As you age you realize how important family life is, and we passed that on to our kids. I think you have to have a family to have a perspective like ours, and maybe to have that drive to work. We wanted the best for our kids."

"And my question is," Vic said, "how long is that going to last?"

Vic insisted I visit their room to watch YouTube videos of the newest models of sod harvesters in action. The high-tech machines impressed me almost as much as Vic's fluency in social media. Thanking him and Connie I set off for Notre Dame, excited to see the famed university.

Pulling into the heart of campus I passed a Chinese tour group shuffling behind a student guide. I heard her say students never walked on the grass in front of the Basilica of the Sacred Heart because anyone who does so will fail their exams. I imagined some crafty groundskeeper long ago planted the seeds for the superstition, because those impeccable off-limits courtyards formed the perfect frame for the gleaming church dome and clean brick sidewalks.

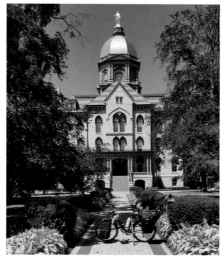

Notre Dame's Basilica of the Sacred Heart

But the peaceful beauty of the place couldn't fend off an abrupt gloom descending over me with surprising intensity. Vic's difficulties remained fresh in my mind. At thirty-six I had rarely felt old—I wasn't old—but watching the scattered summer students stroll by with their slack backpacks, the girls in short shorts and flip-flops, underlined the fact that I, too, was just an observer now, another gawker on tour. Even for a guy riding across the country on a bicycle it seemed clear: the days of endless possibilities, of awe and excitement and reckless, raw passion had left my life, forever. My short ride between St. Joseph's Sanctuary and the sunny grounds of Notre Dame drove that home in a harsh way.

The route east of the university shifted from unimpressive to dangerous. Douglas Road turned out to be a sprawl-piercing thoroughfare with no shoulder and a raised curb, making it impossible to escape drivers who got too close. After grinding out the miles to Elkhart—a town that looked ground-down itself—I stopped at a gas station and asked the cashier permission to use the restroom. The woman looked at me with pleading, almost desperate, eyes.

"I just got it to where it could be used again," she said. "Somebody went in there and did something inappropriate. If you promise not to do anything inappropriate you can go in there. But please, please… "

"I promise," I said, holding up my hands. "Just a regular old bathroom break."

I took the key, feeling a bite of anger that hard-working people on the front lines had to clean up after the kinds of people who do inappropriate things in restrooms.

My ride along the shore of the St. Joseph River mellowed to a cyclotourist's pace again. I pulled into tiny Bristol ready to eat a filling dinner, hoping the town's bar offered a hearty menu—or at least some peanuts in a bowl, since it was the only place still open downtown. Inside, a handful of strung-out looking people sat around staring at their hands, each with an empty stool separating them from the next. The only menu item that didn't come in a glass, can, or bottle was a hot dog, two of which I ordered with muted enthusiasm. A loudmouth towards the back was bragging about all the money he would make repairing RVs. Switching topics, he spoke even louder to be sure the whole bar could hear.

"I know a woman who just got a brand new $50,000 house on Section 8. They just gave it to her—Obamacare. All these ni***rs just sitting around without a job saying '*I'm gonna get that Obama money.*' My kids' mom gets food stamps. She babysits for cigarettes, stays in a place rent-free, and then sells her food stamps for weed."

Vitriol dripped from his words. A woman listening to the rant joined in to complain about having to clean a house she had moved into because the former tenants had used it as a meth kitchen. Compared to the bar's human atmosphere, my dull brown, soggy hot dogs seemed farm-fresh.

In need of something with a wholesome feel to it, I stopped by a small grocery store to buy a bunch of bananas. A stick-thin woman with poorly bleached hair and cutoff jean-shorts stood in front of me in line. On the dirty conveyor belt, she set a 6-pack of Natural Ice beer, a pack of cigarettes, and a Swanson frozen turkey dinner—one of those cheap ones that cost $2. Her mouth had the drawn-in look of a chain smoker, and I knew her voice would be raspy even before she asked the cashier which numbers she should choose for Powerball.

I had encountered a wide spectrum of Indiana that day. The last few miles along Vistula Street felt unclean and burdensome, despite the pleasant agricultural views. Pulling into a campground, I let them gouge me for $32 for a small patch of grass to pitch my tent, and smacked mosquitos at a picnic table until giving up and going to bed.

Day 19
Bristol, IN → Fremont, IN
43/972 miles
Paid lodging

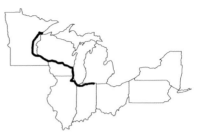

A String Of Wrong Assumptions

In the morning I took advantage of the empty campground laundry room to catch up on clean clothes and emails. A tiny chipmunk obliterated my peace when it burst through the open door, did two circles on the floor right in front of my feet, and then shot back outside before I could even blink in disbelief.

High demand for omelets
or lazy hens?

A brown-skinned woman with a strong foreign accent and Arabic writing tattooed across one of her arms rang up my lunch at a convenience store up the road. I learned that Fatima and her Muslim family had owned the store since immigrating to the area years before. I asked how her rural Indiana customers generally treated her.

"They treat me well. Everyone's nice," she said in a relaxed, genuine way.

I was glad my question hadn't put her off. Nibbling my sandwich at a corner booth I covertly observed the interaction between Fatima and the white restock supply man who entered with his clipboard and scanning tool. Moving together among aisles of chips and coolers of beer, they debated which items the store would need for the following week, and speculated whether a new product might sell. I tried to imagine how the man might have behaved differently had Fatima been a white Christian lady named Jane, but I came up short. The boring normalcy of the scene intrigued me, and that fact itself intrigued me, too.

Continuing east I rolled past field after field of soy, with the cheery sun shining overhead. A trio of raucous children bounced across the street just in front of me and plunged into Wall Lake with splashing squeals. I thought about jumping in behind them, but my dour internal odometer told me I hadn't earned it yet. I kept pedaling.

Traveling along the highway shoulder towards Fremont I continually dodged around piles of grassy manure presumably left by the many horses and ponies in pens alongside the road. I witnessed only one of the animals being put to work, pulling a black buggy driven by a conservatively-dressed man and woman. I assumed they were conducting some sort of funeral event, though I didn't see any other mourners.

An 18-wheeler inched towards the highway from a driveway ahead of me. Feeling certain the driver had seen me and was preparing to stop, I maintained my pace. Big mistake. I heard my rims scrape and squeal and saw the trucker jump in his seat as we both slammed on our brakes at the last minute to prevent my death. The man stuck his hand out the window to say 'I'm sorry.' I returned the gesture but had to cut short my wave to avoid hitting my arm on his truck's warm grill.

At a motel on the edge of town I met two men riding their Harley-Davidsons to South Dakota's Sturgis Rally. They had no idea where they would spend the night at the crowded motorcycle mecca but seemed confident they'd figure it out once there. I couldn't tell whether they believed me when I said:

"I know how *that* goes."

Day 20
Fremont, IN → Spring Arbor, MI
55/1,027 miles
Local hospitality
Martha Hagerty
Chris Eicher
Elwin & Donna Johnson

She Will Fight You
He Will Feed You
They Will Save You

A low sun was still burning off the night's mist when I left the motel in the morning. The mom-and-pop diner in town was just like any other, with one notable exception: the customers at one of the tables looked as if they had stepped out of the 1700s. Two overall-wearing men with beards but no mustaches chatted with their bonneted wives while eating bacon and eggs. I sidled up to the counter on a fixed round stool and ordered coffee from a waitress who called me "honey." Leaning in, I nodded towards the group.

"Are they Amish?"

"They sure are," she said. "They come here a lot, but we don't let them bring their buggies into the parking lot. It leaves ruts."

I had never been around Amish people, and felt ashamed at my surprise to see them sitting in a restaurant behaving like everyone else. The clues from the day before now made sense. I had rolled into Amish country without knowing it.

My sudden and intense curiosity about these folks would have to wait. The interview I had set up with Fremont's Town Court judge was set to begin in a few minutes, so I finished breakfast and got the rig rolling. A block or so down the street I pulled to a stop at a red light. Coming at me from the opposite direction, a black 18-wheeler flashed its signal indicating a left turn. The truck's engine bellowed through downshifts and its air brakes hissed before the driver swung the giant machine in a wide arc across the intersection, overshooting his lane by a few feet. With no time to dismount I

122

took two pathetic hops to the right, dragging the heavy bike with me before swinging its front tire up over the curb. The truck rumbled through its turn, clipping the sidewalk with its 3-foot tall tire and missing me by less than a bike length.

From there, the ride to town hall was a piece of cake.

Martha Hagerty
with her granddaughters outside Fremont Town Hall

I arrived to find Martha Hagerty waiting for me in her office. When I stepped over a disheveled Barbie doll to shake Martha's hand, her two granddaughters jumped up from the carpeted floor and began peppering me with questions. I was happy to serve as their temporary respite from summertime boredom.

Martha's great-grandfather had owned the local feed store, her paternal grandparents ran a restaurant, and her maternal grandfather had established a pharmacy in town and helped build the first high school running track from railroad cinder. Her mother had been a teacher and ran the school library for over 30 years while her father had owned the town's hardware store where she worked when she was younger.

"Daddy was like me," Martha said. "Don't say anything about Fremont, Indiana, because I'll fight ya."

Her granddaughters both giggled. So did Martha and I.

I asked how Fremont had changed during her lifetime.

"Like so many of these small towns, we're feeling a little bit threatened. I think Fremont's survival depends on whether we keep our school. There's fewer students than before, and that means less money from the state. So, we now have to decide whether we want to pay for the shortfall. We have an upcoming vote to raise taxes that I support very strongly. I don't want more taxes just like the next person doesn't want more taxes, and I don't even have children in the school. But we have to keep our school because we need somewhere to grow our children. It's what holds a community together."

"What's going to happen if people vote not to raise the tax?"

"Programs will be dropped, like sports, art, music. We'll have to use volunteer coaches. And I think that's just where it will begin. If we lose our school, we would pretty much lose everything. There wouldn't be people coming in and supporting local businesses. In nearby towns where schools have left and consolidated with others, those towns pretty much just withered up. The buildings stay but there's nothing in them, and they eventually burn down, or fall down, or whatever. Here, we have a little hardware store, a little grocery store, a couple of pizza shops. And we do have a couple of empty storefronts but we're working to get them filled."

"Tell me about how and why you became a judge."

"After I graduated high school and went off to college I moved back here and got married. I was working with the Girl Scouts when an opportunity to clerk for the local judge opened up. The judge hired me on the spot, and I worked for her for 15 years. After she retired I ran for the position and won.

"This is the kind of place where people care about their neighbors, and if they have a tough time... we had two families where the husbands were injured, and the church rallied around them, the community rallied around them. We got them gas cards because they were driving back and forth to the hospital so much."

"Is it hard judging and punishing people who you might see on the sidewalk the next day?" I asked.

"I think people know it's not personal. It's good for people to be judged by someone local. I try to help them understand why I found them guilty, what they did wrong. That kind of advice, and saying hello to people on the sidewalk… it makes people feel important, like someone cares about them. And we do."

"It seems like being a judge in a small town could be a thankless position."

"It is sometimes!" Martha said with a laugh. "I ran for the position because I wanted to help the town—to keep the position here in Fremont. Some factions want to require a law license for Town Court judges but that change could easily mean we lose the position here, which would be another blow to Fremont because the money that the court generates is huge for the town. It pays for streets, it goes for projects that pop up here and there. It goes into a general fund and gets spent on what's needed. So, I'm training my replacement now."

It really amazed me how many of Martha's big life choices seemed centered around what was best for the town.

"You're retiring soon?" I asked.

"Yes, and I'm looking forward to it. My granddaughters are into all sorts of activities and I want to go see them, you know, run cross-country and play ball and swim and those kinds of things."

"Do you feel that you've had the opportunity to fulfill your potential?"

"I've been extremely blessed. I've had all kinds of opportunities given to me, like going to a wonderful college and continuing my studies after that. I was given the opportunity to be a judge, the opportunity to help my town as much as I could, to help the people as much as I could."

"Why do you think you had so many options?"

"Loving parents and loving grandparents are my top two. They never pushed me… I pushed myself. But they were always there. They always backed me. And I think that's so important. People need to be there for their children and grandchildren and back them up. Let them make their own decisions, even if they're not the decisions that you would want them to make, but you can help them if it turns out to be the wrong decision. My mom and dad and grandparents were always that way. And the judge who hired me gave me a chance because she already knew me; she trusted me. That's why I am where I am today."

On my way out the door Martha and her granddaughters all gave me a hug. I suppose uninviting and austere judges' chambers exist somewhere in Indiana, but I never saw one.

Shortly after leaving Fremont's town hall I came to a long, straight unpaved road with no telephone poles or power lines. Two-inch wide tracks ribboned the pale-orange dirt crackling beneath the bike's tires. It had to be an Amish community. Modest white houses with barns just behind them stood between corn and soy fields of moderate size. Front-yard kitchen gardens displayed rows of vegetables alongside tufts of pink, white, and orange flowers, which I assumed served some practical purpose. From my point of view, it seemed unlikely this austere community would cultivate the colorful plants simply for the joy and beauty of doing so.

Hearing the rhythmic thumping of hooves behind me I turned to see a black two-person buggy being pulled steadily closer by a single brown horse. As it drew near, I recognized the man and woman inside as one of the couples from breakfast. My stomach sent up an uneasy feeling. 'These people don't want you here,' it said. 'Don't bother them. You shouldn't be here, spoiling their pure lives. They'll resent you for it.'

They'll scowl at you.

In conscious rebellion against my instincts I looked over and waved as the couple passed beside me. Then I smiled and said in a loud voice, over the clomping of horseshoes:

"It's nice to see someone going my speed for a change!"

Both laughed, and the man said "Oh, yes, it is!" before waving and continuing on.

Maybe they were just decorative flowers after all

That simple interaction wiped away most of my anxiety. Now resolved to speak with Amish folks I greeted everyone I saw, hoping someone would show an inclination to chat. But they were all busy: the man coaxing two yoked ponies through a bare dirt field; the teenage boy in overalls and a blue long-sleeved shirt threshing tall roadside grass with a flat-bladed scythe; the man leading a huge draft horse with oblong muscles that rolled under a smooth, gray skin. Another buggy came into view on the road ahead of me. Three little girls, all wearing dark-blue dresses, sat side-by-side along a raised back seat behind two adults. I waved as they passed. The young girls all giggled, their white-bonneted heads whipping around in succession— one-two-three—to get another peek at the outsider on the odd-looking, overloaded bicycle. They must have seen me turn my head, too, before a light cloud of dust thrown up by the buggy's spoked wooden wheels obscured our mutual spectacle.

When the dirt gave way to pavement I knew I had probably missed my chance to speak with an Amish person. The few whom I had encountered seemed perfectly friendly, but that wasn't enough to make me comfortable rolling up to a random household without some sort of introduction. So I continued on, stopping at a small general store just up the road.

The first thing I learned there was that I had just crossed into Michigan.

"I hadn't known there were Amish people in Michigan," I said to the bespectacled shop owner.

"Oh yeah, they've been here for a long time," he replied. "They got too big in Pennsylvania—not enough land for everyone to farm—so they've been moving into different parts of the country for a while now. They like this area because it's flat and has decent soil. They're good people. Pretty much keep to themselves."

I asked the owner and his visiting friend if they knew of anyone in the community who might speak with me. They were listing off and debating various German-sounding names when the bell on the door tinkled. A plump, red-cheeked woman in a faded brown cotton print dress walked in, glancing at me with guarded, light-blue eyes before moving towards the register. She wore no shoes and had a white bonnet covering most of her dark-blonde hair. Six young children, all barefoot and dusty, shuffled in behind her. Quietly but quickly they moved single-file past their mother, their equally blue eyes darting along the store shelves before honing-in on the candy section behind me. Stopping there they formed a semi-circle in front of a box of Airheads Electric Blue Raspberry Taffy, whispering among themselves. A girl who couldn't have been older than nine held a toddler in her arms but still managed to slap away a small grubby hand snaking toward the treats from within the group. The mother asked the shop owner to use the phone, her accent and somewhat halting manner of speech suggesting English wasn't her first language. She spoke into the receiver with words I didn't understand. The shop owner walked over to the children, none of whom had moved since establishing their vigil.

"Okay, okay. Would you all like to have a piece of candy?"

Their eyes grew bigger, and every child nodded. All six of them.

"Alright, you can each have one piece. Is this the one you want?"

He pointed to the Airheads. More nods. As he handed out the candy, one by one the children said:

"Sankyu. Sankyu. Sankyu. Sankyu. Sankyu."

The little one in the girl's arms did not say 'Sankyu,' but appeared thankful nonetheless. They then exited the store with that sort of tense, heavy step children are forced into when fighting the urge to run.

The mother finished her phone conversation and began filling paper bags with groceries. The oldest girl had returned to help. As I can remember, they bought:

- » A 2-liter bottle of Mountain Dew
- » At least six packages of hot dogs
- » Three 2-liter bottles of Pepsi
- » A few bags of hot dog buns
- » Miscellaneous canned goods
- » A large package of brightly colored frozen popsicles

Their shopping list—well, it shocked me. It seemed so dull, unhealthy… normal. As the mother flipped through a wad of cash at the register I helped the girl load the groceries into a worn-looking cart attached to a horse outside. Threadbare blankets covered the wooden benches where the children presumably sat. Grabbing one, I was draping it over the food to keep off the sun when a jolt of uncertainty rattled my hands. Was it okay for me to touch their blankets? But the little girl smiled and softly said "Sankyu."

Inside, the shop owner and his friend had settled on the person I might interview: an Amish farmer named Chris Eicher. He ran a small produce stand and was used to strangers pulling into his driveway, the men said. They assured me he wouldn't mind speaking with me.

"I hope he's talkative," I quipped. "Those kids just in here hardly said anything to me."

"That's because they probably don't speak English."

Pulling up to the Eichers' farm I took my time dismounting and removing my gloves and helmet while waiting for someone to appear. I worried that looking around too much would be rude and so kept my eyes focused on the small baskets of corn, tomatoes, yellow squash, and other produce covering a rustic wooden table inside the small, partially-enclosed produce stand. A solidly-built boy approached, his flush, uncertain face suggesting he was big for his age. I told him about the project and asked if his parents might be willing to chat with me.

Within minutes every Eicher on the farm was either squeezed into the stand or clambering onto wooden boxes and tree limbs outside to get a better view.

Sensing it would be inappropriate to request a photo, I let my mind absorb the details of Chris Eicher's appearance. Like other Amish men of the area, he wore a hat (his was straw), overalls, and a long-sleeved button-up shirt. Warm wrinkles framed his light-blue eyes, which contrasted pleasantly with a dark beard showing only a few flecks of gray, and a clean-shaven upper lip just starting to reveal a shadow. His hands looked accustomed to work outdoors; his upright posture proved he was not broken by it. I described the project to him.

"Well, yeah, I guess I can talk to you," he said in a resonating and gravelly, but friendly voice. "What is it you wanted to know?"

Chris's pace immediately struck me as slower, perhaps more deliberate, than I was accustomed to. Most of his responses came only after a moment of silence.

"I don't know how much I can help you," he continued. "I only went to school through the eighth grade."

Chris's wife Anna told me they had 13 children between the ages of eight and thirty, with 22 grandchildren. I can't remember how many of those surrounded us but it may as well have been none. While I spoke with the adults there wasn't a push, a pinch… not even a giggle. The young ones just stared. I asked Chris to outline a typical day.

"Well, we get up and I have some coffee, go milk the cow and feed the livestock."

"How early do you have to get up?"

"Before sunrise… around 4:30."

To my ears it sounded like he said four-*surty*.

"The kids come out and get the eggs and then we all sit down for breakfast. Once chores are done I have time to work on other things like getting the produce for this stand or sewing blankets for buggies and calves. We raise and sell them for veal, and we raise ponies for work, too. They don't eat as much feed as the big horses, but if you get them good and tough, they'll pull just as hard."

"Really?"

"Well, they're just fun to have around, too," Chris said, with a half-smile.

"I think a lot of people wonder what language you speak and how often you go to church."

"We speak High German and Swiss in the house," he said. "The kids learn English in school. We go to church every two weeks and don't do business on Sundays. We usually have 25 or 30 families per church— probably no different than your lifestyle."

Chris's answer made me wonder if he knew about the mega-churches and star pastors who dominate Sunday morning TV.

"And you do all of this work by hand?" I asked. "I mean, you use animals to help but you don't use electricity or tractors, right?"

"No electricity, no gasoline engines, but sometimes we hire tractors from outside. I have a unit I can hitch a horse to that does different things like grind meat or run the saw. I can also hook the pump to it to get water."

So, the Amish were innovative and friendly to technology, up to a point—a point that stopped centuries ago. In contrast, my outside world was at that moment frantically pursuing the Next Big Thing. I briefly wondered where, or if, *we* might one day decide to draw the line. On my curling yellow notepad, I scribbled:

=hydrogen bombs

−*eugenics*

−*sentient artificial intelligence*

I asked Chris how the Amish interact with… what do they call the rest of us?

"We say *English*," he said.

The subtle flash of humor across his face told me Chris knew that sounded a bit silly to me. He continued.

"Anyway, I buy and sell things with people all the time. Sometimes if I need to use a telephone I go to my neighbors' house and they always let me use it. We pay taxes on our land like you do, but we don't vote, and we don't receive anything from the government."

"Are you worried that your lifestyle is threatened?"

"I worry some. Things are changing fast. Everyone uses money but it's basically worthless. They print it but it's not backed by anything. Something could happen and the system could just fall apart. We pray every day and hope for the best."

"But since you all are pretty self-sufficient, that wouldn't affect you so much, would it?"

Pause.

"Where do you think people would go if they got hungry?"

Chris's statement hung in the air, almost echoing, and I felt my head nodding. Of course, he was right.

Finally, I got to the questions I guess all *English* people want to ask the Amish: Why do you choose to live like this? Is there some spiritual or character benefit you get from living without modern amenities? Wouldn't it be easier to just connect to the grid… to be *English*?

"We're just plain humans, just like you guys," Chris said, dead matter-of-fact but without reproach. "We make mistakes. But this is the only thing I know. We've always lived this way. I wouldn't know how to do any different."

I sensed a simple but profound lesson embedded in Chris's answer—one I hoped might reveal itself after a few more miles of rolling contemplation.

Northeast of the Eichers' farm I came to Highway 12 where a sign said I had reached the ALLEN VILLAGE LIMIT. Below it on the same post a second sign read ANTIQUE CAPITAL. Forlorn buildings with open holes for windows sat empty along a tired-looking main street. Maybe the lower sign had been added by a well-meaning bureaucrat of the 'fake it 'till you make it' camp, but the town seemed to be buckling under the weight of unfulfilled expectations—more of an antique capital than a capital of antiques.

Further north in small industrial Litchfield things felt more upbeat. Medium-sized metal buildings with vapor-puffing chimneys sported crisp signs with names like METALDYNE and LIVONIA TOOL. A man walking from his truck into one of the plants pumped his fist in the air while giving me a hoot as I rolled by. At the bar where I stopped for lunch two old men were complaining about the flies, but the bartender didn't have a flyswatter because the health code prohibited it. One of the men let loose a series of guffaws, culminating with:

"Well, you might as well just open up the door. Just put a big ol' piece of rotten meat right here and just open up the door and let 'em all on in."

Leaving town I crossed over the South Branch Kalamazoo River, which looked like a creek to me. A man fishing from the bridge next to a NO FISHING FROM BRIDGE sign steadied his rod against the guardrail with one hand while sipping from a can of beer he held in the other. Beside his feet a yellow DeWalt construction site radio spotted with dried cement sang that tonight would be *a real good night*. He said he hadn't caught anything yet.

Arriving in Concord I circled around town a couple of times in hopes that something interesting would happen, but soon gave up and continued east along the Falling Waters Trail. Joggers, walkers, and cyclists were out enjoying the long summer daylight in a way that felt foreign to me—moving for the sake of movement itself, knowing exactly where they would sleep when they decided to stop.

By reflex my eyes began scanning the edges of the rail trail for a suitable camping spot. My thoughts, though, went back to Chris Eicher. I had essentially asked Chris why, given the hard work and tough lifestyle, he chose to be Amish instead of *English*. His response—*this is the only thing I know*—laid bare a foundational assumption in my question I had been only nominally aware of until then: I subscribed wholeheartedly to the notion that we decide who we are.

By extension, I had rarely questioned that we could one day up and choose to be someone different, or to at least follow a different path, if it suited us. From Chris's perspective, though, he didn't choose to be Amish any more than he chose his blue eyes. It was *who he was*—not something he could just change on a whim.

I knew I would never abandon my visceral belief in our power to set forth and forge our identity and place in the world. Nothing is more foundational to the American Dream—however burdensome, exciting, draining, empowering, and fraught with obstacles that path may be. But Chris and the barefoot children from the store taught me a lesson that day that I let sink in. If I ever wanted to even begin to understand folks like them, I first had to consider that their range of choices might not be as broad as mine, their place in the world not as pliable.

Ahead of me the trees lining both sides of the trail gave way to water. Emerging onto the path from a small parking lot, a gray-haired man said the lake was named Lime Lake because it's actually a pit left over from decades of mining by a long-gone cement factory. More pertinently, he also said a pizzeria with a cheap all-you-can-eat buffet was a mile or so north in Spring Arbor. I made a beeline.

Dusk crept up as I finished dinner. Pedaling back towards the trail I passed a ranch-style house with a broad, flat yard of recently cut grass. The front door was open behind a closed storm door, and through the glass I saw a lamp shining inside. Making a mental note I continued on to a dairy farm I had passed earlier just up the road. I flagged down a Hispanic man on his way out of a barn to ask if I could camp overnight behind the buildings. He shrugged.

"I jus' work here, man."

That was distinctly less than a "yes" so I headed back towards the house with the open door and rode up into the middle of the yard, dropping my bike in the grass where it could be seen from inside. With my helmet held humbly in one arm I knocked on the glass. Stepping back so that just one foot rested on the porch step, I put on a smile.

I couldn't know it at that moment, but meeting Elwin and Donna Johnson turned out to be the most fortuitous thing that happened to me on the entire tour.

My saviors Elwin & Donna Johnson
in a photo taken by their daughter in Spring Arbor

After getting past his mild astonishment, Elwin kindly offered me a camping spot next to his big shed in the backyard. I was staking-down my tent when he came outside and surprised me with another offer of kindness: he and his wife Donna had decided I would stay in their guest bedroom instead. I fumbled through my polite protests, but I could tell the decision had already been made. I was grateful for it. Once I was settled we sat down together in their living room to talk.

Elwin's grandparents had homesteaded and set up a branch of the Pony Express in South Dakota, while Donna traced part of her ancestry all the way back to the Mayflower.

"I was born here in Michigan during the Depression—1929—and grew up on my grandparents' 40-acre farm," Elwin said. "My grandma used to tell me about crawling down into their dirt cellar to escape the prairie fires that would sweep over the grasslands. Nothing could stop them. And how they would go for months over the winter without seeing a piece of fruit. She always looked forward to that first train in the spring that would bring oranges and things. My dad worked with the WPA[7] under Roosevelt. Even though he was a teacher, he rode the truck doing highway projects. It was a tough time so the government made work available for lots and lots of people. It was like a sort of welfare but welfare that you had to work for."

"Not like today where you can just sit and draw the money," Donna added.

"Then the War came along and my folks moved to Ypsilanti so they could both work in a plant that made B-24 bombers. I was coming to school here in Spring Arbor at the time, and that's how Donna and I met."

They went on to tell me how they both worked at an air conditioning manufacturer called Acme, and that Elwin had served in county government for over 30 years, in both paid and volunteer positions. He pointed to an empty space on their living room wall.

"Right there used to be a button I would push to blow the siren when I was with the volunteer fire department. I was on the night shift; if you had a fire during the day you'd call the barbershop instead. We had a lot of grass fires back then."

---

7 The Works Progress Administration (renamed the Work Project Administration in 1939).

I asked Elwin why he had gotten involved with the fire department and public service.

"Because it's helping people and it's helping the community. The firemen join and they do it free. And you're all together and you raise your families together. But also when a neighbor has a problem, it's just like the old days raising a barn—helping somebody. I just enjoy working with people to try to improve things, like when I chaired the State Commission on Aging."

"I guess you didn't make much money in positions like that," I said.

"No, but there were some perks," Donna said. "We got to travel a lot to the meetings and conventions, see things. We were at an annual meeting of the National Association of County Administrators in Washington on the day Reagan got shot. We were right there in the hotel."

She then stopped mid-conversation to apologize for not having cooked anything for dinner that she could give me—after already offering a warm shower and soft bed. I assured her I had just stuffed myself with pizza. She went to the kitchen and returned with two ice-cream bars for Elwin and me while he described changes he had seen in the area.

"What stands out to me are the changes in technology. When I was growing up we had no electricity on the farm until I was in the 7th grade."

"Do you remember getting it for the first time?"

"Oh, yeah. I watched my uncle Clarence do the wiring on the house. We were drying walnuts up in the attic and he climbed up there and put a hole in the ceiling and ran the wires. I was fascinated by it. We kept cooking on a wood stove for a few years but eventually bought our first electric stove and refrigerator."

Then Elwin said something else that amazed me.

"The other thing I remember is seeing a black person for the first time. My dad raised rabbits for meat—we probably had a hundred at the time. One day this man and this little boy came walking across the field to buy some, and they were black. They were the nicest people. I was probably in the 5th grade. I don't think I even knew black people existed. I can still see them coming across that field and just being shocked to see them."

It shocked *me* to be reminded firsthand of how much the world can change in a lifetime. I asked what changes they'd like to see.

"I'd like to see people be friendly, help each other if their car breaks down or something like that," Donna said. "Sort of like it used to be. When we were first married, we didn't have a car, and we liked to visit my family about 50 miles away. We would hitchhike to their house, stay the weekend, and then hitchhike back home. That was very common; people would pick you up with no problem. Now you're afraid to go out because of what's going on."

"What do you think has caused that to change?"

"A lot of it is because we don't have families like we used to," Elwin replied. "They don't stay together. The dad leaves them. If you are in a family, you're working together. I don't know how to explain it. It seems like we used to walk down the street and talk to each other, help each other, it didn't matter. Now everyone wants to get paid if they do anything. Don't know their neighbors."

"Are there things you see going well today?"

"Well, there are services for seniors," Donna said. "We have places where we can go and meet and do things. We have little league ball teams, community parks. Places to share things together. There's still a lot of community involvement here. It's like that bike trail you were on. Elwin was involved in getting that built, and now people use it all the time."

"What do y'all appreciate about this country?"

Elwin answered.

"In America, the opportunities are here if you want to do something and you're willing to put yourself forward and work to do it. You got the opportunity to get ahead. Sometimes I worry when I see so many people today who seem to sit around thinking they're owed something. I don't know how to change that. When I came along during the Depression we didn't have a thing. I know what being poor is, and I know what it takes to lift yourself up. We still have that in this country, that promise that if you want to work and get out and do things you can make something for yourself. But only if you put the effort in."

Day 21(a)
Tour interruption
Thursday, August 6th

REAL LIFE STILL HAPPENS

As soon as I heard Donna and Elwin stirring in the kitchen the next morning I went out and told them I had received a phone call overnight, and needed to get to the airport immediately for a family emergency. When I asked Elwin if I could leave the touring rig in his shed while I was gone, he immediately agreed. He then looked at Donna. She nodded.

"We'll take you to the airport, too. Get your stuff ready and let's go."

Sometimes you sort of see kindness coming, but this I had not expected at all. The nearest airport was a full hour away in Detroit, and Elwin and Donna weren't exactly spring chickens, so I protested as best I could. They would have none of it.

As we backed out of the driveway their son-in-law came roaring up in his truck, his face beet red. He sprang out of the door and demanded that his elderly in-laws stop right there, because *how could they even consider* driving off with me, a complete stranger, under these incredibly unusual circumstances?!?

I probably would have done the same in his shoes. But, once again, Elwin and Donna had made up their minds. God had put this test before them, they said, and they were going to do what they felt was right. Trying to defuse the tension I handed the son-in-law my driver's license so he could take a picture of it with his phone. That seemed to help a little bit, but in the end we drove off with him still standing in the front yard, glaring at us with frustration and worry.

I made it home without further incident and worked through the matter over the next few days.

Day 21(b)
Sunday, August 16th
Spring Arbor, MI → Perry, MI
60/1,087 miles
Local hospitality

ROLLING AGAIN

I called to inform Donna and Elwin I was headed back to Spring Arbor. Surprising me again, they insisted on coming to pick me up in Detroit, and by mid-morning on August 16th I was in their driveway replacing an inner tube, keeping my hands clean with a pair of work gloves Elwin gave me. He fired up his air compressor and then sat in a folding lawn chair drinking a glass of tea and chatting with me as I prepped the bike for the road. Their son-in-law came over to visit, too, his former worry replaced by an interest in the project and kind words of encouragement. When I was ready to go he asked that we stand in a circle and hold hands while he said a prayer for my safe passage through America.

The Falling Waters Trail soon dropped me into Jackson. Though deserted on a Sunday, the city's streets showed abundant signs of life. Downtown businesses like Miller's Shoes and Gattshall's Transmissions filled old brick storefronts. Advertisements in fading paint still clung to the sides of taller buildings. Clean, decades-old signs hung over many of the shops, having survived being merely timeworn and outdated to arrive at the eternal safety of antiquedom. Like Red Wing, Jackson had preserved its classic American Main Street and remained relevant to consumers—perhaps by fighting-off shopping malls in the 80s and 90s. Could it likewise survive the present battle against online retailers?

North of town along Cooper Street a tall structure loomed like an out-of-place lighthouse. Only when virtually beside it did I realize it was a prison gun tower. Pulling over near a series of razor-wire capped fences I positioned the bike for a photo, half-expecting to get yelled at, if not fired on. As I was lining up the shot I stumbled back into a tiny graveyard. The Pease Family

Cemetery contained some of the oldest tombstones I'd ever seen, most from the 1850s-60s. Up the road a stone marked the first Indian trading post in Jackson County. I wondered whether any of the Peases buried behind me had traded furs or other frontier goods there.

Mr. Pease was born the year after the United States won its independence and passed away likely wondering whether the country was lost

A few miles later my rearview mirror helped delay the chiseling of my own tombstone. When an elderly woman swerved her car onto my side of the white line, I saw her reflection just in time to abandon the shoulder. She drove right through my heat signature still lingering above the asphalt.

It was along a rural backroad in the middle of a particularly large and deserted group of fields that I finally crumbled under the weight of hundreds of miles of temptation. Checking to be sure no one was around (I looked both ways) I dumped the rig on the side of the road, slinked over to the crowded green cornstalks, and wrenched off a robust and perfect-looking ear. Strapping the contraband to the bike's rear rack I pedaled on, with that extra bit of pep that comes from getting away with something.

But karma has its ways. Finding shelter under a wild grapevine I methodically pulled away the husk and silk from the shiny golden center and went for a bite—nearly breaking a tooth on the rock-hard, completely inedible kernels. At least the pea-sized grapes all around me were half-decent.

Down the road I came across a small apple tree surrounded by windfall in that ugly state between crisp and cider. The fermenting fruits lent the air sticky, sour-sweet odor. It felt supremely hedonistic to grab a decent find, take one bite out of the best spot only, and then throw it away and grab another. Trying to clip my shoes back into the bike's pedals I found the cleats completely clogged with applesauce.

Near a town called Perry I encountered a message spray-painted right across the road in blue letters: IF I DIE ALL I KNOW IS THAT I'M A MOTHERF*****G LEGEND.

That rogue declaration to the residents of Shiawassee County struck me as both stupid (it's not *if*, pal) and probably the most legendary thing the idiot would ever do. Shortly thereafter I started at the sight of a roadside deer with an arrow shaft protruding from its flank. Standing up on the bike's pedals, I made ready to swerve or brake if the wounded animal came running at me, but it didn't move—probably because it was a rubber bow target.

In Perry, a group of pizza shop employees tried in vain to help me find a place to camp overnight. When I walked into the V.F.W. post up the road the bartender looked at me with wide, almost shocked, eyes that did not convey kindness. I asked if I could pitch my tent on the corner of their property. She said "Yes. Not a problem." That was it. I thanked her, and thanked her again a few minutes later when she walked out after closing the bar. Again, she said "Yeah, yeah, not a problem," in a quick, blunt sort of way. I wondered if the wall she threw up had been built over years of visits from unemployed or homeless vets appearing suddenly at her bar, expecting help.

After dinner and a shower at a nearby truck stop I returned to the V.F.W., timing my entrance into the parking lot so as to not be seen by passing cars on the main road, and keeping a low profile before crawling into my shelter hidden behind the barbeque trailer. As the night cooled, the dew grew so heavy it soaked even the gear stowed inside the tent with me.

It felt good to be back on the road.

Day 22
Perry, MI → Ortonville, MI
53/1,140 miles
Local hospitality
Rick Beardslee

AIN'T NO DAMN WAY

I rolled northeast along Lansing Road to the hum of I-69 traffic nearby. The sole bit of morning excitement was a two-mile leapfrog race the rig and I had against a mailman and his boxy white truck, passing him when he paused to deliver mail, and then getting passed by him between his stops. I tried pedaling fast enough so that he could fill only one mailbox at a time before I got around him again. I doubt the mailman found it as much fun as I did. In fact, I doubt he even realized we were racing.

To my mind, the name Flint seemed synonymous with the shifting fortunes of American industry. I wanted to see for myself how things were changing, and how that change was affecting people there. The treasurer of UAW Local 598 had invited me in for a visit. Growing up in the Southeast, I hadn't stepped foot in a union hall before, nor had I ever chatted with a unionized worker about organized labor. My conversation with Rick Beardslee was a superb introduction.

Rick Beardslee
at Flint's UAW Local 598

142

High-energy Rick began summarizing his background before we had even sat down.

"I been with the Flint Assembly plant for 31 years. Grew up in a small farming community about 40 miles away. Graduated high school and married my high school sweetheart; married 36 years last week. Got 3 kids, all doing great—none of 'em are a menace to society, you know."

He laughed, took a breath, and continued.

"I'm a hard worker—my dad taught me how to work. He was a blocklayer, and when I was 12 years old he had me mixing mud and hauling blocks for him. I wanted to be a builder but I couldn't make money at it at the time. So, I took a job at a machine shop, working five tens and going to school at night for machine and tool building. I think my starting wage was $4 an hour.

"Back then, Flint was still doing pretty well. The plants were going strong and employing something like 60,000 people. I would meet guys who were working for GM, and these guys were getting paid to go to school, and at the same time making three times what I was earning at my shop."

"For the same kind of work?"

"Yeah, oh yeah. That's just the difference between being on the inside and being on the outside. But I put in my application and got a call from both Buick City and the GM truck assembly plant. Buick City was a massive operation at the time—it might have been the biggest in the world[8]—but the best decision I ever made was to go with GM, because just a few years later Buick City shut down, and now it's completely leveled. There's nothing there."

"What's the GM plant like inside?" I asked.

"The assembly plant line is miles long, snaking back and forth inside the buildings. Parts are made all over and then the whole assembly process happens right here, from raw metal and frame at the beginning to a brand-new truck full of gas and rolling off with new tires."

I pressed him for details and we spoke for a good 20 minutes about the different processes and stations it takes to build a truck.

---

8 Buick City operated for over 100 years and was, indeed, the largest in the world until surpassed by Ford's Rouge River plant near Detroit.

"So, working at the plant is still a good way to earn a living?" I asked.

"Well, things have changed a lot," Rick said, "and a lot of it depends on how you get hired. Since the 2007-08 bankruptcy all the big three have been hiring people as temporary workers. Now you can have two guys working side-by-side on the line, one a temp worker and the other on the inside, with the guy on the inside making twice the wage of the temp guy and getting healthcare and retirement on top of that. It creates a lot of tension and division in the plant."

Of course it would. And the result is two groups of workers together in a union that no longer represents a unified body with perfectly aligned interests. Rick continued.

"In the old days our goal was to work hard, make some money and then get a comfortable retirement. If you got hired after 2007-08, you don't get a retirement. Now you put your money into a 401K of your choice and they'll match some of that. But the thing is, how do you put any money away into a 401K making $14 an hour and trying to raise kids living in Michigan? Nobody can do that. So, that's how this generation is missing out on that American Dream to build a house, have a family, have a retirement. It happens a lot where these kids come to work at the plant as a temporary worker, working for just a paycheck and nothing else, with hopes of getting brought in during the next round of hiring. They'll work here and go to school at night for years, and they're just getting strung along on that hope. And if they don't get hired, or have to quit, then they just wasted all that time for nothing but a paycheck, not building anything. We've been working on helping kids in that situation."

I asked Rick to describe his view of the state of the industry, generally.

"Well, it's tough because we've got all these foreign products coming in. I don't know if you want to get into that, but that ain't fair. They don't have to pay nothing to get their stuff over here but for us to sell our stuff over there, it's tremendous. And that stuff is all done in Washington, with the lobbyists and those guys making those rules. Sure, we've got Nissan and Toyota plants building cars down South and employing guys down there. They're making a decent living, sure, but the profits—the real profits and growth that comes from it—that's all going across the ocean."

"What's the solution to that unfair trade imbalance?" I asked. "For us to raise tariffs on foreign imports, or for us to make foreign countries take away tariffs on our exports? I guess I could ask if you think we should favor protectionism or free trade."

"Aw, man… that's a tough one," Rick began. "For me, I don't drive foreign cars. I try to buy American, I try to buy Michigan. I was raised that way by my dad. He'd say 'Why the hell are you going to buy those cheap boots at Walmart that came from China?' But I understand that times are tough, people ain't got money. If you're living in Michigan making $14 an hour trying to raise a family—there ain't no damn way."

"Can you think of some good aspect to importing foreign products into the U.S.?"

"You know, I do have to say that the foreign automakers helped us improve our own product. When they first started wanting to sell their cars here, they had to have good quality to get their foot in the door. And I still hate 'em to this day, but they did force the big three American manufacturers to raise the bar, take another look at engineering and things like that."

I asked Rick to describe what unions do for working people.

"The whole idea of unions with Walter Reuther in Detroit was to try to get the wages and the standard of living up for the blue-collar worker. We know we're not going to be millionaires. We're the ones who make all the stuff, work all the time, pay all the taxes, but yet are the ones who are always crapped on. You would not believe all the things that have been achieved by the unions since the 1950s. I'm going to give you this paper right here that lists our achievements. I'm going to get it blown up and put on my wall."

He handed me the leaflet, the contents of which I never did see (it disintegrated in a rainstorm that soaked my bags a few days later).

"Some people say unions and their bosses are just a bunch of crooks," I said, suspecting Rick would relish the challenge.

"That's definitely not the case. Was there some funny business in the past? Sure. Everybody is human. Money and greed can take hold of anybody. But you want to talk about crooks? Even though wages have gone down with the use of these temporary workers, have you seen the price of a truck go down? Never. I've seen over the past 30 years how it's always the little guy, the laborer, the worker, who's doing wrong—that's the story, at least. The whole system is skewed against the working guy. The people up top get hold of power and do everything they can to keep it and grow it. Why does the middle class, the worker, always have to be the one who pays the most percentage of his wage in taxes, limping along, while the guys on top have five Mercedes?"

"We already have a minimum wage," I said. "Do you think there should be a *maximum* wage, then?"

Rick winced.

"Yeah… I don't know about that," he said. "I know if you get involved in that then that takes away our capitalism. If they've done all of this on their own and they're smart enough to get it, yeah… but how much is too much? Because all that getting of what they got is costing the little guy something. It's tough. I mean, how many millions do those guys have to make?"

"Well, if you could make the call, what would it be? If you were emperor and could say the CEO of GM can only make X because that's a fair wage for someone who does that kind of work, what would X be?"

Rick laughed, in the release-of-tension way rather than the boy-that's-funny way.

"I… right… I… well… I always put it this way: I'm not Harvard or MIT educated, but if those people are making this huge amount, and I been bustin' my butt since I was 12 and I'm only making this little bit, what is different between them and me? But other people will say 'Well, that's how capitalism works; they deserve it.' I didn't say they didn't deserve it."

But it appeared to me he did say that, basically. Rick seemed torn between his class-conscious outrage at the wage disparity among labor and capital, on the one hand, and his strong libertarian instinct, on the other.

"What worries you, Rick? And what changes would you like to see to get the country on the track you want for us?"

"Well, I think one of the scariest things is that to keep the peace and to keep everybody happy you gotta have jobs and you gotta have money. These days you have to have dual income families—nobody can stay home and raise kids no more.

"Another thing is this immigration issue. I know our country is built on diversity and letting people in but I think we're getting a little out of hand with that. You've got all these different religions moving in. You can't be American no more. It's always *their* rights, but what about the Americans' rights? I think people should learn to speak English or go back home. If your culture was so good back there then what the hell are you here for? That scares me, I guess. I wonder what it's going to be like for my young grandkids. Having grandkids changed a lot about how I think. There's no reason for it to be a crazy world, and it won't be if we fix some things."

"How can we strengthen American manufacturing?"

"Quit buying foreign things. You know, the East and I call it the Left Coast, them guys don't care about Midwest manufacturing. That's just the way it is. And if you got no ties with America you'll buy all the Nissans, Kias, BMWs, whatever the heck you want to."

"What are the values that define us?"

"Number one, of course, is our freedom. To let that slip away, either by being overrun by somebody else or because of greed for money, I shudder to think of what could happen. Also, in America we still have smart people who know how to work.

"And also, for me, faith is important. I'm not an angel but I am a man of faith. And I've always had told to me that if you don't stand for something then you'll fall for anything."

"Do you see any solutions coming from Washington?"

"I think a lot of our politicians are just phony bastards, to be honest. They're just in it for themselves and their families to get lifetime benefits, insurance, that type of thing. It's just a shame that our country has gone to hell because of it. But I still love our country."

🚲 🚲 🚲

I did not see much of Flint, but my chat with Rick had been a hundred times as informative as anything my eyes could have told me. Having heard all about the inside of the GM plant, I pedaled up the road to get a glimpse of the outside.

Headed south from Flint past bungalows with postage-stamp yards, I was soon back on rural Michigan's unpaved roads, trying to enjoy the views of picturesque hilltop farmhouses. Motorists with pebbles tinkling in their wheel wells made that difficult, kicking up clouds of dust as they sped by. A busy highway then brought me into Ortonville, a small town that looked like the perfect place to stay the night if I could find somewhere to sleep.

It didn't take long. I was cruising my standard *let's see what happens* circuit along the town's main street when a man pulled up in a car and asked if my name was Rob. He didn't look too disappointed when I said "No," next asking if I was headed to the library. This time I was smart enough to say "That depends… " and that's how I found out this fellow Rob would be at the library presenting a cycling guide he authored.[9] I asked the man if he knew of "any place I might be able to stay the night." Dave was his name, and he said he'd help me figure it out, one way or another.

Of course, I went to the library. I enjoyed Rob's presentation as much as the touring rig seemed to enjoy being surrounded by a dozen or so bike-friendly people all admiring his setup. Afterwards, Dave invited me to his house, where he helped me hang my tent to (finally) dry out before we coated it and my bags with the silicone spray I had bought earlier that day. I met his wife Sharon and we all sat around their kitchen table chatting while I stuffed myself with the dinner Sharon had prepared. She refused to let me help clean up and led me to their guest bedroom once I began to nod.

If hearing from Rick and many others about the country's numerous problems made me feel down on America, the unexpected kindness shown to me again and again by folks like Dave and Sharon reminded me of why those problems were worth fixing.

---

9   Rob Pulcipher's book is *Dirt Road Washtenaw*, named for nearby Washtenaw County. Ron also wrote a Falcon cycling guide called *Best Bike Rides: Detroit and Ann Arbor.*

Day 23
Ortonville, MI → Dearborn, MI
47/1,187 miles
Couchsurfing/Warmshowers

FORDS ARE NOT BUILT IN DETROIT

Before leaving Ortonville, I crossed my fingers and stopped by the post office. A package there on the General Delivery shelf had my name on it. Inside was a set of flags to replace those I had lost near Chicago. I fixed up the new flagpole in the grass outside, proud to see the tour route flapping once again from the rig's rear end.

The stretch along Highway 15 towards Detroit was busy and narrow, making me doubly glad I had repaired my attention-grabbing banner. I was relieved to take a break in Clarkston, one of those nice towns that stay afloat with money from elsewhere, such that it can justify offering things like a cupcake shop. Further south the street lost its shoulder so I decided to ride along the broken, bumpy sidewalk. Stopping later I found myself a sandal short—one of my Tevas had vibrated off the rear rack. Probably a dozen times during the tour I had been confused and even incensed at seeing *just one shoe* on the side of the road, as in "How does someone lose *just one shoe?*" Now, I was that dolt. I slung the remaining, useless sandal into the garbage can outside a Subway restaurant.

A few roadside lakes offered the last vestiges of scenery before Detroit's outskirts began taking shape. I stopped to gather my courage with a milkshake at a hot-dog place in Redford. The lone waitress went back-and-forth between serving customers and reading her Bible. She said she had moved there from Jackson for a man.

"But I finally realized he wasn't ready for marriage," she said. "Now I'm just waiting for a signal from God to tell me what to do next."

I told her I had biked through Jackson, finding it to be a very nice place. Would she be moving back?

"I don't think so. People from Detroit are moving there—all the drug dealers and prostitutes. It used to be peaceful, but now it's ruined."

Goes to show how little you can tell by just passing through.

Cycling into the city was miserable. I received more honks over the five or so miles down Beech Daly Road than all prior honks from all other states combined. I finally let down my guard in the tranquil Dearborn Heights, where I had arranged to stay with a young couple through one of my apps. When I told them I would be riding past Detroit's Ford plant the following morning they politely corrected me: the plant is in Dearborn, not Detroit.

Another lifelong misconception crushed by bicycle tires.

Day 24
Dearborn, MI → Monroe, MI
56/1,243 miles
Campground
Rudy Nelson
Paul at the bus stop

HALLOWED HALLS; HOLLOWED HOPE

Detroit—from the French, meaning *narrow waterway connecting
two larger bodies of water*
Traditional synonym: *American auto industry*
Modern usage: *??*

Other than my recent trip through the airport, I had never been to
Detroit. I reminded myself that whatever brief experience I was set to have
there would, at best, offer just a small insight into the city's overweight role
in the nation's story. But when the rig and I rolled up to the south side of
Ford's Rouge River automobile plant, that sort of expectation-management
evaporated in a sense of awe. It felt like making contact with one of America's
vital organs.

I really enjoyed seeing Ford's Rouge River plant
but, of course, this carbon-free purist could only scoff

The compound was a sight to behold. Light 8am traffic allowed me to cruise along slowly while gawking at the railroad cars, tall chimneys, and manufacturing writ-large dominating the landscape. Small delivery vehicles hummed among stadium-sized buildings bristling with steaming pipes. Turning up the east side of the plant I crossed the Rouge River itself along a bridge with decorative turrets at each corner and a metal surface slippery with morning drizzle. The occasional metallic clang and the hiss of trucks' air brakes joined with a distinctly chemical, but not noxious, smell to saturate the senses with *industry*.

Leaving the plant behind, I caught sight of the UAW Local 600 union headquarters where I would be visiting with Rudy Nelson, a man who had been retired from automobile factory work for about as long as I had been alive. It surprised me to find the building surrounded by geometrically-adorned mosques, and shops with signs in the striking Arabic script.[10] I decided to stop by some of these places after the interview to see who might speak with me.

At the union hall several officers greeted me as I made my way back to see Rudy.

Rudy Nelson
in the Hallowed Halls of Local 600

"My father worked at the Ford Motor Company," Rudy told me. "He migrated here from the South during the time that Ford had come up with

---

10   I learned Dearborn, Michigan is home to the largest Muslim community in the U.S.

the $5 workday. He got hired in the early 20s and he then got me a job at the plant many years later in 1949.

"Just to give you an idea of how things have changed in the auto industry—I can remember working on the line in the Dearborn assembly plant back in the early 60s during the time when our industry just cared about one thing: *production*. Not quality—quantity. I remember the foreman saying 'I don't care if you fudge this up, just get it out of here!' We had great automobile designs, but the quality was never there. It wasn't until the Japanese starting making quality automobiles that our side said 'Wait a minute, nobody's buying this junk no more, so we gotta start putting out quality.' "

Rick in Flint had said the same thing a few days before. Rudy told me he remembered seeing the Japanese walking along the line, learning from Ford's processes.

"Why did they let the Japanese come see things in the first place?" I asked.

"That's a good question, 'cause they used to crawl all over the line. I could hardly do my work! I had one of 'em ask me—I was putting in the brake booster up under the hood of a car—and he asked me 'What is that you're putting in there?' I told him it was the engine."

Erupting in hoarse laughter, Rudy slapped the table with a loud pop. His jolly demeanor probably had a lot to do with the fact that he was still kicking high at nearly 90 years old. I asked how working conditions at Ford had changed over the years.

"We used to be known as the 'working poor,' " Rudy said. "We had a job but we weren't middle class. Then the union came in and bargained and negotiated, and really brought us up into the middle class. During my years there we won a pension, paid healthcare, and a good wage. And conditions improved a lot. My father worked in the foundry, and that was one of the worst jobs at the plant because of the shakeout. They'd take those engine blocks out of the core and just shake 'em and all that smoke and soot would go everywhere. I can remember my mother would have the bathwater waiting for him every day when he got home because you couldn't hardly see him he was so black with soot.

"I've really seen the process change in my lifetime. Back when I started, the Rouge River plant was like a small city. It had its own railroad, its own power plant, and water treatment plant. There must have been something like 65,000 people working there. We had a hundred guys at different stations just assembling the motors. But then automation came in. They started bringing in those robots and stuff. And when I left, you could be inside one of those buildings and throw a brick and not hit nobody [more laughter]. That's how much it dwindled down, you know, with the technology and the computer age, things like that."

Rudy went on to tell me how Ford had made the change from fitting the person to the job to fitting the job to the person. He said he remembered when 'ergonomics' was a new idea.

"These guys down in the plant today can't squawk at all, 'cause they got it made!" he said.

I asked how many strikes he had been part of.

"I think it must have been two strikes that I was on. And that's what I tell these young people working today. They all think that everything they have is because of the goodness of the company, without knowing anything about our struggles. I tell them they need to come here and walk down these halls, what I call the 'Hallowed Halls of Local 600.' They can learn about us being out there in the rain and the cold and the sleet, huddling around these big barrels of fire trying to keep warm. But I've always said that Ford's been good to me because they put a lot of bread on my family's table. Especially when they came out with that Mustang. We were working a lot of overtime back then, seven days a week. That was actually the last car I worked on before I retired."

"What have unions done for the country as a whole?"

"What they've done for the workers was done for the country. I know, especially in the black community, unions have really raised the standard of living for workers. For blacks, there couldn't have been anything better than a union membership. We sat together with whites at the union hall meetings, and—even though it took a while—they now have many black members at the executive level."

"What are some of the changes you've seen in the area?"

"I was born and raised in the city of Detroit, and then moved to Highland Park to raise my kids when I had my own family. It was like a small city inside of Detroit. This little town, it had about 35,000 people. It was a very rich city because they had three major manufacturers there, and that generated enough revenue that we had free junior college after high school. It was known as the city of white streets, the city of tree-lined streets. In 1957, 58, 59 it was awarded one of the cleanest cities of its size in the United States. But if you go through there today—it looks like Beirut. Torn down, burnt-out houses and things like that. It makes tears come to my eyes to drive through there. And it's pretty much that way all over Detroit right now."

Rudy continued.

"Now, what caused that? There's a couple of things, I think. First: freeways and malls were built. People in the city, rather than patronize local stores and things, started getting on the freeway to go to the mall where things might be a little cheaper. And the other thing that hurt the area was white flight to the suburbs."

"Were the neighborhoods more mixed when you were growing up?"

"Oh yeah. Back when my dad was working here, it was just a melting pot of people. Blacks coming up from the South to get a job, Europeans coming over, and everybody working side-by-side.

"To hear people talking about the prejudice in the South, I never saw that growing up here. We went to school with white kids. But over the years all those people left and a lot of the poor blacks, probably on some kind of government assistance, kind of let things get run down. So, I finally moved away because things were falling down and getting torn down all around me. I wasn't going to live out there in the middle of a empty field!"

"Why do you think poverty took over in those areas?"

"Back then, blacks didn't have access to the trades, to apprenticeships, like whites did. They could get a job in the factory, but they couldn't go beyond that. The union worked to change that, and it did in the early 70s. But, by then, some of those people didn't have any boots to pull up! I just can't say that if a person is poor that it's all their fault. I can't say that. I believe that if a person is given an opportunity, like everyone else, if given a chance, that they can better their lives and be productive citizens. I really believe that."

Rudy raised his index finger.

"But, like I said, it has to start with that chance. It just hurts me sometimes to know that we've got kids going to school and they're hungry. How are they going to learn anything and they haven't had nothing to eat!? I raised six children—five boys and one girl. And I realized back then that I couldn't raise my kids just in the confines of my own house and make them productive citizens. I saw that they were more influenced by their environment, and so I had to get out there and help make that environment better so that my kids could benefit from it. That's the reason I was involved in little league baseball, basketball, I was a Scout leader for eight years, I was the PTA president. I even tore down my garage and built a basketball court so that all the neighborhood kids would come to my backyard instead of being out in the street! Parents got to be involved in kids' lives, you know."

I asked Rudy to tell me a story before I left.

"I remember when I was fastening bumpers to the frame with bolts and I was in the hole my first two days—'in the hole' means I was going slower than the line. There was an old guy working across from me doing the same thing. On day three I had almost caught up and was getting close to his speed and I asked 'Hey Pops, do I got it?' He said 'Nope, you don't have it.' On day four I had caught up to him and was doing it fast and I asked him again 'Pops, I got it now, don't I?' and he shook his head and said 'Nope, you still don't have it.' And I thought 'What is he talking about?' Well, on day five I was working so fast I was two stations ahead and so I jumped over the line, ran and got a drink of water, and came back and kept working. Pops looked over and said 'You got it now.' "

A few blocks from the union hall I approached three older men sitting on folding chairs in front of a mosque to ask if they might chat with me for an interview. One of them, wearing the sort of skullcap I'd often seen worn by Muslim men,[11] didn't even look up at me and said something to his companions in a foreign language I didn't understand. The only man among the group who acknowledged my presence told me to come back later and maybe someone else would chat with me (which I took to mean *don't come back*).

Over the course of a few blocks the neighborhood transitioned from Muslim to Latino, with Hispanic markets replacing halal grocers. Like everyone else, I was curious about the deterioration of Detroit, and found myself evaluating the state of disrepair of every building and house I passed. But, so far, I had not ridden through anything resembling devastation. People went about their business among gritty buildings and streets, just like in other city outskirts. The corner of one block even boasted a community garden.

The subdued tempo downtown seemed out of character with the confidence projected by the district's opulent architecture. Buildings from an era before minimalism sported American flags, sometimes four or five flapping in a line. I took a seat at a new-looking picnic table in a central plaza full of food trucks to chat with whoever arrived for lunch. The first man to join me shook with Parkinson's disease. He asked if I had ridden through the city's blight, saying the area was not doing well. Echoing that sentiment, the young couple I spoke with next said the city's tax base had shrunk drastically, and what improvements were happening weren't being spread around equitably.

After five or ten minutes searching for a place to use the bathroom I rolled past a massive hanging fist memorializing black boxer Joe Louis, the world heavyweight champion from 1934-1951—a time when Motor City had been winning, too. But rattling jackhammers and hard-hat men directing traffic around new construction were not the sounds of a city stuck mourning its past or resting on its laurels. Detroit was not done.

---

11 My friend James later told me it's called a *taqiyah*.

How doth thou fare, O' Spirit of Detroit?

Headed away from downtown I passed a young white man with a buzz cut, probably in his mid-20s, sitting alone on a low wall at the edge of a parking lot near a bus stop. Wanting to hear one last Detroit story I pulled over and in my most nonchalant, small-talk voice said:

"Hey, whats up man? I'm riding this bike all over the place trying to get to know the country. What's going on here in the city?"

"Horrible. It's horrible," he said, his eyes dropping to the sidewalk.

His response threw me.

"Why? What's going on?"

"Drug problems, man. Drugs everywhere."

Noticing his missing teeth, I looked him over. He appeared unhealthy overall but not deathly thin underneath his black jeans and t-shirt. I wondered if he was actually miserable, or just a skilled actor preparing to hit me up for dope money.

"What kind of drugs?" I asked.

"Heroin. Crack."

"Are you having problems with drugs right now?"

"Yeah. Heroin."

"Why did you start using in the first place?"

"When my mom died I started. I was hurting."

"I'm sorry to hear that. And you're still on it?"

"Yeah."

"For how long?"

"Years."

"Where are you headed right now?"

"I'm going to see my grandma downriver. I was hoping you could help me out with some money to buy a drink."

There it was. But I sensed more than just a two-bit hustle.

"Well, I can't give you any money but you're welcome to drink as much of this water as you want," I said, handing him my scuffed red water bottle after removing the lid. He didn't hesitate, gulping down almost the entire thing before handing it back. He told me his name was Paul.

"Have you tried rehab?"

"Yeah, but there are more drugheads there than in the streets. It's all drugs."

His eyes teared up and he put his face in his hands.

"I don't even know where to go. I don't know what to do."

"Do you have a plan?"

"No, no plan. I'm just here going it day by day. I don't know what to do. I don't know what I'm doing."

Wiping his eyes, Paul looked up at me with a face that was despair manifest. I remained silent for a moment, realizing the stupidity of my initial binary assessment of him. I had been searching for clues to determine whether he was a junkie panhandling addict or a real person in genuine need of help. So stupid. Of course, Paul was both.

With that understanding, my empathy found a foothold.

"How much do you spend on heroin every day?" I asked.

"Twenty dollars. I haven't eaten in two days. I spent all my money on heroin."

Feeling a pang of shame for not thinking to ask if he was hungry, I pulled a bag of trail mix from my blue pannier and handed it to him. He started eating handfuls of it immediately, and continued to do so while we talked.

"Do you have a job?"

"No."

"Where do you live?"

"Homeless."

"So you make $20 a day panhandling or something?"

"Yeah, sometimes."

I just asked him outright: "Do you have to steal sometimes, too?"

"Yeah."

"Do you break into houses?"

"Nah. Shoplift."

"How much does it take for you to get high?"

"I don't even get high anymore. I just take it so I don't get sick."

"Have you tried some of that synthetic stuff?"

I was well beyond my area of expertise.

"Yeah, Suboxone, but I can't really get it. I throw up in the morning if I don't take heroin."

We spoke for a while longer. I did my best to give Paul a pep talk, conscious of trying to straddle the line between preaching from a position of ignorance and offering support to someone who desperately needed it. I said I was sure his grandma wanted to help him, but she wouldn't be able to if he wasn't willing to do the hard work to help himself. I told him he could probably find a job if he moved away and started somewhere new, emphasizing that *he* was the only person who could fix his life, which would be hard to do if he stuck around a place where his friends were addicts, too. I was just going off what I had learned watching my dad succumb to alcoholism, and what sounded right, mostly. I had never been addicted to anything, had never had to steal to get money, had never gone two days without eating, had never lived in the streets, had never been at the end of my rope. Whether I had the right to give any of that advice, I don't know.

I didn't ask to take Paul's photo or get his full name. He did want people to hear his story, though, in hopes that "even one person who reads this stays away from drugs."

So there it is.

Leaving Detroit to the south rounded-out my view of the city. A headwind blew dirt into my mouth that ground between my teeth while I dodged glass, trash, wires, crushed CO_2 canisters, and other broken junk all over the side of the road. A series of burnt houses, some with caved-in stairs, confronted me with evidence of what I had heard. Many of these sat next to empty lots where the wrecks had already been torn down. But the lots had been planted with grass, and the grass was mowed. And many of the other houses were fine, some with flowers, and all of the mostly black residents I waved to waved back. Further south I passed through a Polish neighborhood with small houses also adorned with flowers, where things looked okay. There was no swanky suburb on this side of Detroit, but I definitely didn't see too much of Beirut, either.

The storm cloud I had been racing finally caught up, but since my new rain jacket made me sweat I just let the rain soak me. At least 99% of the next 30 miles was unnoteworthy. The interesting 1%:

» an abandoned hospital (I think);

» a kid practicing karate in his front yard, who stopped practicing when I rolled by;

» a huge, decrepit building with a patchwork of busted windows that looked like a Tetris game;

» a massive landfill across from a cornfield;

» two nuclear power plant cooling towers, belching steam, surrounded by soy fields and barns;

» seeing the inside of a supermarket for the first time in weeks, which was overwhelming.

Once settled at the Sterling State Park campground I unsuccessfully tried to heat a can of soup directly on my campstove, and drank instant Starbucks tea made from a packet of powder someone had given me. I found out later it was loaded with caffeine, but at the time it seemed like I had been kept awake all night by roaring thunder, mosquitos that had somehow infiltrated my tent, and visions of a changing city with millions of stories I would never hear.

Day 25
Monroe, MI → Lindsey, OH
50/1,293 miles
Local hospitality
Richard Watkins & Nina Hayes

OBSTACLES & OPTIMISM

I awoke to the macabre scene of my own blood streaked across the interior of my tent walls—signs that my nighttime mosquito-swatting had been true, if late.

Lack of sleep and a heavy wind sapped the pleasure from what might have been a nice trail ride along Lake Erie's marshy shore. Even a Revolutionary War battlefield failed to rouse me. I finally gave up on an agreeable morning, figuring I'd try for a fresh start after lunch. For that, I stopped at a café in Monroe and asked the owner if he knew of someone in town who might chat with me for the project. Instead of a simple 'no' he said: "You're in the wrong place."

Rolling into Ohio offered little excitement except seeing the state's cool, nonconformist flag. The road through northern Toledo bisected golf courses salted with white-haired white folks—a world coming to a jarring end when I crossed some unseen, abrupt border into a neighborhood steeped in poverty.

Giant, once-beautiful gabled houses, some with spires, languished in states of disrepair. The area's few storefronts all hid behind iron bars. An 18-wheeler with only five or six wheels slouched in a vacant lot. I came to a side street my gut told me to avoid, so I did the opposite, turning down it in search of an interview. After a few minutes of wandering around I found a young couple sitting on the top step of a front porch, and said hello.

Richard Watkins & Nina Hayes
on Nina's front porch in Toledo

Richard Watkins was a rising high school senior; Nina Hayes, his girlfriend, was going to repeat her freshman year for the third time.

"What happened the first two times?" I asked.

"I don't like to deal with people," Nina said. "I like to keep to myself. I don't know... I just don't got that much motivation about school."

"So, you just don't show up a lot of days?"

"Yeah," Nina answered, "but I'm going to do way better this year. I know I am."

"Why the change? What's given you the motivation?"

Nina looked at Richard.

"Him. I never had nobody to make me go to school, but now I know I can go and have a friend there. Just having somebody with me will be nice."

"I want her to finish school so that she can have a life," Richard said, "have a career... so that we can live and not be failures."

"My sister dropped out of school when she got pregnant and now she has a two-year-old," Nina said. "I thought, if she can get away with not going to school why should I make myself do it if I don't want to? Plus, my mom works a lot and a lot of times she don't know if I go or not."

"How much does she work?"

"Yesterday she had a 12-hour shift. Sometimes I see her, sometimes I don't."

When Nina told me her family had recently moved to the neighborhood, I asked why.

"Because we needed a bigger house. There was six of us living in a small house with just two rooms. Now, it's me, my three sisters, my niece, my mom, my sister's baby-daddy, and now my boyfriend. And three dogs. And one of the dogs is pregnant."

"How is your family making it by with just one income earner?"

"My sister's baby-daddy works, too. And we get food stamps."

"Do the food stamps help a lot?"

Both Nina and Richard said "Yeah."

"If it weren't for the food stamps would you guys be going hungry?"

"Yeah," Nina said. "We almost do sometimes. I mean when we run out of stamps my mother always makes sure she has dinner for us, but that money could be going towards something else besides food. It could be going towards bills that we need to pay, or stuff that we need in the house or for school. But it's always the food that has to get bought first."

"What do you say to people who think there should be no such thing as food stamps?"

"Then they should try to live on our streets and see. They would understand if they could see how we're living."

"Why don't you try telling them how you're living, here in the interview?"

"Well, I'm not saying I live bad," Nina continued. "I have a good family; I love them; they don't treat me bad. It's just that we struggle a lot. We don't get stuff that other kids might get. We don't always get things we need; we don't ever get things we want. It's real hard to see my mom being stressed out over trying to take care of the family. I want to help her, but I can't get a job without the right paperwork, and my mom doesn't have the time to take me to do all that. And she doesn't have a car; she takes the bus to work, so she can't just take me there any time. She needs a ride, and most people will want gas money and she don't got it."

"Sounds like it's hard to get a foot ahead."

"Yeah. And every time we get a foot ahead something sets us back. The pipes bust in the house, we need something new, someone gets hurt, stuff like that."

"There are lots of people who say that if you study and work hard in America, you can get ahead in life. What do you both think about that?"

"I believe in that," Richard said.

"I believe in that, too," said Nina. "But it depends on what career you choose. Like Richard, he can draw real good, and he might want to be a artist. But that would take lots of time and money to go to college and he don't have that."

Richard said he planned on attending a local community college for engineering, if he can.

"What's your biggest obstacle to doing well this senior year and going on to college?" I asked him.

"Just doing it. 'Cause a lot of the time I feel like I can just wait until tomorrow. Like my homework don't got to be done; I can just wait until tomorrow. And then a lot of times it doesn't get done. And that's a lot of my problem, is the work. I just don't feel like doing it. My dad is hard on me sometimes, but I've finally started to realize that he just wants me to do better than he did when he was in high school."

"What other impediments to going to school and being successful do you two feel like you face?"

"If I feel like I can't look decent because I can't afford clothes and stuff, I don't want to go to school and have everyone see me," Nina said.

"There's a lot of shootings around here," Richard said. "A lot."

"The other day the boyfriend of one of my best friends died," Nina said. "He got robbed and they shot him."

"When people read about you and your story, what would you want them to know about what young people in your situation need to be successful—to fulfill their potential?"

"You need to go to school," Nina said. "For real, that's the only way you're gonna get out, get to be something. I feel like if you're struggling, or you're poor, that should be a real good motivation for you to want to go to school and get a good job, so you don't have to go through what your parents went through and you don't have to keep living the same."

"I personally feel like at our age we don't really need anything from anyone else, like in terms of people giving us things," Richard said. "I feel like the only people that can help us is ourselves. Alls we got to do is go to school. It's just up to us, in my opinion."

It struck me they said this just after Nina had told me she didn't feel like going to school. I silently hoped they, especially Nina, would see that irony, too.

"Some people think it's cool to get food stamps and get food for free," Nina said, "but it's not cool if you know the reason you're on them: 'cause you can't support yourself to buy your own food. I know my mom wouldn't use them if she didn't need them, because then she'd be taking them from somebody else who did need them. It's hard to get signed up for food stamps, especially since they're trying to drop that law that says you can't get food stamps if you smoke weed. And a lot, a lot, a lot of people smoke weed."

"How can they afford weed if they can't afford food?" I asked.

"That's actually a really good question," Nina said. "Some people feel like they need weed; a lot of people feel like that. I ain't gonna lie, I feel like I need it because of my stomach problems."

"But where do people get the money to buy pot if they're on food stamps? I don't understand."

"Hmmm… there's different ways to make money," Nina said. "You can scrap, cut lawns, fix somebody's house, do anything to make some extra money. And they feel like if that's money they made on the side, that's not part of their paycheck from their job, then that's money for them to spend on themselves. Because some people feel like they work so hard they deserve something. And they do. They deserve a little something, instead of being stressed all the time. And weed does help with some of that stress. It can help relax you."

"Do you think there might be more healthy, cheaper ways to deal with that stress, like going for a jog, playing basketball or something?"

"I guess so," Nina said, "but to do that you would need energy, motivation, and when you come home from work you're so tired you just want to relax. And with weed, you just need a blunt to relax you and that's just $5."

"Yeah, but think about it," Richard said. "It does add up."

Richard told me he needed his birth certificate and ID to get a job, but he didn't have the $40 it would cost to get the documents. When I challenged him he admitted the truth was he really just had trouble saving money; if he had five or ten dollars he would want to spend it on something right then.

"How do you guys feel like the system has treated you? Has it helped you or does it hold you back?"

"I feel like it really helps us," Richard said. "If it wasn't for the food stamps and welfare that people get, regardless of the people who use it and don't need it, those of us who do need it, it really helps us. Like, a lot. Who knows where we would be at if it weren't for that help?"

"So you guys don't feel like there's anything holding you back?"

"No, not really," said Nina.

"Because like I said, it's up to us," said Richard. "That's why I plan on going to school, graduating, and going to college. Then trying to make something of myself."

"You gotta get that ID first," I said.

"Yeah, I know man."

At a McDonald's on the edge of town I met a trucker who gave me some good advice:

"I'm going to tell you what my wife tells me when I have to go cross-country: enjoy the trip; enjoy the ride."

It surprised me how much I enjoyed the ride away from the city and into open land again. The rig and I cruised along with healthy soy fields to our right, a beautifully-mowed golf course on the left, and the cleansing, golden sunlight of the late afternoon behind us. Our cue to begin thinking about where to spend the night, that shift in color may also have signaled the crop dusters to return home. I saw one swoop down and vanish behind some cornstalks. When I stopped to peer after it down a grass landing strip I heard a buzzing behind me, turning just in time to see a blue prop-plane fly directly overhead. It landed just 75 feet or so from a simple metal hangar, whipping its tail around in a fluid motion and rolling right into the open door.

I decided to end the day in the small town of Lindsey, a place probably owing its existence to the railroad that used to run along the trail I had ridden in. Defunct warehouses and grain silos still lined the old right-of-way. The only place for food was a small grocery store I slipped into just before it closed. The Hispanic mom and daughter owners made me some fajitas and let me eat them inside.

My foil-wrapped dinner was almost gone when a lively woman named Ann entered the store. She had been cycling the trail herself and had seen the touring bike propped against a bench outside. Learning I was headed to her hometown of Sandusky she said she would be away but that her husband Mike would be happy to host me when I arrived the following day. She also promised to arrange an interview with a local. Exiting the store I didn't even have time to begin worrying about where I would sleep before a woman in a mini-van pulled up and told me her retired father-in-law had been on several bike tours, and lived across from her just down the road. She said I could camp on their land and get a shower at the house.

Flipping through scrapbook pages at the kitchen table an hour later, the father-in-law reminisced with his family and a stranger from out of town.

Day 26
Lindsey, OH → Sandusky, OH
50/1,343 miles
Local hospitality
Miss America 1963 Jackie Mayer

Through Highs & Lows
Do Your Best And Be Yourself

My morning coffee came served by none other than Lindsey's mayor herself. I felt honored, even after learning she served coffee to any customer who ordered it at her small downtown café. Outside, The Men Who Drink Coffee[12] made room for me at their table, and we chatted until I finished the refill the mayor had silently poured. At the cash register I learned one of those men had already secretly paid for my breakfast.

Hopping back onto the rail trail the rig and I enjoyed a smooth ride to tidy Fremont and then on to the likewise pleasant town of Clyde. I was there applying sunblock under a tree when a grade-school aged boy walking a small black puppy stopped to talk with me. Upon learning about my cross-country interview project he said "Oh cool" before spontaneously sharing everything he knew about his new dog and its short history.

Highway 101 carried me 10 rural miles northeast to Castalia, where I had lunch in a bar. The only other customer was a man who told me he had also done some bike touring, with his wife. When I asked if they were planning another tour he said probably not, since he had not seen her in two years.

Just up the road, Sandusky gave me the immediate impression it had been the perfect place to live 60 years before. Too big to be a town but on the small side for a city, its size probably had made it somewhere you could get anything you needed while the kids could still ride their bikes anywhere they wanted to. The classic and well-maintained municipal buildings downtown

---

12 If you're up early enough, you, too, might catch a glimpse of these groups of retired men (nearly always men) discussing the world's problems over coffee at gas stations, fast-food restaurants, and cafés. I encountered them in every state I visited. They are an American institution: The Men Who Drink Coffee.

spoke to a robust past behind the SPACE AVAILABLE and FOR LEASE signs now hanging in vacant shop windows. An older woman at the thrift store where I bought a two-dollar pair of bike shorts summed it up this way:

"Used to be on Friday nights when you came into town you would circle and circle and never find a place to park. But when they built that mall outside of town and people stopped coming down here to shop, it hit local businesses hard. Then when the auto industry slowed down that put the nail in the coffin."

While many of Sandusky's storefronts sat empty, the same couldn't be said of its boat slips. All types of pleasure craft bobbed in the Lake Erie marinas I passed on my way to see the rollercoasters on a spit of land called Cedar Point. Once there I learned that watching other people have fun from the wrong side of the fence is a poor choice of activity. Turning south towards Ann and Mike's house, I pedaled along a narrow causeway lined with modest vacation homes, and dunes made from grains of sand clinging to pallets, riprap, and old Christmas trees.

Checking my route while headed east on Highway 6 I saw the road I needed was just a stone's throw away behind a line of trees to my right, but to get to the turnoff I would first have to pedal a half-mile in the wrong direction (and then a half-mile back). A much quicker option would be to go straight through the woods, cross a railroad track, and then cut through somebody's yard.

My chance came a minute later at a gravel drive running across the tracks. Without stopping I peered to check whether my road was visible on the other side. It was not, but I almost—almost—took the shortcut anyway. At the last moment I chose to keep rolling along the highway to avoid winding up at someone's back door by mistake. As I turned my head away from the tracks my ears casually registered a low humming in the background. Bursting through the trees a split-second later, a train barreled past at full speed. The conductor had given no whistle or warning at the unmarked crossing. Had I decided to make that turn I know I would not have stopped at the tracks to look. It would have been the touring rig's final mile.

That story was enough to prompt Mike and his friend to take me to a bar in town for local brews and the famous Friday-night fried perch. We then returned to Mike's house for the interview he and Ann had arranged with a very special Sanduskyite.

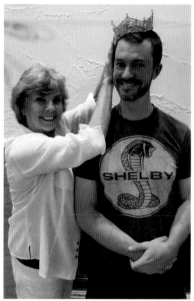

Miss America 1963 Jackie Mayer
placing her crown on the undeserving author's head (she insisted)

"I grew up with a mom and dad who loved life," Jackie Mayer began. "They were very motivated, and they encouraged all of us to have goals and go after them. So, they supported my enrollment at Northwestern University and my dream of becoming an actress, and when I got the opportunity to travel the country and sing with Fred Waring and the Pennsylvanians, they supported that, too. My roommate during that tour was Miss Minnesota 1960 and she told me that if I wanted to raise money to pay for school then I needed to go into a pageant affiliated with the Miss America Foundation, since it was a scholarship organization. So when our tour ended nine months later I decided to sign up for a pageant in Sandusky that was put on by a local radio host at a restaurant. I wasn't sure if I was going to win but I had a 50/50 chance, because there were only two of us!"

She laughed.

"But I won, and then I competed in the Miss Ohio pageant and I won that one, too. So, a few months later I was in the Miss America 1963 pageant, and I just decided I would do my best and see what happened. I really thought Miss Wisconsin was going to win. She was so kind and considerate. Well, she was my runner up."

I had never in my life spoken with a pageant winner—let alone Miss America—and hoped my questions were not going to sound… well… dumb. Jackie seemed like a gracious woman.

"Was it difficult to transition to being Miss America? It sounds like it was pretty quick."

"It was. It was really quick. Usually, women are in five or six pageants before they ever win a state. After winning I traveled around the country doing lots of different appearances. Every single day was a different appearance. I'd get up early in the morning, take a flight someplace and on that same day be doing a couple of things like luncheons and going to hospitals to meet with the patients and staff, and then doing press conferences, and a dinner and then maybe visit a pageant that night. It was busy, busy, busy. But it was a fantastic time. I grew up. Being Miss America just made me, I think, more aware of everything. I couldn't get sick, but if I did get sick I couldn't show it! I had to be happy; I had to be smiling."

"What do you remember most about that year?"

"My favorite part of it was the hospital work—visiting with the patients and just seeing their eyes light up when I put the crown on their heads. It was so exciting to see their joy. After that, I returned to college and then transferred to Washington & Jefferson where I was the only female student there. I finished my last courses at Pitt and finally graduated in 1968. And the only reason I was able to do that is because of the $10,000 scholarship I had won in the Miss America pageant."

"Is that your answer to some of the criticism we sometimes hear about pageants generally?"

"Yes. The Miss America pageant is a scholarship program. We have women who are not only pageant winners, but who are doctors, and lawyers, and veterinarians, and judges… I mean it's amazing who our sisters are. We do have a sisterhood, and they are just outstanding women."

"How do you think preparing for and participating in pageants affects a girl's development into a young woman?"

"It can be tough on young girls who don't win, because often times these kids aren't prepared to deal with the disappointment. Unlike losing a softball game or something like that, in a pageant you're on your own. I think these young girls are better off out on a playground somewhere getting dirty. Once they're a little older, I think competing in pageants is a very good way for a girl or young woman to develop character."

"So, tell me more about what you did after Miss America."

"Well, I went to school, had two children, and then had a stroke that left me paralyzed on my right side and unable to speak. I was 28 years old. It was devastating. At first, I didn't know what had happened to me. My son was five years old, and my daughter was just nine months old, and I was unable to care for them. I had to learn how to speak again, starting with my ABCs."

"Wow," I stammered, momentarily stunned. I had not been expecting to hear anything like that, and was unsure how to continue—so I just asked the first thing that came to mind.

"Do you remember what it was like not being able to speak?"

"Yes. It was frustrating, very frustrating, because you want to say something but you cannot get it out. And I still have some of that, where I cannot think of a word. So, often times I just sort of explain the word and it comes to me. It took me about five years to start talking well again. My son was my teacher. He would teach me the ABCs and counting. As my daughter started learning to talk she and I would have speaking competitions. Sometimes she would be able to say something better than me! Anyway, we worked very hard at it, and my family taught me that if I was afraid to fail then I would never try and I would never get better. So, I told myself that I would try and be prepared to fail, but that eventually I would get it right."

"Did you ever get to the point where you said 'Okay, this is as far as I'm going to recover' ?"

"I don't think I ever felt that way. One time after many years of not seeing my doctor I visited with him and he told me 'Jackie, I can tell you now, you have a lot of guts. I *never* thought that you would recover as well as you did.' And I told him 'You gave me hope.' And that's what people need. You need hope. You have to be realistic, but you have to have hope."

Jackie's inspiring message resonated during a moment of silence. She continued.

"So, that's one of the reasons I started working with stroke survivors, a lot of whom can't talk at all. I visit with them in long-term care facilities and hospitals and just try to talk with and communicate with them, even if they can't always respond. And the people here in Sandusky have been so appreciative of that and good to me. They even named a highway after me. Route 2 is the Jackie Mayer Miss America Highway."

"You went from being on top of the world to being in what I'm sure was an incredibly tough situation. How did that change or shape your outlook on things?"

"I think that there was—there is—a purpose for my stroke and for me getting better. I believe in God, and I believe that he brought me back... he helped bring me back. I had to do it myself. Sometimes people will say 'You can't walk, you can't speak.' But you just have to go at it and say, you know, *I'm going to walk*. Of course, it depends on the damage, too, but so much rests on you and your will to improve. Now, my life has meaning because I can help other people. My parents taught me that you have to give of yourself to others to have real meaning in life. And also believe in God, because he will help you get through all the situations that you face."

"One last question, Jackie, that I just have to ask you. If you could give two or three basic pieces of advice to a girl or young woman preparing for a pageant right now, what would they be?"

"First of all, be yourself. You can't put on because the judges will know that you're putting on. I… well… "

Jackie remained silent in thought for a few moments. It made me happy she wasn't just giving a stock answer to a question she had undoubtedly heard before.

"Judges will score you differently. You might get the highest score with one set, and then get first or second or third runner-up with the next set. What you should work for is to be proud of the effort you've put into it. So, be yourself and enjoy the moment—and do your best. That's all you should ask of yourself, and that's all anybody else should ask of you."

Day 27
Sandusky, OH → Cleveland, OH
57/1,400 miles
Paid lodging
Dayna Clingain

A Chance To Blossom & Bloom

After a rough morning ride along Highway 6 I needed a break. A park picnic shelter offered a brief respite until a group celebrating a kid's birthday set up the party at a nearby table. *Well, at least I'll get to chat with the moms and play around with the kids,* I thought. But the group orbited around me as if I had deployed an all-in-one impregnable force field and invisibility cloak. I kept smiling, but no one smiled back.

In quaint Vermillion the restaurants' savory smells tempted me, but because of my careless sandal mishap a few days before, I resisted. I had decided to "earn" the price of my replacement footwear by not eating at restaurants until I had made up the cost, subtracting $6 from the ledger each time I skipped a decent meal and ate ramen or something cheap like that instead.[13]

Under a perfect sunshine at Lorain's Lakeview Park people strolled among busts and other monuments scattered around a superb rose garden. Other parts of the town had looked run-down and neglected in a way that contrasted sharply with the cheery public space. I guess the park tenders had realized that no matter what state the world is in, one can always stake out a little piece of it and make that beautiful.

Arriving into Cleveland along Lake Avenue was as smooth as it gets. Houses lining the clean street looked older but well-kept. A spotted deer hopped around in one front lawn. It took little effort to imagine the area as an upscale neighborhood in the city's industrial heyday, with a curved-steel car parked in each of the concrete driveways now faded with time.

---

13 An insane scheme that quickly crumbled under the weight of excuses and exceptions.

The city's jagged edge served as an extended homage to rugged work. Riveted bridges spanned waterways filled with gruff-looking ships and barges. In comparison, the atmosphere downtown at first seemed frivolous, with its passive parks and young people acting the fool on their way to the next bar. I circled around for a while before stopping at a mobile hot dog stand where a white, middle-aged woman with graying wispy hair and deep blue eyes stood feeding a stream of hungry Clevelanders.

Dayna didn't want a photo
but Cleveland didn't mind

"My family came to America from Northern Ireland when I was just a child," Dayna Clingain told me while tending her cart. "I know this might sound silly, but I believe my family was led here by God protecting us from what happened in Northern Ireland a few weeks after we got here. It was Bloody Sunday. British troops fired on and killed a group of Irish protesters. They marched right down the streets where we had lived. It tore the entire city apart."

Dayna recounted a tough childhood that she escaped at 20 years old by running away with a much older man. She got pregnant, bounced around from place to place, and tried to go to school.

"I was two months shy of finishing my degree in media relations in New York when I had to come here to Cleveland in '89 and help my mom try to recover from a double mastectomy followed by a failed reconstructive surgery. After that, I got my nursing certificate and worked until a few years ago. I was fired from the nursing home where I worked, even though I had done everything right. My last job was taking care of a woman in exchange for a place to stay but that didn't work out. I ended up homeless for a while."

I asked Dayna how Cleveland had changed during her time there.

"What stands out to me is that there are no homeless people around the Tower City area like there used to be. When I first came to Cleveland, the people on the 22 bus line were all poor, poor to the extent that they literally all stunk. I used to make little personal hygiene kits and give them out to the people on Public Square, with soap, a washcloth, little Nivea creams, a hand towel, toothbrush, and toothpaste. They weren't very expensive because I used the little sample sizes."

"Why did you do that?"

"I just felt in my heart that I wanted to help people. Many of those people out in the street needed psych meds; many of them needed a lot of physical care. It was just really bad. Now there are more services for them, more shelters, and they're getting more of the care they need."

A man approached and asked directions to the liquor store. Dayna didn't miss a beat.

"Next block on the right. I'm an inner-city minister also. I was trained in crisis intervention at the Inner-City Renewal Society here. I've worked with the church in telecare, which offers counsel to people who are abused or have other problems. God leads them to us so they can call in for help. I helped start that."

A young, unfit-looking black guy had approached and was checking out the rig. He started throwing out questions about touring while I chatted with Dayna, saying he was thinking of doing the same thing. I sort of blew him off at first since I was in the middle of an interview and also, I think, because my subconscious told me he didn't look the part of a serious cyclist. I never would have noticed my assumption had he not asked something that seemed particularly insightful. I've since forgotten what it was, but it made me pause and consider that his interest might be genuine. When I finally gave him a chance I saw him looking at me with an awe and admiration I would expect reserved for some sort of hero. I might have been the first cyclotourist he had ever met, someone who was living his dream. And I had basically ignored him because I was busy, because he was chubby and, I have no doubt, because he was black. I had never encountered a black cyclotourist—but that was no excuse. I felt ashamed, changing my demeanor immediately to convey an encouraging enthusiasm about his plans to tour on his own someday. After a few more questions he thanked me and went on his way. I watched after him for a moment, feeling certain I saw a bounce in his step. In my gut I noted a deep sense of something. It might have been hope that this young man's big bike tour through America would be just as rewarding and open and inviting as mine had so far been.

I turned back to Dayna.

"What changes in the city would you like to see?"

"In the middle of the city square in Northern Ireland's Londonderry —it's called Ebrington Square—there are steps down to public bathrooms. And there are chambermaids who keep the bathrooms clean and maintain them. It's a lovely idea, a great idea. When they were doing work on Public Square here I was hoping they were going to put in something like that because now if you try to go into a restaurant people will tell you there's no public bathrooms. At the Renaissance Hotel when I was selling hot dogs on the corner over there they knew who I was and so they let me use their bathrooms there. But there are so many places that frown on people trying to use their bathrooms. We could really use clean public bathrooms where everyone could go. Another thing is that Cleveland's shelters close very early. I've seen people not make it in time and wind up huddled in the doorway in the snow like little chicks together trying to keep warm.

"Also, I would like to see all of these empty buildings on St. Claire Avenue turned into something productive. There are people who are very talented, who know how to cook. The economy is down, why not give people a chance? I wish people could go up to a business that's closed, like a coffee shop for sale, and make a deal with them. 'Cause I know I'm going to do it. And I'm going to say to them: 'Your store has been sitting there empty for how long? You've had virtually no business there, so there's no income there. Now, if you allow me to open the doors for a month, I would give you a percentage of what I earn. And then you can begin to charge me rent once I get a steady business going. Now would you go for that, or would you not?'

"I think that's fair, and it would begin a business. It would put people to work. You see, Cleveland is a very wealthy city, but in all of its wealth, it is very poor. Because wealth is no good if people don't stop to think. There are empty buildings all throughout the city that could be used to give people places to live, places to work. Because if you give someone a chance, it allows them to blossom and bloom, whereas they might not have ever had that chance before."

Like that of Detroit, central Cleveland's almost regal architecture appeared conceived and delivered in an era of abundant self-confidence and aspiration. The large grassy courtyards, Fountain of Eternal Life, and imposing columned buildings suggested an admirable but naïve certitude that the city would continue marching forward steadily and boldly. Spanning an entire side of the Cleveland Public Auditorium, a chiseled inscription read:

A MONUMENT CONCEIVED AS A TRIBUTE TO THE IDEALS OF
CLEVELAND—BUILT BY HER CITIZENS AND DEDICATED TO
SOCIAL PROGRESS, INDUSTRIAL ACHIEVEMENT, AND CIVIC INTEREST

A few blocks from there a man about my age flagged me down. He had done some cyclotouring himself and we swapped a few stories. When I told him I was still looking for a place to stay the night he said his trick was to call up police stations and say he had no money and nowhere to sleep. Often, he said, officers would arrange for him to stay in a Motel 6 paid for with "ministry" money—funds earmarked to help battered women and children escape for a few days from an abusive situation at home. I made note of his advice only as a reminder that exploring the country by bicycle does not automatically immunize one from making selfish, morally repugnant choices.

The Rock and Roll Hall of Fame
I had been expecting a giant guitar or lightning bolt

After visiting the pyramid-shaped Rock and Roll Hall of Fame I spent a long time flipping through my phone, trying to find free or reasonably-priced accommodation. I finally accepted I had just two options: an expensive hotel room or a park bench. The latter would have left me tethered to the bike all night while chilly, vulnerable, dirty, and ill-at-ease. Still, it felt like a blow to the gut to pay $130 for eight hours of peace when I had a tent and sleeping bag within arm's reach. Recalling Dayna's stories then punched me even harder. I was agonizing over a choice multitudes of people didn't even have to begin with.

Exiting the hotel lobby to explore Cleveland's nightlife I met three gray-haired ladies on the sidewalk out front. **Debby, Shari, and Peggy**— sisters, if I remember correctly—were headed out for a big night on the town themselves. They said I could join them so long as they got a mention in any eventual book. It was a deal I couldn't turn down, and I'm a man of my word.

Day 28
Cleveland, OH → Kent, OH
45/1,445 miles
Couchsurfing/Warmshowers
Jim Zeller

—BOOM—

The rig and I enjoyed a trouble-free departure from Cleveland, passing through the familiar band of run-down neighborhoods before coming to a cleaner area of restored brick storefronts. The sign announcing SLAVIC VILLAGE sent me into a snowballing inquiry, trying to imagine what it might have been like back when that name had meant something to people, back when the white Slavs had their own neighborhood, when they were not 'just Americans.' It brought to mind that not so long ago *white* was not the uniform, all-encompassing ethnic designation it is today; that the word *diversity* had once been a substantive term meaning 'diversity' instead of mostly just a safe synonym for 'not Caucasian.' I figured these days one didn't have to be a Slav to live in Slavic Village, and wondered which of our present ethnic or racial labels, so sacrosanct today, would be the next to get emblazoned on government-funded signs hanging cheerily above people having brunch at sidewalk tables.

Not far south of the city I met up with the Ohio & Erie Canal Towpath Trail. Riding up a pedestrian bridge, I heard a yell to my right.

"Are you going to Canada?"

Two young men stood in a building materials storage yard below.

"Rochester, New York," I yelled back.

"That's awesome bro!" one of them replied, lifting his fist into the air.

I returned his gesture. It was one of many quick, enthusiastic displays of encouragement I had received over the past month. But this one raised a question for the first time: What is it about forward motion that Americans love so much? I didn't come up with an answer, but I knew whatever the reason, this man and others like him counted on me to keep moving. So I did.

Murky water flowed towards Lake Erie at a snail's pace through the 185-year-old trailside canal. Once a state-of-the-art feat of engineering, the waterway served several decades as the region's primary artery of commerce, a fact richly illustrated at a superb little National Park Service interpretive center I came across by an original canal lock. I arrived just as a park ranger was opening the floodgates with a metal hand-wheel to demonstrate how the system had worked in its day. I felt a little guilty for stealing his audience's attention with the flashy touring rig and its squeaky brakes.

Soon, the canal was replaced by the free-flowing Cuyahoga River. The spectacular summer day steadily drew more and more cyclists to the trail, from the dangerously-fast spandex class to oblivious families riding three or four abreast. My extra-wide, lumbering setup forced me to focus hard on avoiding a collision. A guy zooming around someone else nearly hit me head-on. But, even with my frayed nerves, I refused to acknowledge the little voice in my head saying riding the highway shoulder would be safer than trying to navigate a recreational bike path.

A couple of hours later I arrived in Kent, bumping over a set of railroad tracks before emerging into a new-looking, crisp downtown. My remaining sunlight budget favored stopping for a beer before heading over to explore the virtually deserted Kent State campus.

Jet-black squirrels darted around the hilly grounds while I searched for the memorial to those killed by National Guard soldiers in 1970, in what became known as the Kent State Massacre. I first found the area where the young people had died. Now covered by a modern parking lot, the exact spots where the perforated bodies came to rest had been cordoned by lighted posts, with the decedents' names engraved in stones set in the corners. A short distance away, the memorial itself bore an unassuming but heavy message chiseled into its flagstones:

INQUIRE   LEARN   REFLECT

Jim Zeller
enjoying a summer evening out in his hometown of Kent

My host for the evening had helped me connect with lifelong Kent resident Jim Zeller, who took a break from listening to live music with friends to chat with me outside a downtown coffee shop. He had just retired from 30 years of work as a salesman for a local paving company and was now doing odd handyman jobs for friends, mostly just to keep busy.

"I was born right near here in 1951, and I've lived in Kent most of my life," Jim said. "Both my parents grew up in Kent. Dad started at Kent State and dropped out immediately to go fight the Germans, and after that he became a schoolteacher, and my mom took care of us and the house. With twelve kids in the family we had to live pretty frugally growing up!"

"Wow, twelve kids! Do you remember wanting for things?"

"Oh yeah, I wanted for everything. I never went hungry, but at the same time I never had nice clothes, shoes, things like that. The best clothes I got were hand-me-downs from my cousins whose father was a doctor. I learned carpentry and handyman stuff when I was young because we had to build additions onto the house for the growing family. I lived at home until I enrolled at Kent State."

Looking down at the coffee cup in his hand, Jim fell quiet. A few moments passed. His abrupt silence confused me, but I also kept quiet, waiting for him to continue. His eyes, not moving from his cup, began welling up. I asked if he was okay.

"Yeah, just getting a little emotional."

"What's wrong?"

"May 4th, 1970. I was a freshman."

I hadn't known Jim had been there, then.

"I didn't know any of the students who were injured or killed," he continued, "but it's a really big thing for people from around here."

I had no training and little life experience in discussing traumatic events with people, but it seemed like Jim wanted to talk about this. The memorial came to mind.

Inquire.

"Were you part of the movements or demonstrations?" I asked.

Learn.

"Not at all," Jim answered. "I came out of class and there was an army sergeant standing by the door with a machinegun. The demonstrators stood on one side, the army on another, in kind of a stand-off. I stood around and watched the whole thing, like tons of people were doing. Then the National Guard started marching on 'em, shooting tear gas. Some of the demonstrators were throwing teargas back. I decided to leave the scene. Five minutes later as I was walking across the front of campus I heard the shots.

"I thought it was fireworks. I had seen all the soldiers there with guns but, when I heard all the shots, I thought... somebody's let off a string of firecrackers. I couldn't believe that it might be gunshots. I don't think I was alone in that.

"Anyway, a few minutes later every ambulance in this part of Ohio was on its way. Lots of sirens. I went down to the pool hall where I hung out and heard on the radio that students had been shot. And everything that happened over the next couple of days is part of history: closing down the school, a curfew."

"Students were protesting the U.S. invasion of Cambodia, right?"

"That was basically it. It started down in the bar district with some rabble-rousing. Then on Friday night somebody decided to drag a barrel out into the middle of the street and set it on fire. Some of the kids ran through town and broke some windows. And then the big thing was on Saturday they burned down the ROTC building on campus. The National Guard moved in on Sunday, and the students were shot on Monday."

I asked Jim how he thought that experience might have informed his worldview. He shrugged and said "I really don't know," without looking up or offering anything further. Time to change the subject.

"Tell me about your views on America today. How do you feel about our direction, generally?"

His slouch and long face instantly dissolved in a laugh.

"I'm kind of a leftist liberal, I guess, but I don't think you have to be a leftist liberal to think that it might be a good idea for everyone in the country to have access to good healthcare, just like every other advanced country in the world. You don't have to be a liberal to think that students should have free college education as opposed to $100,000 in debt, like my daughter and son-in-law are facing now. And I don't think you have to be a radical leftist to be pretty upset at the enormous income disparity in this country. If you look at the statistics you see how crappy the minimum wage is today compared to what people were earning 50 years ago or whatever. The top 1% has wealth in the multiples of what everyone else has."

Jim seemed like he was warming up, so I decided to challenge him with some provoking questions.

"Why is income disparity a problem? Isn't it true that the rich people are the ones who are smarter and who work harder than others? Don't they deserve to be richer?"

"The statistics on income disparity are sickening," Jim replied. "It's the same here as it is in Saudi Arabia or Iran or somewhere like that. When you got people with billions and billions of dollars, like the Koch brothers, trying to get what they want, they're usually going to win."

"But much of the country is conservative," I said. "They like things as they are, or maybe it's more accurate to say many would like to see things be as they believe they were at some point in the past. You seem more focused on things you want to see change."

"For a liberal, keeping things the way they are, or trying to make things the way they supposedly were, is the biggest problem. I look back at FDR, for example. He created Social Security, put millions of people to work, enacted all of these reforms and changes that we take for granted today. I bet the conservatives of his day hated his agenda, but we see today how many of the changes he set in motion have been good for America."

"I've heard people say that some of those changes have resulted in a welfare state that is abused by able-bodied people who live off of government checks rather than working for a living," I said.

"I've got religious fundamentalist conservatives in my family who spend a lot of time complaining about having to work for their money while people on welfare supposedly live like kings for free. I don't know if Jesus Christ was God or God's son or just a regular person, but I do know what his message was, and I believe in it: turn the other cheek, do unto others, love your neighbor. The Religious Right doesn't seem to believe in the part of Christianity that teaches about helping those less fortunate."

I asked Jim if he could explain how members of the same family could end up with such diverging political views.

"I know lots of very, very bright conservatives, including those in my family. So then if they're so smart, how can they believe some of this s***? Well, I think it's basic psychology, the chemistry of inspiration, the way the human mind works. It's similar to the process that can cause someone to join a cult. A pretty normal person one day and then—BOOM—all of the sudden they're over the edge. I've read articles that explain how the brain can fool itself into thinking it's having some sort of revelation, when what's actually going on is a chemical process that provides feedback and rewards. I don't know what causes that initial choice but once you decide that you're a little bit right or left then—BOOM—everything you do after that is just supporting and rationalizing the belief you chose. And you're so sure of yourself."

"You're talking about confirmation bias."

"Exactly. And also the way that so many people have problems just not knowing all of the answers, being unsure of things. They *need* to know. Like with my agnosticism, I guess I'm okay with the fact that some things are really unknowable. I think that viewpoint makes someone less susceptible to dogma or groupthink, and more open to changing your mind."

It was fully night by the time Jim and I wrapped up. My host's home lay just outside of town. Along the shoulder of a dark but mercifully calm Highway 251, the silent miles offered ample time, and solitude, to REFLECT.

Day 29
Kent, OH → East Palestine, OH
57/1,502 miles
Urban camp
Ailis Murphy & Will Benton

ANOTHER GO, TOGETHER

I was cruising down Industry Road before many Buckeyes left home for work. A man walking his dog waved and said hello as I passed and then, from behind me, shouted: "Have a safe ride!" Hoping to interview someone at a monastery my map showed in the area, I felt my heart jump at a set of castle-like towers rising from the woods. They turned out to be grain silos. I never found the abbey.

Healthy fungus near Limaville

Plan B was to search for an interview in the nearby town of Limaville, but the only sign of life there was an old mobile home serving as the town's post office. I kept moving. A raucous flock of blackbirds, surely numbering in the thousands, fussed and darted over my head among the trees of a

wooded stretch near a reservoir. After miles of fields and barns I pulled up
to a place called the Greenford Cupboard, where I met owners Ailis Murphy
and Will Benton.

Ailis Murphy & Will Benton
in front of The Greenford Cupboard

Ailis sat down with me at a small table while Will tended the counter
and the couple's baby slept. She had always enjoyed cooking, growing up
helping her mom and grandma prepare meals.

"So, I decided I would enroll in culinary school, and went off to
Kentucky for my first semester. A few months later I got pregnant. I thought
about quitting school, but my family helped me realize I needed to get my
degree more than ever now that I had a baby coming. Well… the baby ended
up passing away when I was nine months pregnant. He had leukemia. So, I
came back home and had him and we had his funeral. That was actually six
years ago today."

Ailis fought back tears, and I am sure I did, too. The story, the timing, everything was sudden and surreal. I felt like an intruder in her grief.

"After that, I didn't want to do anything. I kept failing classes, didn't want to get out of bed, that sort of thing. I was trying to cope with the depression, not really understanding what was happening. But I still knew I had to finish school, for him. That was the whole point. It took me a little while but I did graduate with an associate's degree in Culinary Arts."

"Was the baby's father around at the time?"

"He was. But things kinda fell apart after that and so I moved back here and stayed with my parents for a couple of years. I met Will and got pregnant again, and the day we told my parents my dad walked out of the room. Five minutes later he came back and was like 'Everything happens for a reason. The Greenford Cupboard is up for sale and I've always wanted to buy it, and I know you guys could make it work.' That was one year ago. So, we decided to give it a shot. I quit my job and we came straight over here and got to work fixing it up. I had my big belly at the time, and Will had a broken hand, all wrapped up with pins. It was… a challenge."

Something about Will, who was in earshot, told me he had led a tough life. Maybe it was the tattoos on his arm, or the way he wore his hat. I asked him if he had been in a fistfight, half-joking.

"Yeah, with a door. I learned my lesson."

In solidarity with Will and every young man who has ever made a testosterone-fueled poor decision, I showed him the missing pinkie knuckle on my right hand.

"What types of challenges did you face when starting a business while pregnant?" I asked Ailis.

"It was really, really hard," she said. "I went into labor a month before my due date while I was making this guy a sandwich. He was like 'How long is this going to take? I'm really in a hurry!' And I'm in tears; my contractions are five minutes apart. We had to close down the store and I had her two hours later. They released me from the hospital two days after that and I came back here and worked. I didn't take any time off. She sat back there in her little car seat. People would ask 'Aw, how old is the baby?' and I'd say

'Oh, she's four days old' [she laughed]. It works out great having her here with us while we work. I guess until she starts walking!"

Ailis asked Will if he wanted to take a break and chat with me. They swapped places and Will picked up.

"Yeah, it was overwhelming at first, and it took a lot to realize, for me at least, that it was all for a good thing. I realized that stress and worry aren't really beneficial in the long-term, but a business is."

"So, you've got tattoos," I said. "I think it's fair to say someone who didn't know you might look at you and think 'This guy doesn't look like a friendly neighborhood deli-owner,' at least not out here in rural Ohio. Don't you think customers might find you a little intimidating?"

"Yeah, exactly. I definitely know what you mean. And you gotta make up for that with your personality."

He pointed to a nude woman on his arm.

"Like this one. I got it a long time ago. I try to keep it turned away from the customer, or sometimes I'll even take a marker and draw a shirt on her. Some people are a little stand-offish to me I think because of my appearance but once I talk to them and let them know I'm not a big jerk or something like that they usually warm up pretty well."

"Did you have a time in your youth when you were kind of running around with a rough crowd?"

"Oh yeah. All the way until I was 22-23 years old I was involved in drugs, not making money the right way, you know. I won't sugarcoat it. I was a pretty crappy person, and I've done some crappy things to people that I love, and I still feel really bad about that. Luckily, they still love me back. All I can do now is focus on today and try to make sure they know that it wasn't personal towards them and that I grew up and now I'm here for them. When you have kids you realize that you have somebody depending on you, and there is nobody else for them to count on."

"Do think you would have turned your life around without having children?"

"If you got the drive inside you to change yourself, then you're gonna change yourself, you know what I mean? Like, you actually have to want it.

If you're out there doing the wrong s***, you gotta decide in your soul that your life and the lives of the people that count on you are more important than that, and that these people need you. Be it a child or a significant other or anyone, maybe even a pet [he laughed]. Anything can make somebody decide that they need to do better."

"Do you have any advice for young guys who might be in the position you were in, who are maybe thinking of making a change?"

"Yeah: if you have a vision just hold on to it and keep fighting until you actually achieve it. And don't give up. You know, there will be days when it seems like it's all for nothing, and those days are really tough, but the next day could be the greatest day of your life. So, if you stick it out and keep trying and keep working, it does get better. Stuff's always going to happen, but you gotta have bad to appreciate good. It's just *keep on fighting*, you know? That's it. With everything."

"You've got a lot of responsibilities," I said. "Family, a new business; you've got to smile at people and say you're sorry when they complain about a cold sandwich. That's probably not how you used to live life. What benefit do you get from all of this? What makes your life better now than it was before?"

"Now I have a family to appreciate. That's my number one joy, is holding them two girls whenever we get a few minutes together. That's it, that's what it's all about to me—just being close to them."

"Is the joy you feel from that greater than any kind of joy you used to get from things in your life before having a family?"

"Oh yeah, for sure. There's no comparison. This is like a spiritual fulfillment. The other was like a physical, material fulfillment that doesn't last forever. I think that relationships go beyond the world we live in. I think that afterwards they continue to exist, and it's really important to me that focus be put on them."

"Was that transformation for you painful or hard, or did it come pretty naturally once you became a father?"

"It wasn't really painful but there was a lot of anxiety. A lot of unknown stuff, kind of jumping into things in a sink-or-swim fashion. So, that was the tough part, dealing with that anxiety."

"Are you optimistic now?"

"Definitely. I'm a lot more optimistic than I used to be. I see a good picture at the end of the tunnel, I can say that."

"What do you worry about now, as a business owner and a family man?"

"Really, with this place and with the baby, it's the immediate things that keep me occupied. Instead of worrying about things that might happen, you have to take care of the things that pop up and need attention right now. That's where it's at for me and Ailis."

Battling a series of hills and trucks out of Greenford I charged towards the East Palestine post office, where a package of replacement gear sat waiting for me in the General Delivery box. I had until 4:30pm, and was cutting it close. Throwing a private tantrum at 'those lazy, early-closing government offices' I checked my mounted phone to be sure I was on the fastest route. In mid-scroll I ran smack into the rear bumper of a parked Jeep Cherokee. Hard.

The shock of the impact jolted but did not injure me. After a moment or two of collecting myself, I looked up and heard the words "Oh, crap" escape my mouth.

Through the Jeep's rear window I could see someone sitting in the front seat. Someone sitting there, in the middle of the day, in the only parked car I had ever hit in my life—I mean, *how likely was that*? Before I had time to make any decision about what to do, the young bohemian driver leaned out the window and asked if I was okay. I felt my muscles relax.

Looking over his Jeep we didn't see any damage. I apologized, thanked the young man for his understanding, and began pedaling away. Turning the handlebars a few feet later I watched my red water bottle shoot out into the street from its under-frame caddy. The collision had bent the rig's front forks so much that the wheel fender no longer cleared the bottle lid. When I stopped to disassemble and evaluate everything, the driver walked over to check on me. He had been parked in front of his parents' house, and his retirement-aged father soon joined us.

Dad was a friendly, surly fellow. He told me I was in a town called Columbiana, home of the late Harvey S. Firestone, founder of Firestone Rubber Co. I inadvertently set him off when I mentioned the early-closing post office.

"Those #$@! lazy government workers are all the #$@! same. All of those bastards over there in Washington and Congress need to be hung!"

His pronunciation of words like 'those' and 'over' caught my attention.[14] The *o's* sounded to me like *oe*, like a cross between "oh" and "ewww." It likewise caught my attention that I had found Dad's unique accent more noteworthy than his angry demand for the mass execution of our political leaders.

Down the highway a lifted pickup rumbled by with a large Confederate flag flapping from its bed—the first one I had seen on the tour. Another Dixie banner hung from the front porch of a small house nearby. I assumed these people did not have deep family roots there in Southeastern Ohio; otherwise, their Union-soldier ancestors would be turning over in the grave, and the flags would be espousing something other than 'heritage.'

Arriving in East Palestine I cast a sour glance at the closed post office but figured the municipal police station would still be open, at least. I looked forward to some friendly local assistance in finding a place to set up camp. When I strolled through the station's front door a man in a polo with an embroidered badge glared up at me from his desk like I was Public Enemy No. 1.

"*Can I help you*? You need to go back outside."

The officer's acerbic attitude was so unexpected I assumed he had made some kind of mistake. Ignoring his orders I explained my cross-country cycling tour and asked if he knew where I might be able to pitch my tent. This time he looked at me like I was an idiot, said no, and again barked that I go outside. I didn't budge—but not so much from defiance. I believe it was more like 'Pardon me, but there must be a misunderstanding here. You're supposed to be helping me.' Soon, every officer in the station was shooting unfriendly questions and challenges my way. I finally accepted that the East Palestine police force was either having an agency-wide bad day, or it was

---

14 My first contact with what I later found out is called the *yinzer* accent of the Pittsburgh region.

the least helpful, most ill-tempered, poorest excuse for a group of public servants on Earth.

The sole female in the room must have surmised the best way to get rid of me was to answer my question. People sometimes camped under a bridge on the south edge of town, she said.

Those vague directions brought me past a cemetery where I decided to set up instead, before the last of my daylight was gone. I pitched the tent and poked around outside for a while, indulging in the sensations one can access only when alone in the evening, trespassing at the edge of a graveyard a thousand or more miles from home. The half-moon seemed brighter than it should have been, backlighting tall clouds into striking 3-D relief. Bats swooped and chirped over the open field of mowed grass. A propeller plane visible only as flashing red dots buzzed overhead. A dog howled somewhere but never barked. Faint decorative lights twinkled in front of nearby gravestones. A shotgun blast erupted in the distance. A light breeze blew from the north; it was the first time on the tour I had felt a real chill. Finally, I crawled into my sleeping bag without the slightest doubt I was entirely alone.

A minute later that certainty crumbled. Through my tent wall I saw one of the gravestone lights vanish and reappear, vanish and reappear—as if blocked by something passing in front.

No stranger to the mind-tricks and hallucinations that go with solo camping, I sat up and peered through the translucent nylon to be sure I wasn't willing a wraith into existence. Sure enough, like a will-o'-the-wisp the light came and went in quick, irregular intervals, very much unlike its constantly-lit companions. My mind filled those gaps of darkness with human legs advancing towards my camp, leaving me two choices: sit, cower, and wait; or get outside and immediately confront whoever it was. I palmed my knife, stepped out into the grass wearing just my boxers, and headed directly at the light with a deliberate gait. I had advanced a few steps when a breath of wind rolled across my back just as I caught another movement from the grave. The gray moonlight painted the outline of a small American flag fluttering gently in front of the headstone, hiding the dim light for just a moment before revealing it again.

After a while my heart rate slowed enough for dreams to come. I was watching my late father walk unhurriedly towards me from a tidy burial plot, his hands in his pockets, when he vanished in a bright flash. Opening my eyes, I found the tent awash in light. A police cruiser was beaming a spotlight at me from the drive encircling the graves. Thrusting my hands out of the tent, I motioned for the officer to wait a moment, and reached for my shorts. The spotlight then shut off. Had it been one of those discourteous town cops I would have figured his bulb had burned out. But this was a sheriff's deputy, so I instead assumed the officer was affording me the courtesy of privacy while I got dressed. Grabbing my license I approached the car, keeping both hands away from my waist. At the officer's open window I explained myself and promised to be gone first thing in the morning. When he asked if I had gotten permission to camp there, I lied and said yes.

"Alright, no problem then," he said. "Just checking for kids messing around out here, you know."

The remainder of the night was uneventful.

Day 30
East Palestine, OH → Pittsburgh, PA
54/1,556 miles
Couchsurfing/Warmshowers

Steel City, Still?

Finishing an early McDonald's breakfast an hour before the post office opened, I loitered at a table charging electronics and eavesdropping on The Men Who Drink Coffee. One of them said a boy in his granddaughter's class had upset her by stealing some of her drawing pencils. He then shared the exquisite advice he had given to her:

"I told her to tell him: 'I'm going to smack you so hard your mother's gonna feel it, and then I'm gonna smack her, too.' "

After retrieving my package I pedaled southeast, the undulating topography certifying the rig's first trip into the Appalachian foothills. Zoning into NPR and BBC podcasts I laid down the rolling miles until I felt hungry again, right near an exit ramp and a sign for ALIQUIPPA. That turn led to one of the most disturbing sights I would encounter on the tour.

I had stumbled into a post-industrial wasteland. Looming beside the ramp, a decrepit brick building with empty eye-socket windows urged the visitor to move on. Broken bottles and torn mattresses littering the floor inside revealed a structure empty, but not abandoned. A demand graffitied across the nearby underpass was about the only thing suggesting hope hadn't been completely abandoned, either.

A languid line of trucks crawled both ways through a large gate just up the street. A sign said the place used to be the Aliquippa Works of the Jones & Laughlin Steel Corp, which at one time employed over 14,000. Many of those commuting workers had likely arrived each day via the nearby train station, a boarded-up but still striking building with a decorative brick work and terracotta-style roof obviously designed by architects, instead of accountants.

On the opposite side of the highway, Aliquippa proper was the closest thing I had ever seen to a ghost town with people still there. I pedaled along the deserted Franklin Ave. in disbelief. Virtually every storefront in town sat vacant, with pieces of tape and torn bits of poster pocking the empty windows. A few trucks and pedestrians, and an independent café, seemed to be all that stood between the town and unmitigated desolation.

Sitting in a motley mismatch of chairs outside the café, several black men seemed to be idly passing the time. One of them, holding a plastic grocery bag, stood up and approached a pair of white hipsters lunching at a sidewalk table. The young couple pursed their lips and nodded politely as the man produced a pair of small speakers and a metal shampoo caddy—an actual shampoo caddy that you hang on the showerhead—and launched into his pitch. I stopped and secretly observed to see if the man's presentation would work, ready to request his contact information for some future joint business venture if it did. Alas, he didn't clinch the sale.

From Aliquippa south, the roads grew steadily busier and more frequented by heavy rigs. A large industrial island in the middle of the Ohio River teemed with trucks. I lucked out one wasn't on a bridge with me when a gust of wind yanked my rain jacket from the bike's rear rack and deposited it into the middle of the lane. Burly tugs with tires hanging from the sides of their decks pushed loaded barges across the water below. Chimneys spiked the sky everywhere. Back on the mainland I caught sight of two spotted, reddish deer with glistening noses, staring at me from wooded cover a few feet to my right, as rumbling dump trucks jarred my other side.

Getting into Steel City challenged my own mettle. A bus nearly ran me over before I ascended another bridge along a narrow pedestrian walkway littered with dirt and trash. I had just picked up speed on the downhill side when my right front pannier caught against a concrete outcropping, jerking the front wheel and throwing me into the bridge's chain-link fence with a loud jingle. I readjusted the rig's crooked handlebars before continuing on.

A mean-looking neighborhood across the river did not seem like an ideal place to leave the bike unattended, but I needed a break. A teenager just inside the entrance to a small urban supermarket unlocked the door when he saw me coming. My first thought: 'Gosh crime must be bad here if they have to keep the doors locked.' I was chatting with the friendly cashier when someone said to her "Ready to go home?" I then realized it was just closing time, and the door-unlocking exercise had been the same 'just this one last customer' routine taking place at that same hour all over the Eastern Time Zone. That instant and pure insight into the invisible workings of bias, both generally and in my own head, illuminated how an assumption can be both perfectly rational and distorting of one's perceptions at the same time. Sitting outside on a chipped concrete staircase sipping Coke I contemplated how best to navigate the world utilizing all of my instincts, experiences, and learning, without being blinded by them. I ran out of soda before figuring it out.

Like in Toledo, decades of neglect had left streets lined with shells of formerly elegant homes. A steep hill brought me down to the strangest place: two old brick buildings in a sort of gulch surrounded by cliffs and shaded by two bridges soaring overhead. One of those was built right into the solid stone, with rock morphing into mortar and block at different places along the natural wall. At other spots, the exposed cliff faces looked like massive stacks of inch-thick stone pancakes—hundreds of layers of pancakes. Just around the corner from that anomaly a veritable fortress slumbered behind impossibly tall walls. A line of geese waddling down the sidewalk beside the structure softened its austerity, a little bit. A man there told me it was a federal prison "where people go when they're bad, so don't be bad." He walked away chuckling at his own wit. Between the penitentiary and the Ohio River I found a bike path that brought me all the way downtown.

A view of Pittsburgh
from the spot where the Allegheny and Monongahela Rivers merge to form the Ohio

It must have been dorm move-in day at one of the local universities because young adults towing around photo-taking parents flooded the public spaces downtown. Navigating the crosswalks proved tough, and pausing to stare at my map or soak in the city without getting in someone's way was nigh impossible. Seeing an empty plaza sandwiched between two tall buildings I ducked through the gates and stopped to get my bearings and breath. I shared the shady little refuge with a handful of passersby and the bronze statue of a businessman, while a few yards away, Pittsburgh buzzed.

Once adjusted to the urban pace I set out again in search of an interview, but no one wanted to talk with me. People were either hurrying home from work, sightseeing, or trying to hustle the first two groups. Turning towards my host's house I began a series of climbs that left me exasperated a city would pack so many hills into itself. The slow going gave me time for long stares at the numerous old brick smokestacks and grimy foundry buildings, some of which displayed the name of this-or-that brewery, or arts center, or shared workspace. Regardless of the specifics, each sign said basically the same thing: wholesale change.

I finally arrived, huffing and puffing, at a small two-story rowhouse. A young man opened the front door.

"I guess no one told you cyclists call it *Hill* City," my host said.

After a quick change of clothes I hopped back on the bike and followed him to a beer and burger joint where we met up with his likewise bike-nerd friends. None of them knew anyone employed in the steel or heavy manufacturing industries, but they had no problem listing acquaintances who worked in a sandwich shop or tech startup. I enjoyed my evening with those guys, but at the same time I think we all recognized how thin a bond we shared. Those early twenty-somethings just *hanging out* worked odd jobs, lived together in groups and shared bongs, drank the cheapest beer on tap, biked because they loved it and because they had to, and weren't yet concerned with saving money or building a career. They lived for the moment, not worrying too much about the other side of the hill—while I often struggled to think about anything else.

Day 31
Pittsburgh, PA → West Sunbury, PA
47/1,603 miles
Local hospitality
Alan Brzezinski
Mark Fallen

Pouring, And Throwing, The Heat

A few days earlier I had emailed a local nonprofit for help connecting with a steelworker. The good folks there put me in touch with former crane operator Alan Brzezinski, who had retired outside of Pittsburgh but agreed to chat with me by phone. After a relaxed getaway from the city I searched for a place to make the call.

Before the bike tour I had always taken for granted the luxury of having a quiet, private spot to use the phone. But over the past few weeks simply hearing and being heard had been a struggle—forget about avoiding strange background noise or eavesdroppers. I had added "hassle-free phone call" to the list of things I missed from normal life.

A fast-food place in its mid-morning lull seemed like my best bet for a peaceful conversation with Alan. Taking just three steps inside the door I froze in my tracks, reasonably certain I had just heard the word "diarrhea" from somewhere near the cash register.

"I've had some stomach problems," said an elderly man in a Members Only jacket, apparently on familiar terms with the cashier.

"Yeah, I have too," replied the heavyset woman behind the counter. "Some people here have even had to miss work because of it. It's been really hurting us."

A sudden craving for a bear claw and carton of milk pulled me back outside and towards the Dunkin' Donuts next door.

Alan Brzezinski (in a photo sent to me by his wife, Denise)
supporting striking workers at a plant in Vandergrift

"I was a C student," Alan told me once our call was connected. "Wasn't fit for college and couldn't afford trade school. But this was 1971. The steel industry was booming; there were lots of jobs. I went to work at the United Engineering foundry. My first paycheck was $186 take-home."

"What was Pittsburgh like back then?"

"It was nothing like it is today. When you would come through those tunnels, the skies would be bright orange from the furnace fires. It was a sight to behold. It was sooty. And a foundry was a dirty, dusty place."

Although I had heard Rudy in Detroit talk about a foundry, I didn't *really* know what one was.

"It's where you pour molten metal into molds to make stuff—we call it *pouring the heat*," Alan said. "So, first you make a mold with sand. Then you insert the nails to keep it together before baking it in the oven so it gets hard. Then you pour in the heat and let it cool. Sometimes you insert a 'hot pot' into the mold—a carbon rod with 440 volts—to keep some things from cooling too fast. As the metal cools the impurities float to the top and get cut off. After 2-3 days the thing is cool enough to break away the mold, but it's still cherry-red. So here I am, 21 years old, and they're teaching me how to take a 50 or 75 ton crane with this dump-truck sized ladle full of molten steel and pour it into a hole the size of a 16oz Styrofoam cup. I had to be that good. I had a police siren on the crane. I would turn that on and everybody would get the hell out of the way."

"How did the decline of the steel industry affect folks around here?"

"In the early 80s automation and more efficient use of larger batches of steel meant we could do more work with less labor. From 1980-83 things got really bad. There were lots of layoffs. They had also opened up the market and the Japanese were sending us steel. I can tell you that in the city, the skies weren't orange anymore. Larger companies were losing money but had enough to wait it out, but the smaller companies went under. Thousands and thousands lost their jobs. And most of them were never going to find another job that would pay as much as the steel industry did."

"Did you lose your job?"

"Yep. We had saved enough to put a down payment on our house right before the crash. My wife worked in a restaurant at $50 a week plus a few tips. We lived off of her income. We got help from our families… my father-in-law bought us diapers for the kids because it was 'something less you had to buy,' he said. I collected unemployment until it ran out, and our Local started a food bank helping unemployed workers with 5-pound blocks of government cheese, butter, and canned meats. The boxes and cans were black and white. Everyone knew it came from the food bank."

"That sounds pretty tough."

"It was coming from all sides. Our bank sold our mortgage to a company in Texas. The local bank understood our situation and worked with us on the payments, but the corporate bank didn't care. Mom-and-pop stores were shutting down because the new mini-malls were going up outside of town. Those malls slowly wiped out these towns."

I asked Alan how he saw things going today.

"I'm worried about this area, worried that my grandkids are going to move away because they won't be able to find jobs here. I don't think anything is going right at the federal level. Politicians are just in it to get reelected. They are out of control with the fighting and bickering. We're seeing spending that is ludicrous. We're paying farmers *not* to grow crops? That's ludicrous, just ludicrous. And we have immigrants who are taking jobs from locals and a government that doesn't take care of its own first. It's a mess."

"Is there anything good you can point to that came from all these changes?"

"You know, if there was one good thing that came from all of it, it was that my wife Denise and I were forced to learn to get along since I was at home a lot. It brought us closer together, and we still get along well. We just celebrated our 43rd anniversary yesterday."

North of Pittsburgh the continuous hill after steep hill made for an exhausting body/mind dynamic: a slow, physically taxing climb, 10 seconds of rest when cresting the hilltop, and finally a fast, mentally challenging descent on the other side—then repeat. The land eased into a rural character, but one very different from the vast expanses of commodity crops I had pedaled through virtually every day up until then. Here, the rolling countryside offered only an occasional flat spot big enough for large-scale agriculture.

A precipitous drop brought me into a lively town called Butler. After a chat with a local newspaper reporter I bought a milkshake, which I tried carrying while steering one-handed up the steep incline away from downtown—a lunatic's gambit ending in predictable fashion. Undeterred, the rig and I climbed steadily along Highway 308 for several miles while garbage trucks rumbled past, to and from the local landfill. When a light rain began falling I donned my jacket, hoping I wouldn't regret it as I struggled uphill.

Arriving in West Sunbury I rode straight to the baseball field where West Sunbury Little League coach Mark Fallen had agreed to meet me. Practice was just getting started. A few moments of watching the field was enough to see that one of the best players there was a skinny blond girl—the only girl on the team. Her dad caught and returned her fast warm-up throws. She was really good.

Mark greeted me and we chatted on the spectator stands while minivans and trucks dropped-off kids and gear bags.

I forgot to get Mark's picture
so he sent me this selfie he took with his kids in West Sunbury

"I've lived in West Sunbury my whole life except when I went to college in Butler," Mark said. "Dad worked construction and also at some of the mills; Mom owned a Dairy Queen until she passed away."

"Did you ever get tired of ice cream?"

Mark laughed.

"I did not. I'm still in love with it, and my kids are in love with it. I got a kid who plays hockey and her reward is a bowl of ice cream."

"That says something about ice cream."

"There's so many different flavors, you just can't get away from it! Anyway, these ballfields have been here as long as I've been here. We didn't think a lot about what we were going to do when we grew up—we just played baseball. Every day in the summer we would come out here, and hopefully one of us had a ball. And if we didn't have a ball we'd be out in the farmer's field behind the diamond looking for balls we might have forgotten to get from the day before. You can play baseball one-on-one, believe it or not."

"What got you into coaching?"

"First of all, I love kids. When I decided I wanted a family I told my wife we had to have 10 kids. I just love 'em."

Calling over a young blondish boy, Mark put his hand on the child's head.

"But this is the reason we stopped at three."

Mark laughed, assuring his son he was just kidding.

"I most enjoy coaching kids about his age, around 7 years old. That's when they seem to be the most moldable into ballplayers, into people. I feel like that's when it's easiest to get through to 'em. Getting them to understand it's not about doing the silly stuff you see on TV, you know, like cheering or dancing as you're running the bases and stuff. Getting them really into playing the game of baseball. You can teach these young kids what's right and what's wrong. I'll probably never quit. Hopefully, I'll be coaching my grandkids one day."

"How do you think being out here and coaching baseball benefits these kids?"

"Well, I wish I could say I make a big difference in these kids' lives and that I'm really molding them into good players and good human beings, but I can't. All I can say is that while they're out here they hear the right things, not just from me but from all of the coaching team we have."

"Do you think they get anything out of it other than just learning how to play a sport?"

"I think if they're coached properly they'll grow as people, too. Teaching somebody to respect a game is just like teaching them to respect anything else, right? So it carries over. And you preach hard work. You're not going to get anywhere without trying; you're not going to get anywhere without effort."

Mark told me that although the area was a safe and beautiful place to raise a family, the lack of economic opportunity made it difficult to keep young people around.

"The fracking industry has started coming into town recently, though," Mark said. "That's who paid for these two new dugouts we got here. That industry in this area has been growing and is pretty significant now. And that's all fine by me. Good companies treat the environment and the community how they should be treated. They're open about what they do; you don't have to pry your way through stuff to figure out what's going on. It's good for the local economy. You can see driving through here that a lot of the farms in the area have wells going up."

"So you're not worried about fracking ruining that sense of safety and the beautiful countryside that people enjoy here?"

"Well, the safety, no. From my perspective, if you get a responsible company and you hold 'em responsible they'll take care of it. See, you can run your business with integrity or you can run it with only profit in mind. Good companies recognize that the community is what's helping them make money, so they want to help out the community, too."

"I guess eventually you did have to think about what you were going to do when you grew up," I said.

"Yeah, and after working construction with my dad I knew I wasn't going to do that. My whole idea behind going to college was to get out and get a nice cushy job. What you realize though is that you're built for what you're built for. I work at a foundry now—not exactly a cushy job."

He laughed again. I hadn't known that about Mark, and was surprised at the coincidence after having spoken with Alan earlier. Mark supervised a 40-employee shop that fabricated raw metal into bases for hospital equipment, brackets for monitors and screens, military items, and dozens of other things. I asked him about the challenges faced by small-scale industry.

"Well, it's always employees. I don't think that's changed over the years. You know, finding a guy who wants to work in a foundry is not an easy thing to do. And if you are able to find guys who want to come to work, and are willing to take the proper testing to come to work, then finding one who can be successful in a foundry is just as challenging. Heavy industry around here just isn't what it used to be and so a lot of guys are looking for something easier."

"It surprises me you're having problems finding guys to fill positions," I said. "I've heard people say jobs are scarce and lots of people are looking. I think most people believe that if there's a good-paying job out there available for a young guy who doesn't have one, he would jump on it."

"Yeah, you would think. I can't argue with that for a second. We say the same thing when we sit down to review our attempts to hire every week. I mean, that's how bad it is. It's so bad getting people to work we have to sit down once a week and figure out what we need, how do we need to prioritize our work based on how many guys we have that week. When people say there's not jobs out there, I'll challenge them. I've been trying to fill five positions for almost six months. We're a union shop, have a great benefits package; it's just a good job."

"Are drugs causing problems?"

"At the shop? No. For hiring? Yes. Out of ten guys we interview, four of them don't show up for the drug test."

Mark looked over at the ballfield.

"Anyway, I gotta get started with baseball. You can help, you can sit there and watch, you can talk to other people, whatever you want."

I wanted to do all of those things, but I was freezing. As I feared, accumulated sweat had soaked my jersey while I climbed into town wearing my jacket. The sun had gone down, dropping the temperature just enough to turn a slight summer-evening chill into a shivering fit for me in my damp clothes. I tried to warm up in a pizzeria, strapped the Styrofoam leftovers box to my rear rack, and then met with Mark again at the town's laundromat after practice. We chatted for another half hour or so while I washed clothes before a tall, thin, fairly old fellow strode through the door, jingling a ring of keys and cursing a lot. Butch owned the laundromat and had come to lock up for the night. Mark had already offered to let me sleep in the league's dugout but I was still cold, so I asked Butch if I could spend the night on the floor beside the dryers. He squinted at me for a moment before raising his bushy eyebrows.

"I don't see any reason in hell why not."

Sleep Like A Baby
Run Like A Criminal
Visit Like A Neighbor

I was ready to go when Butch showed up early the next morning to unlock the door. He asked how I had slept.

"Like a baby," I lied.

"That's a f***ing hard floor for you to sleep like a baby."

After rolling north a spell I descended into a hamlet called Boyers, which, so far as I could tell, consisted entirely of a small store and its gravel parking lot. I stopped in and asked the middle-aged man behind the register if he had any orange juice.

"No, I don't. I guess I stopped carrying it when I stopped drinking it myself. Found out it was giving me heartburn. I suffered from heartburn for years. I'd wake up and have my OJ with my breakfast every morning and take the prescription pills my doctor gave me. That seemed to help some, but boy when I'd forget my meds I'd suffer. So, one day I decided to take matters into my own hands and see if it might be something I was eating. Well, the first thing I cut was OJ. The first day I felt a little better, the second day a little better, and by the third day, I didn't have any heartburn at all. I'd been going to the doctor for years and he never even once suggested I do anything like that. Doctors can be so biased by pills, you know, not even realizing that they should do basic doctoring first."

Two things struck me about the man's story. First, he was right. He had realized that placing trust in an organization or professional is no grounds to stop thinking critically for ourselves. Second, he had just shared his personal health story with a completely random guy on a bike who hadn't asked for it, probably so that I might learn something from his tough lesson. I loved that.

Leaving the store (with a pink lemonade) I was soon pedaling along unpaved roads between hay fields, completely alone. That peaceful backdrop made it especially jolting when a shrill scream erupted from the weeds to my right, startling me so bad I almost fell off the bike. The brush crackled, the scream melted into a hiss, and a little brown demon ran up a berm before turning to glare at me with beady, black eyes. By demon, of course I mean groundhog.

At the top of a hill, a sweeping panoramic view of mowed fields and farmland unfolded through a break in the trees caused by a dirt drive. Parking in a roadside ditch, I stepped over a chain stretched across the entrance to get a better look.

I had just snapped a photo when a puttering sound floated up the sloped bank to my left, growing louder by the moment. I retreated back through the woods. As I was pulling away a man on a tractor drove right by where I had been standing. With his dark sunglasses, long beard, and black t-shirt tucked into his jeans, he looked like the kind of fellow who probably had a shotgun tucked under his seat, too. I felt pretty sure he hadn't seen me, but to be on the safe side I waited until I was out of range before stopping again to check my map in an empty church parking lot.

The kind parishioners had obviously left their red porta-potty unlocked for wayward travelers just like me. After a short break I began readying to get rolling again when I realized my sunglasses were missing. I couldn't manage without them, so I walked in circles, checked my pockets, checked my bags, checked everything until finally accepting my excuses had run out. Lifting the potty lid, I took a long, unpleasant look inside. No sunglasses (thank God).

Then it struck me: I had probably dropped them in the farmer's field when I bolted. Cursing myself back up the hill, I found the man still making passes on his tractor, his back to me and his engine rumbling. Sliding through the trees like a snake, I spotted the reflective blue lenses in the grass and snatched them up before leaping back onto the bike I had left pointing downhill. I had been fast—faster than buckshot. The tractor rolled on.

Risking it all for this epic shot

Ready to eat my stiff pizza from the night before, I found a tree-lined gravel drive that would get me a few feet away from the road and offer some shade while I lunched. I had been there just a couple of minutes when a woman in a truck pulled in. I thought *oh crap* and tried to drag the bike out of the way without dropping the rumpled tinfoil and half-eaten slice in the dirt. When she drove up and lowered her window I was prepared to hear 'Can I get around you?' at best, with 'Get off of my property!' also being likely.

Instead, the woman smiled at me.

"You're alright, no problem. How's it going? Do you need anything?"

Diana & Gordon Pettit
on their back porch in Polk

Diana Pettit (pronounced *Pet-it*) invited me up to her house for a cold root beer. She called to her husband Gordon, who emerged from his workshop to peer at me with crushingly skeptical eyes. Diana managed to convince him to join us on the back porch anyway. Hundreds of crickets hidden in the nearby forest squeaked a background summer melody, probably fooled by the deep shade into thinking it was evening. Fighting with a bee for control of my bottle, I asked them about their roots in the area. Gordon's brow slowly unfurrowed as he began warming up with his answer.

"One of the Pettits was an officer in the Civil War," he said, "and received this tract of land as compensation for his service, so it's been in the family for a very long time."

"We were both born in Pennsylvania and we've lived here almost our whole lives," Diana added. "Gordon services woodworking equipment and I keep the company books."

"What changes in the area here stand out most to you?"

"One is a lack of work," said Diana. "Now that things are going abroad people are unemployed, people are moving away. Most of the big manufacturers around here are shutting down, so the major economy is gone. This community is going to be poorer in five years, and as beautiful and wonderful as this place is, it's going to be really tough for those of us who stay. But don't get me wrong—I'm not saying everything is going in a bad direction. People are still loving. People are still kind. But as people get older and without young people staying or coming in, that sense of community is going to change."

"What would attract young people here?" I asked.

"Sadly, not much, other than how beautiful it is from a nature perspective," Diana replied. "For those young people who want to be green, live on the land, this place might be attractive to them."

"Our biggest and highest-paying employer in this county was a company called Joy Global," said Gordon. "They make shaft mining equipment, specifically for coal. Well, the way things are today if you say the word 'coal' they're going to throw you right out on your ear. Other parts of the world are still using coal, big-time. So why would Joy stay here and manufacture their machines to ship them overseas when they could just move production to the countries that use those machines? You know, people don't realize how much of a domino effect a big plant closure can have. Everything is intertwined."

Diana, who had been nodding while watching Gordon speak, said: "The local restaurants go under, things like that."

"And we're not competitive anymore," Gordon said. "China makes something for $50 that costs us $80 to make. So, that means you're going to have to put a tariff on the Chinese product to get it to $80. And then that money is going to be used to help displaced workers in reeducation and so-forth. It's as simple as that. I think our politicians maybe... possibly... are figuring that out."

"But isn't a tariff a type of tax?" I asked Gordon. "A tax the consumer has to pay. So are you for raising taxes, then? It sounds like you view the jobs problem as something politicians need to fix. Do you put any blame on the manufacturers and companies themselves for moving production overseas?"

"You can't blame a company for leaving if they're in a situation that makes it not viable for them to earn a living," he answered. "If they can make things cheaper overseas, they will."

"Why is it cheaper to build things overseas?"

"From what I understand it's the lower cost of labor."

"And EPA," Diana added.

"In our industry," Gordon continued, "OSHA and the EPA[15] are just absolutely killing business. Now, I believe we ought to have a safe and clean environment to work in. But it seems like our government can't find the right balance."

"So, you guys think right now we are putting too much emphasis on worker and environmental protection?"

"It's not common-sense stuff," Diana said. "It's over the top. For instance, he visits a company to work on their machines and every time he goes through that door he has to spend an entire hour in safety instruction. He hasn't changed, the rules haven't changed, nothing has changed, but he always has to do the same safety training each time."

"What I'm talking about," Gordon said, "is when OSHA shows up for a pop inspection and walks through the shop right off the bat handing out $500 fines because there's an extension cord lying on the floor. That's not conducive to helping a company do business. That's conducive to a bureaucrat trying to justify his job."

---

15 Occupational Safety and Health Administration, and Environmental Protection Agency, both federal agencies.

"What benefit do you think the government gets from hurting business?"

"They don't get anything!"

"So then why would the government be trying to do that?"

"I have no idea. But that's just sure what it comes across as."

At the same time as Gordon's heated answer, Diana calmly said:

"It's just what it seems like."

A complete amateur at interviewing people, I was learning that folks often answer questions in a way speaking to the state of how they feel, rather than their literal view of the facts of a situation—like when Vic Kegley back in South Bend had told me he didn't think America was doing *anything* right. Of course Vic could think of things we were doing right; of course Gordon didn't believe the government was hell-bent on shutting down all business. They were both just very frustrated. Diana's even-voiced comment helped crystalize that lesson.

"Do you guys think agencies like OSHA have a place in the world?"

Both said yes. I turned to Gordon.

"Say you were the boss of OSHA. As a guy who comes out of industry, what general framework would you put in place?"

"Well, the first thing I would probably do is try to in-line my inspectors. I'm not going to send somebody that inspects woodworking shops to go and do a chemical plant, or vice versa. Next, unless it is a gross violation of safety rules, I would put in place a warning system that allowed businesses to fix problems before getting fined. Safety is important, it really is, but I get pretty upset when I've been doing this for 29 years and a guy from OSHA comes up and tells me I'm doing it all wrong."

"Earlier we mentioned the EPA," I said. "Do you feel like that's being done incorrectly also?"

"I've seen some larger companies simply fold up and go away because they can operate overseas without all these environmental rules and regulations," Gordon said.

"But there's no doubt that the EPA has a place, right?" I said. "I mean, there was that river in Cleveland that caught fire because of all the pollution being dumped into it. I've heard people tell me on this tour about how dirty and dangerous their rivers used to be when they were kids. Most of that was pre-EPA. We hardly ever see things like that in this country nowadays. But that's still China today, isn't it? Lax rules, dirty environment?"

"That's why we have regulation," Gordon replied. "That's exactly why. But where do we stop? Why do we gotta keep adding and adding and adding and adding guidelines and rules?"

After a few moments' pause I realized it wasn't a rhetorical question, so I tried answering.

"I don't know, but I imagine someone at EPA might say 'We keep adding regulations because we still have threats to human health and the environment.' "

"I'm just worried about it getting so bad that the economy just collapses on itself."

Gordon's statement surprised me.

"Are you really worried about that?"

"Yeah, for our grandkids, we really are," said Diana.

It was clearly something they had discussed before.

"We're in a situation right now where kids aren't going to have a better life than their parents did," Diana continued. "And that's sad."

"What makes you think that's the case?"

"I think most of it is just that society is falling apart. Half of marriages end in divorce nowadays. Who suffers for that? The children."

"I think it's a breakdown in morality in society and the lack of good employment in the country," Gordon said. "And that goes clear back to what we've been talking about. If you've got a president of a company who comes from a broken home and doesn't have any morals, he's not going to have any morals when he's running that company. And now we have to have OSHA and EPA and all that because alls that president is interested in is making a buck. He could care less about anybody else. It really boils down to morality, and morality comes from the home."

"Yeah, but hold on there," I said. "The EPA was started in the early 70s in response to problems being caused by people who had been raised by these families in the 30s and 40s. That was before this high divorce rate, right? I mean these guys who grew up in traditional households were dumping poison into rivers and spewing coal ash into playgrounds."

"Well, you can't legislate morality," responded Gordon. "If a guy doesn't have a conscience, it doesn't matter what you do, you cannot make him moral. Our whole system of laws is based off of the Ten Commandments if you really break it down. You take those Ten Commandments out of the law and you don't have anything."

Shortly after leaving the Pettits I soared downhill in a flight lasting a full minute, which I paid for with a 29-minute climb up the other side. The slow ascent gave me plenty of time to think more about my chat with Diana and Gordon. Hearing their perspective on what they saw as the general decline of morals in America helped me understand that much of their frustration was with the *necessity* of more regulations, rather than the regulations themselves.

The highway into the town of Franklin was dangerous because its downhill grade had me rolling along at the worst speed a cyclist can do: too fast for drivers to easily pass but just a few miles per hour slower than they wanted to go. They piled up behind me before racing around in quick spasms.

Once in town, though, relaxing came easy. Plopping down on a bench in Franklin's centerpiece Fountain Park, I crunched on the apple Diana had stuffed into my pannier and thought back to my months backpacking the South American continent years before. In scores of Latin American towns and cities I had lounged in leafy squares, usually eating some sort of tropical fruit and waiting to see if anyone would stop by to chat. No one did in Franklin, but it was such a nice afternoon I found myself stuck to the bench anyway. The miles could wait until tomorrow.

Day 33
Franklin, PA → North East, PA
78/1,713 miles
Couchsurfing/Warmshowers

SIGNS

A gauntlet of lonely, unpaved roads slowed the morning departure from Franklin. The steeper sections forced me to seek traction in old automobile tracks through the loose gravel. So complete was my solitude over a half hour of pedaling that I didn't even have to dismount for my morning bathroom break.

Along this quiet stretch I happened upon an anomaly among the trees. Surrounded by a simple wooden fence at the end of a dirt drive sat a squat, white building with a tall cone pointing skyward from its circular roof. The mysterious structure stuck out like a sore thumb from the surrounding rural monotony. My bored brain yearned for it to be a forgotten Cold War missile silo or a secretive extra-terrestrial research installation, but a somber metal sign told the truth: LOSS OF HUMAN LIFE MAY RESULT FROM SERVICE INTERRUPTION of the Federal Aviation Administration control facility.

The roads flattened out some around midday. I was admiring a real-life monster truck parked next to a house trailer half its size when a man walking by paused to say hello. His gray beard and ponytail, t-shirt, faded jeans, and incomplete smile made his appearance unremarkable for the area, save for one thing: his modern-looking, rectangular eyeglasses. They lent a smart contrast to his style. Over the next few minutes I learned how the gravel crusher behind his house converted raw material into a finished product, a process that began by separating the stones into two sizes: large and small.

Up the road a plump woman with a perm waved from a church parking lot, fluttering her fingers in a way that seemed like flirting. The sign out front said:

GOD'S GARDEN
LETTUCE BE KIND
SQUASH GOSSIP AND
TURNIP FOR CHURCH
WORSHIP 9 AM

Shortly thereafter I came to another sign, this one announcing the Erie National Wildlife Refuge. Since arriving at the edge of the Pennsylvanian Appalachians I had nurtured a lukewarm hope of seeing a black bear. That hope skyrocketed now, and my greedy eyes redoubled their scanning efforts along the edges of the trees. With its level fields of wildflowers and low brush I figured the area had once been farmland, something confirmed near the center of the sanctuary by a long-abandoned roadside hayshed, just one good storm away from oblivion. At the top of a tall hill I paused to take in a spectacular eastward view of barn-speckled fields and forests tinged with blue. But no bear.

North of the refuge several unstaffed produce stands with honor boxes awaited customers' cash. I opted instead for a cheeseburger at a bar in small Mill Village. A pink sheet of paper taped to a mirror above the register listed a half-dozen names below a bold heading written in Sharpie: NO SERVICE. Next to it, a sticker with a drawing of a handgun read "IF AT FIRST YOU DON'T SUCCEED, RELOAD AND TRY AGAIN." Somehow, a woman and I became engaged in a conversation about hunting. I asked if there was a problem with the deer population in the area.

"Yeah," she said, with mild disgust. "The Amish people."

"Are they not doing their part to keep the population under control?"

"No, that's not it! They hunt nonstop!"

Her answer served as an almost comical reminder of how oblivious I sometimes was to my own subconscious bias, and the difference in perception between the urban and rural world. Being mostly from the former, I had never even questioned that if one said 'problem with the deer population' it meant that there are *too many*.

"Yeah, the Amish get around the game limit rules because they say the deer cause crop damage and they have like 20 kids to feed. They get other exceptions, too. They're carpenters, but they don't have to follow code like we do when they build things. They don't pay the same taxes, either, because they don't open up their own companies to do business because their whole extended community uses the same one or two companies. They're definitely a problem around here sometimes."

Another revelation. I had never considered *English* people might harbor grievances against the Amish.

At the outskirts of Erie I pedaled by a subdivision of neatly arranged, mostly white houses. Rising above the lots, a lone grain silo served as a stoic trophy from the old farm the residents had conquered. My interview with a local shipbuilder fell through, leaving me time to relax with a milkshake on State Street and enjoy the classic car show filling downtown with Mustangs, Camaros, and Chevelles. The sweets shop window beside my outdoor table shuddered again and again as they rumbled past. After that break I glided down to Lake Erie, falling under the shadow of a monolithic smokestack towering above everything. A man cycling by with his son said it had been part of a coal-fired power plant, long since gone.

Awww, look at that teeny-tiny bike at the bottom

With the day winding down I headed towards my hosts' house in a municipality called North East. The countryside along Highway 5 was soon overtaken by grapevines, acres and acres of them, rising and falling with the topography. I had not expected to find grapes cultivated just a few miles from the Canadian border. The repeating pattern of linear rows was a beautiful thing to see under the fierce orange light of the setting sun. I arrived in time for dinner with my hosts, and spent a while playing with their two bright homeschooled children and friendly yellow lab named Pinball, before turning in. I felt tired but not destroyed, which made me proud because at nearly 80 miles—80 *hilly* miles—it was my longest touring day to date.

Day 34
North East, PA → Angola, NY
57/1,770 miles
Local hospitality
Doty Wagner & Jessica Albney

BIG & SMALL

I had just pulled onto Highway 5 to begin the day's ride when I passed a roadside produce stand in front of a white farmhouse. A tall and hefty older man wearing denim overalls was exiting a small blue barn, bellowing answers back inside to questions I hadn't heard. He looked and sounded like he didn't have time for any nonsense, but I gave it a shot anyway.

"Do you have time to come talk to this young man?" he belted towards the house behind him after I explained the project. A woman in a plaid shirt stepped out to meet me.

Jessica Albney & Doty Wagner
at the Wagners' farm in North East

Doty Wagner and I sat down at a picnic table, a few feet from boxes of home-grown fruits and vegetables she had for sale.

"I grew up here in North East," she said, "but on the other side of the tracks. Back then if you lived on that side of the tracks you were a nobody. Now, all the beautiful subdivisions are on the same road I grew up on.

"My husband David's family owned this farm. He was the fifth generation, so my kids are the sixth generation to grow up here. One day I came here with a friend who was dating one of David's friends and on my way up to the house I fell into a snowbank that covered me almost to my head! David was playing ice hockey down on the pond and saw it happen and came over to help me out of the snow. That's how we met."

Doty's daughter Jessica Albney pulled up in the driveway and came over to join us. I was explaining the project to her when Doty volunteered, pretty much out of the blue:

"We both had weight-loss surgery about a year ago. It was a gastric sleeve procedure where they make your stomach smaller. I lost 104 pounds and she lost 128."

Not exactly what I had expected to chat about, but…

"Wow! That is a radical change in a year," I said. "So, you just don't get as hungry now?"

"You don't really get hungry at all," Doty continued. "They take out seventy to eighty percent of your stomach, mainly the part that produces the hormones that make you feel hungry. Now we almost have to eat just because we know we're supposed to."

"Is it something you would recommend for people facing serious obesity problems?"

"Yes, I absolutely would," Doty said, firmly.

"Do it," said Jessica, immediately after Doty had spoken. "It will save your life."

"What was the recovery from that surgery like?"

"Actually, pretty easy," said Doty.

"I'll be honest," said Jessica. "I was kayaking two weeks later. I shouldn't have been, but I was able to."

"What do you guys say to folks who might think 'You don't need surgery, just stop eating and exercise' ?"

"You know, I've been called a cheater," Jessica said. "The way I look at it is: you do what you have to do. It's not like you get the surgery and suddenly everything is perfect. There are some side effects. It's a lifestyle change. The doctors give you this tool and now you have to use it. And I have the willpower—I know it. If I have to eat like a bird for the rest of my life then I'll just eat like a bird. I am not going back."

"I wish I had done it years ago before my weight had done so much damage to my knees," said Doty.

"How do you guys feel now?" I asked.

"I feel amazing," said Jessica.

"I look in the mirror and it's hard to believe… ," said Doty, trailing off.

"Have your friends and family been supportive?"

"Yeah, but you get that jealousy, too, from friends who are still heavy," said Jessica. "Now that I've seen both sides of it, I've been thinking of becoming a counselor for people before and after their surgery. I feel really motivated at this point."

"Can I ask y'all this: how does somebody get that big? I think a lot of people wonder that."

"I think some of it is your genes," said Doty. "What I've also learned is that, for some people at least, there's a problem with the flow of serotonin in the brain, so you constantly think that you're hungry."

"And you just can't resist eating?"

"Yeah, you just can't resist—even if you fight like crazy."

It was the first time I had ever heard about any of that. I wanted to learn about their livelihood, too.

"So tell me about your farm."

"Well, we have 42 ½ acres, which is actually a very small farm around here. We have mostly grapes that we planted back in the 70s. We also have pick-your-own cherries. People love picking those cherries with their families."

"What was it like growing up here?" I asked Jessica.

"If I ever wanted anything, I had to work for it. But I wouldn't change a thing. I compare myself to a lot of women I know now, and I think my work ethic is better because of growing up on the farm. I know women who can't keep a job, don't want to work. They probably never had to work when they were kids."

Doty told me about her son losing his engineering job because of the sharp drop in oil prices, and it made me wonder:

"What about you guys? What are the geopolitical events that most affect your business as small farmers? What helps you and what hurts you?"

"I don't think there's anything that helps us except this new healthy trend we have now," Doty said. "People are more interested in foods raised on local farms by local farmers."

Jessica looked at her mom.

"I think what's hurt you is that my generation doesn't can vegetables."

"Yeah," said Doty. "We can't sell bushels of things very easily anymore. That used to be common, but not anymore. You've got both parents working now so nobody has time to can vegetables and things."

"Why don't you guys can the produce yourselves and sell it like that?" I asked.

"Well, we would have to be inspected and get permits and all that. They're so fussy anymore. We would have to stop letting the dogs in the house, things like that. We'd probably need to build an entire separate kitchen."

"What challenges do small-scale farms face today?"

"Pricing is a big one. We need the same amount of equipment for 40 acres as bigger farms need for 400 acres, pretty much. And they get price breaks when they buy seeds and things in bulk. We don't get that discount. So, big farms can beat us on price any day."

"But you guys have been able to survive."

"Because we're very, very careful with our money. I think we missed out on a lot of the fun because of it. We tried to do things now and then. We managed to take the kids to Disneyland once."

"But we didn't go on vacation every summer, either," said Jessica. "It's just as well because a farmer doesn't have time for that anyway. It's a 'you don't own the land, the land owns you' kinda thing."

"Can young people who want to start farming from scratch make a go at it these days?"

"I think if someone has a farm handed down to them, yes," Doty said. "I think they could make it. If they have to buy one, I have to say no. It's not economical."

"I'm sure y'all see a lot of people romanticizing life on a small farm," I said. "What are some of the difficulties people might not know about?"

"I don't think people realize we don't have a steady income," Doty answered. "Like when I went to work at a local company people asked me 'Why would you come to work here if you're a farmer? Farmers are rich.' Sure, we're rich in equity, but that's all it is, really. You don't have a lot of money in the bank, and if you are able to put some money away one year you end up having to take it out another year when everything fails. We have had a year when we haven't had a single crop. And we don't have any retirement to speak of because we're always having to put back into the farm."

She said one of her biggest fears was getting hooked on the pain medication she had to take before doing basic farm chores, because of her knees.

"A lot of people go to work for a company they hope helps them figure out healthcare, retirement, things like that," I said. "How do you guys figure out those things?"

"It's tough," said Doty. "We had our retirement to worry about, and I realized the only way we could get good health insurance was if I went to work at one of those companies, so I got a job at Welch's. And I made sure I didn't make waves at work so that they didn't have any reason to pick on me or get rid of me. I just did what I was told even if I didn't agree with things because I knew once my husband started having health problems I was going to need that insurance, and that was the only way I could get it."

She described some of the children's farm injuries: a leg run over by a harvester, a finger smashed when setting fence posts.

"Workman's compensation never wanted to pay our hospital bills, even though the kids had received wages like any other employee," she said.

In summary: Doty's independent farming lifestyle meant she constantly had to fight a system neither set up nor inclined to take her family into account.

Northeast of the Wagners' farm I watched Lake Erie pop in and out of view to my left. Seeing all the grapevines near the lakeshore still surprised me. I remembered something Tom MacKay told me about Park Point's weather on Lake Superior—that in the fall and winter the big body of water kept it a good five to eight degrees warmer near the shore when compared to just a half-mile away. I wondered if that was also the case here. Doty had told me most wine grapes grown in the U.S. were grafted hybrids: European varieties above ground with American roots below. That sounded vaguely familiar, if backwards, to me.

A ship beached on the Lake Erie shore near Barcelona (NY)

Crossing into New York state I paused to enjoy the beachy attitude of Dunkirk. A pier extended into the lake from a touristy boardwalk within sight of a defunct coal-fired power plant. I questioned whether that spot would have the same pleasant, summery feel with white plumes of vapor and the sounds of heavy machinery in the background. I also questioned whether, without those things, towns like Dunkirk could carry on and continue to boast their pleasant, summery feel.

It seemed like a subject best contemplated over a milkshake. A pretty, college-aged girl with dark hair and tanned legs was sitting against a post near an empty ice-cream shop, her nose in a book. Seeing me headed towards the entrance she jumped up and just barely beat me inside. While she made my chocolate shake I filled her up with stories from the road (mostly true). She watched with awe as I fixed the hot water valve on the shop sink, and her pure laughter followed easily behind my jokes. If I had glanced in a mirror, I'm sure I would have seen the advancing gray in my beard obscured by a boosted ego and a satisfied nod.

My hosts back in North East had already resolved the where-to-sleep-tonight puzzle for me by calling ahead to their parents in Angola, NY, a place that happened to be the perfect distance away along my planned route. The semi-retired couple received me warmly with a big dinner, and left on the back-porch light so I wouldn't have to pitch the tent in the dark.

Day 35
Angola, NY → Canada!
46/1,816 miles
Campground
Various Canadians

O, (POLITICALLY DIVERSE) CANADA!

Grapevines and cherry trees gave way to vacation cottages as I cruised east towards Buffalo. Near the edge of the city the signed bike route matured into a dedicated bike lane, carrying me through a series of working-class neighborhoods and public housing tenements. Whether an effect of the perfect sun, smooth road, and easy Sunday traffic I'm not sure, but even the abandoned brick buildings near the city's downtown seemed at peace and in their place. The ride into Cleveland had been easy, but rolling into Buffalo was almost a treat.

My route brought me right into some sort of festival taking place in a park beside the Niagara River. On display in the grass were three august Mercedes-Benz recreational vehicles with floating balloons strung from their oversized mirrors. I stopped and walked through all of them, just to see what the next level of cross-country travel could look like. I'm sure the rig would have turned up his nose, if he had one.

I soon came to the Peace Bridge, with Canada visible on the other side. The excitement at cycling across an international border for the first time was my excuse to ignore numerous admonitions painted on the sidewalk to WALK YOUR BIKE. Rolling down the river, a tenacious southerly wind whipped the flags marking the countries' boundary.

Between the stars & bars and the red maple leaf
flies the sky-blue banner of the United Nations

Pulling up to the border gate kiosk on a bicycle felt silly. When the agent inquired about weapons I politely responded that I had none, counting my knife as a tool. Pressing further he asked about pepper spray, and I remembered the small can of HALT! dog repellant stowed in my front pannier. The agent said "You're not in trouble because you told me about it," and sent me to get checked at another station. Alone among some twenty empty inspection bays, the loaded touring rig looked vulnerable to me for the first time.

The agent there looked over the pepper spray and said I was okay because "A cyclist is allowed to have dog repellant." Appearing satisfied, he returned to the station office, but soon emerged again with a female agent who told me they would have to inspect all of my bags.

"I need you to step away from the vehicle, sir," she said, pointing to a bench. "Come over here and sit down."

I suppose I had escalated the situation by telling them I was unemployed.

After some light rifling through the rig's panniers the agents let me go. The process had been more unpleasant than necessary, but I didn't let that spoil my enthusiasm. I had hatched a plan: instead of interviewing an American about America, on this day I would seek short chats with several Canucks to learn what outsiders thought about us. Getting Canadians' opinions about their socialized healthcare system especially interested me because, as far as I knew, that was one of the biggest differences between our countries.

The first person I stopped to talk with was a man walking his dog along the riverfront. When I asked him to summarize the differences between our two countries, Rodney's response was succinct to the point of being abrupt:

"The color of the money," he said. "That's it."

It was one of the more anticlimactic moments of the tour.

Next, I saw Jim Olsen cleaning out his garage and pulled into his driveway to ask him the same.

"In the U.S., gun violence seems like it's an everyday thing, but nudity is a huge scandal," he told me. "Over here it's the opposite."

A few minutes later I rolled up to an older couple watering flowers in their front yard. The man, named Bruce, said he had dual citizenship but if he had to give up one of his passports it would be the American one, because in Canada he gets better healthcare and there is much less gun violence.

I had lucked out with my atypical interview plan because it just happened to be a Sunday, and a gorgeous one at that. Folks were scattered all along the grassy bank of the Niagara on my right, or in front of their houses doing something outdoors on my left. And nice folks, too. No day could have been better for doing this.

"Canadians are overly polite," said the next woman I spoke with. "Americans are rash but more patriotic. If you move to the U.S. from another country you assimilate. You become American. Not here."

Her husband, who wouldn't give his name ("I never get quoted and I never make a promise") said:

"Some of the most giving people I've ever met are Americans. They'd give you the shirt off of their back if you needed it. At the same time, Americans are much more politically divided and, I hate to say it, but more politically ignorant than Canadians. They follow either Fox News or MSNBC; they don't ever see the entire picture or look at things from a wider perspective."

Next, I came across a group of seven or eight young guys and gals who had been out cruising around on their motorcycles. They were relaxing on blankets spread over the grass at a small riverside park. All of them sort of spoke to me at the same time, but one young woman expressed a thought the whole group seemed to agree with:

"Sometimes, Americans come off as rude or conceited. Many of them don't see us as a real country or, if they do, they make fun of us. Some of the things about Canadians we hear on the radio coming from America are just bad. We consume so much American television, music, and movies I guess we are more aware of America and what's going on there."

Disagreement arose among the group, too. One of the guys complained that American malls don't accept Canadian currency, even though Canadian merchants usually accept the U.S. dollar. When I challenged him on whether that was a legitimate grievance a couple of the others gave the guy a hard time. Then, another of the guys surprised me when he said he'd much rather go to a concert or similar event in America as opposed to Canada because he felt we had a greater police presence in the U.S., better security, and better and more organized facilities.

My final question concerned our respective healthcare systems. Another young woman in the group spoke up, and everyone there agreed with her.

"I kind of feel sorry for Americans because of your system. You're always worrying about insurance and deductibles or whatever. Here, if we get sick or hurt we just go to the doctor or the hospital and get treated. It's no big deal and we usually don't have to pay anything. We see on the news how you guys have so many people who can't get treated or who get worse off or die because they've waited too long to get treated because of how much it costs. Or when the doctor prescribes something, but your insurance won't pay for it, so you have to pay some ridiculous amount to get the medicine you need or go without. It's really sad to me. I don't understand why you guys do it that way."

It didn't take long to recognize the absurdity of my initial approach, thinking I would uncover some uniform "Canadian Point of View." Of course our northern neighbors held a wide range of viewpoints. The earful I got from a middle-aged white couple up the road underscored that. I found John and Gina sipping beers in lawn chairs behind their _imported_ red Corvette.

"When Americans have a dollar, you'll go spend that last dollar to get ahead," John said. "That's something I admire. Canadians are way more conservative. They'll stick that dollar under their mattress and be afraid to spend it. Maybe that's because we're taxed to death here in Canada. I like your way of doing things a hell of a lot better than the way we do them here. You guys tend to call a spade a spade. Canadians speak really soft and easy, but close the dining room door and then you'll find out what they really think."

I told them a few of the things I had heard from their compatriots so far that day.

"It's not true that gun violence is higher in the U.S." was John's response. "You have more people than we do, that's why it seems higher. People are getting shot all the time in Toronto.

"And on healthcare—our system was the best, but not anymore. Now, we keep bringing in immigrants, not from countries in Europe like Sweden or places like that, but from India and Pakistan. Those guys know the system better than we do. They want to come here for three months and then get a pension and healthcare. Some of these Muslims have five wives, and they petition the government and get payments for each of those wives. I'm all for immigration—let 'em come. We need good skilled people to come here and work. It's not a racist thing; I just don't want these people coming here and not working, or coming here to change the way we do things. I mean, we can't even say *Merry Christmas* anymore without offending someone!"

Of all the things I heard that day, this was the most surprising. I would have never, ever imagined I would hear a Canadian reference the War on Christmas. A Canadian!

"We have to say Happy Holidays," John continued. "And they've taken down Christmas trees from places because the Muslims don't like them. And they even let this woman have her ID made in her burka because she didn't want to take it off. They tried to avoid that but she took it to a human rights court and won. And they get in the driver's seat with those things on and you know they don't have any peripheral vision! Canada is bending over backwards for these immigrants. We're a minority in our own country now. There's no patriotism in Canada like in the U.S. If I could move there I would do it in a minute, because you guys call a spade a spade."

I was absolutely dumbfounded. They laughed when I told them I had never really considered that Canada had both conservatives and liberals, too.

"I'm a first generation Canadian," said Gina. "My family moved here from Italy. We had Italian food in the house. We spoke Italian. But my dad always told us that we were guests here in this country, that we had to respect their ways, their language, and when we went outside we had to speak English and be Canadians. Today, immigrants keep their nationalities. They say: 'I'm Afghani' or 'I'm Pakistani.' They never say 'I'm Canadian.'"

I asked what they thought generally about a public versus a private healthcare system in macro terms, given that they seemed more conservative than most of the folks I had spoken with that day.

"I still think that a government-run single-payer system is the best way to run healthcare," Gina said.

John agreed, with the caveat he mentioned before. He wanted to see measures put in place to curb abuse. It was the only criticism I heard all day of Canada's system: it was so good that unscrupulous people used it *too much*. I wondered what a dozen miscellaneous Americans would say about our healthcare system if asked by a random cyclist on a given Sunday afternoon.

🚲 🚲 🚲

I was in my tent at the edge of a soybean field that night when a series of distant booms startled me awake. Sitting upright I peered through the mesh walls, but the darkness gave away nothing. More booms followed. I knew I was near Niagara Falls—was it a fireworks show?

I never found out.

Day 36
Canada → Middleport, NY
37/1,853 miles
Urban camp
Jennifer & Jesse Bieber

So Far, Everything's Alright

A morning person's whistle carried me through striking camp and readying the rig. I had two reasons to be excited: seeing Niagara Falls for the first time, and spending the night on the road for the last time. No matter how much I had enjoyed the past few weeks, visions of a normal day at home increasingly crowded my dreams.

Following the bike path across a small dam I pedaled towards a plume of vapor rising in the distance. Forgotten gray buildings sat dormant along the river's edge, in stark contrast with the increasingly kinetic water just a stone's throw from the bike's wheels. The river turned from dark blue to white as it boiled over rocks, producing a hiss that was nearly drowned out by the roar from up ahead. After passing through a bellowing, refreshing cloud of mist, I arrived.

The mighty Niagara Falls
looking towards the United States from Canada

Reams of prose have already described the splendor of Niagara Falls, so I will simply summarize them: magnificent… and so *loud*.

With its Hard Rock Café, Planet Hollywood restaurant, and numerous souvenir shops, the viewing area catered heavily to tourists. I worked my way down the promenade at about the same pace as a group of young Chinese women sweeping their selfie sticks in wide arcs to see the falls from their smartphone screens. Watching them as we walked, I never saw any of them take even a moment to contemplate the long-famous spectacle other than as a backdrop for social media posts. I imagined the shop and restaurant owners at the bottom of the path would be happy so long as the women made their friends back home envious by hashtagging their #niagarafallsadventure, and were ready to spend money at the end of their walk. I wasn't bothered by the businesses there generating revenue at such a unique site, but it did trouble me that those traveling thousands of miles to be there, too, were not really there at all.

Crossing the Rainbow Bridge back into the U.S. I was greeted by a surly Customs & Border Patrol agent who barked that I wasn't supposed to have biked in the pedestrian lane—that instead I should have waited in a long line of exhaust-spewing automobiles. His attitude fell far below the 'Welcome Home!' I would have appreciated, but at least he did hold open the door so I could get the unwieldy rig back into my own country. I hurried through the town of Niagara, which looked to be holding on by a frayed thread. Ill-kept houses gave way to 18-wheelers rattling inches from my panniers along an industrial stretch of highway.

In Lockport I watched a few small watercraft rise and fall in the mostly inert locks of the Erie Canal. Above the loading ramp a decades-old FALLOUT SHELTER sign fastened to a brick building seemed more quaint than ominous. These icons had once been among the most consequential elements of American culture and commerce. Now, they remained largely because removing them would be too much trouble.

From there I joined the Erie Canal Towpath Trail. Despite the trail's fame I saw just two other people over the five miles to tiny Gasport, where I met up with the town supervisor of nearby Royalton, Jennifer Bieber, and her husband Jesse.

Jesse & Jennifer Bieber
at a small park next to the Erie Canal in Gasport

"We both grew up here," Jennifer told me. "I'm 7th generation, my kids are 8th generation Town of Royalton. I grew up on a dairy farm—and he [laughing and pointing her thumb at Jesse] married the farmer's daughter. The picture on my desk is of him at age five sitting on my dad's tractor. Now we have our own little farm and we've been married 27 years. I work full time for the phone company. My town supervisor job is my other full-time job—but with part-time pay, is how I like to describe it."

She laughed again.

"And Jesse is the town historian. But he was appointed before I was elected so there was no funny business there."

"What does a town supervisor do?" I asked.

"Signs a lot of checks. Takes care of the budget. Makes sure everyone gets paid."

"Do you enjoy it?"

"I love it. I just love it. I wanted to be a part of the solution. I wanted to be able to help people solve their problems. It's where I grew up and I want to do some good here."

"What kinds of things do you deal with on a daily basis?"

"I get calls like 'What day does my recycling get picked up? Who do I need to call about my neighbor's yard not being mowed? What do I do if I want woodchips? How do I connect to city water?' Things like that."

"We don't hear about woodchips and city water on the national news much," I said.

"No, but these are the things that actually affect people's day-to-day lives. I don't think it's too much to ask in this day and age that everyone has access to basic things like clean water and internet. Our kids come home from school to do their homework and they need internet access but, unfortunately, they don't have it in a lot of places. That's important."

"To what extent do you think people are concerned with what's going on in their communities, relative to what's being discussed in the national news?" I asked.

"Out of 7,700 town residents," Jesse said, "how many people do you think come to a board meeting every month? One, two maybe. It's sad. People just don't… I don't want to say they don't care, but it seems they're just content with the status quo sometimes."

"With meeting attendance that low, do you ever feel like 'Well if nobody cares, why should I care?' "

"No," Jennifer said. "No, I probably care sometimes to a fault."

"How do you do it, time-wise?"

"I spend my lunch breaks at the phone company working on town stuff. Sometimes I'll go to the office before I go into work, or I'll stop by at night after work. I have a great secretary, so I call her on a daily basis and we make it work. And, anytime I need to send out a press release or something, I've got the perfect proofreader right here," Jennifer said, patting Jesse on the back. "And he's always right there to send it back corrected!"

"Do you plan to stay on?"

"I'll do it as long as I get reelected, I think. I had a medical issue in 2009—a brain tumor. And I thought 'Oh my gosh, what if I can't do this? I just got elected and I've had to get brain surgery. What am I going to do if I don't recuperate?' I was so excited when I got released from the hospital and I could still talk and I could still think and so I thought 'I want to go do something; what can I do right now?' I went straight to my second board meeting! So now I have a big scar across my head. The tumor is still there but every year I just go through the tunnel to make sure nothing's growing and, so far, everything's alright."

"That's some serious dedication."

"I mean, I don't know every single one of the 7,700 residents who live here, but I consider anyone that lives in this town to be part of my family... part of my extended family. We have some great people here."

"Depending on what you're doing," Jesse said, "sometimes public service makes you really realize how good you have it. No matter how bad things are with you, you can always find someone who has it worse."

Jennifer went on to describe how she had called her senator to complain that her insurance company made her buy drugs through the mail instead of filling prescriptions with her local pharmacist, whom she had known forever. That was important to her, she said, because the pharmacist employs local people and supports the local economy. I asked if they were optimistic about the direction of the country, and whether anything worried them. Jesse answered.

"I'm optimistic about the town, at least."

They both laughed. Jesse continued, in a more serious tone.

"Once you get past that, I don't know. I mean, it's scary. To be honest with you I don't know where this country's headed. I don't feel it's the right direction, but maybe it is going to be okay and I'm just wrong."

"What about our direction worries you?"

Jennifer picked up there.

"Here in New York State we have really strict gun laws, but it's really rural out here where we live. If I call 911 nobody's coming for at least 20 minutes. We're on our own. If somebody's coming at me or after my kids or my animals and they have a gun, it's not going to do me much good to have a baseball bat. We need to be able to defend ourselves."

"For me," said Jesse, "I'm one of those people who worries about their own government—whether it's getting too big or it's getting misguided. All it takes is for everyone to get into a tizzy and... you know, I hate to throw out comparisons to... post World War I Germany, but... I see where... I know everybody's getting all stirred up with their nationalism, but I'm worried because I don't know how far everybody's willing to take it. I'm afraid that, you know, you get that mob mentality sometimes and there's no controlling it or stopping it, and before you know it you have *Kristallnacht* in the United States, with people going against immigrants! It scares me that it could come to that."

Jesse looked at his wife.

"In Germany when the Nazis went after the Jews and they broke all of the windows in the storefronts and everything. That was the 'night of the broken glass' that they call *Kristallnacht* in German. And it was the big precursor to the internment of the Jews."

The heavy thought kept everyone silent for a moment.

"How do you think your passion for and knowledge of history influences your views of what might happen in this country?" I asked Jesse.

"I think the vast majority of people out there don't care about history," he said. "And they don't have a clue about things that have happened, or why they happened, or that they could happen again if we don't learn from our mistakes."

"Do you see our division being reinforced by anything? Is there any way out of it?"

"I think what fuels most of the division in this country is ignorance— on both sides. And people are not willing to sit down and discuss the hard issues of why people are doing what they're doing, be it rioting or what have you."

"It sounds like in your view the biggest threat to our continued prosperity or our future is ourselves, essentially."

"That's it in a nutshell."

"Oh, I agree," Jennifer said. "But don't get us wrong. I think we both understand that our society has evolved in so many ways for the better. But there still are these big issues we haven't worked out yet."

As we said our goodbyes Jennifer gave me a patch with the Town of Royalton official seal.[16]

---

16 Later, affixed to my sleeping bag stuff-sack, Jennifer's gift took its place among the small but elite group of commemorative patches that actually get sewn to something.

Though the sun had set the light lingered on, so I decided to squeeze a few more miles from the day. The towpath was completely deserted, which may have been why there were still several decent picks among the windfall scattered near a trailside apple tree. Pulling into Middleport at dark felt like winning the lottery. A simple municipal campground with showers was available for towpath travelers, and I had company, to boot. Two other touring bikes leaned against a bench next to the canal. Suspecting I'd find the cyclotourists at the Irish pub around the corner, I hastily pitched the tent and rode that way to find out. There they were, both near the beginning of their tours. After a few beers we returned to the campsite together, where my jolliness turned to confusion. My tent had vanished. On the grass next to my now bare ground tarp was the small nylon sack where I kept the tent stakes. I nudged it with my foot, and my heart sank at the metallic clinking sound inside. In my rush to meet the other cyclists I had forgotten to stake down the tent. It had blown into the Erie Canal.

A cabin light glinted through the port window of a boat moored nearby. Knocking on the hull felt silly, but it did the trick. A man emerged and lent me a long pole with a hook on the end that he happened to have on hand. With the other cyclists keeping watch I swished back and forth a few times in the opaque canal, just enough so I felt like I hadn't given up too easily. That done, I resigned myself to the fact that my last night on tour would be spent out in the open under a beautiful, dry sky, nearly free of mosquitos but full of stars.

I guess it could have been worse.

Day 37
Middleport, NY → Rochester, NY
55/1,908 miles
Couchsurfing/Warmshowers
Chris Whitman

GOTTA BE ALL-IN

The final day of the Great Lakes States route began under a ceiling just starting its transition from gray to blue. I arose with a quick brush of my face to shoo away any lingering spiders. As my head began swelling with tour-end logistics and tantalizing visions of having my own bathroom again, I reminded myself, out loud, to *be present.*

Pretty soon trail dust had coated the black touring rig in a fine, white powder. Seeing few other people, I stayed entertained by half-heartedly scanning the canal banks for hints of snagged nylon tent fabric. Boredom more than hunger nudged me into a small town called Holley for lunch and socialization. At Sam's Diner a man with gray hair under his mesh cap described how farming in the area was changing. They had endured a lot of rain that summer, he said. His use of the word 'endured' puzzled me. I had thought lots of rain was a good thing.

"That's what you would think," he said, "but it's like my dad always told me: a dry season will scare you, but a wet season will kill you."

The plants get lazy with all the water and don't put down deep roots, I learned.

"So, if the fungus doesn't get them," the man continued, "the wind blows them down, and if that doesn't happen, then any short dry spell will kill them because their shallow roots can't reach the moisture stored in the soil below."

I asked him how things were changing in the area.

"Things are always changing," he said. "Not getting better or worse, just changing. Farms are growing, but around here they're limited in size by the canal because there's nowhere to cross over with your farm equipment. I guess that's one thing that has really changed. Today, a piece of equipment costs you at least a hundred thousand dollars and takes an inch-thick manual to learn how to use it. Back when I was a kid, my dad built a cabbage picker out of spare parts he had lying around. The man who bought his farm is still using it."

After a couple of dozen more miles I hopped off the trail at Emmerson Street, passing numerous manufacturing plants on my way into the heart of my final destination: the city of Rochester.

Ever fond of his portraits, it pleased the rig to learn
a cycling enthusiast and photography legend had put Rochester on the map

Like Detroit, Sandusky, Cleveland, and other formerly vibrant cities I had been through over the past few weeks, Rochester showed signs of a proud past and an uncertain present. The soaring beauty of the Powers Building merited a few minutes of gawking. Crossing the Main Street Bridge I did a double-take at the statue of a winged Mercury perched atop a tall tower to the south. These and other superb details had surely been dreamt-up, or at least financed, by those kings of industry now much less relevant to the city. The most famous of these, Kodak, had been founded by cycling enthusiast George Eastman, a pioneering cyclotourist himself (at a time when, like the farmer's cabbage picker, riders fashioned touring gear from spare parts lying around).

I wandered for a while, stopping for beers at different bars along Alexander Street in hopes of meeting someone for conversation. At the bottom of pint number three I figured I should give up if I wanted to make it to my hosts' house without falling over. I succeeded in that, and when I shared with them my dismay at ending the tour without finding an interview, they huddled for a moment, and then said:

"We've got the perfect person for you!"

Chris Witman in her Rochester living room

Within a half-hour my hosts and I were seated on a series of modern sofas in the condo owned by their friend Chris Whitman and her husband Steve. Chris was born and raised in Rochester, and returned to work in the biochemistry department of the University of Rochester after graduating Syracuse. She eventually found a job that allowed her to travel the world selling advanced manufacturing equipment.

"I worked there for a long time and eventually got the crazy idea that I would try to buy the company," Chris said, "even though I knew nothing about that side of it. So, I went back to school and took some business classes and talked to everybody I knew. I recruited a few partners and we wrote a business plan and went to a bank and convinced them to give us a loan, and we got some investors, and we went out and we bought the company! I had little kids at the time, so this business plan was written late at night on an early Apple computer. It was a very har... kind of a fun time."

She had corrected herself last-minute, with a smile.

"We had zillions of problems in the beginning, one thing after another. But over the course of 10 years we grew the company from about 8 million dollars in sales to about 100 million dollars in sales. We were able to get extremely good at making these thinfilms for the read/write heads for disc drives. Eventually we took the company public, and after another year or two one of our competitors bought the company from us. After serving for a while as president I left and decided to do it all over again.

"The second time around, though, I thought I might invest in companies but help somebody else be the president or CEO. So, my new goal was to serve on the board, showing others how they could run things. I got together with some guys in Rochester again and we started investing in early-stage companies, almost all here in the region. This was in the early 2000s. So, we now have a portfolio of companies, some of which didn't make it, some that did, you know. That's what angel investing is all about. You don't get a 100% yield.

"At the same time I was investing I was working on some community projects, trying to get our community to work better together. While I was growing my business I had spent a ton of time looking at other communities, like in Silicon Valley, Austin, parts of Asia. And I came to see that Rochester really had an opportunity to strengthen itself. So I got involved in the formation of a public-private partnership in our region. That's worked out pretty well and has brought some businesses to the area.

"Along the way I found more deals than I could possibly invest in, so we put together a group of folks and founded something called the Rochester Angel Network. One of the reasons I wanted to see these small companies grow is because here in Upstate New York, creating jobs is what's needed. Like a lot of Northeastern communities, Rochester has seen some decline. There's been some large companies that have not kept up. So, creating good jobs that include health benefits and safe environments in the city of Rochester is the kind of thing Steve and I are passionate about."

Steve, who had been listening quietly, smiled and gave me the thumbs-up, clearly content to let Chris have the floor.

"It seems like many young people come out of college with ideas about making the world a better place," I said, "and they don't think about business.

They think about joining an NGO, or starting an NGO, or traveling across the world to help poor people somewhere. I was kind of that way. But it sounds like you view job creation here in the States as one of the fundamental ways to improve folks' lives."

"Yep. Wealth creation is all about people having a job to begin with. And then, to have a job that isn't a minimum-wage job. NGOs are great, but sustainable wealth creation means people have jobs and careers, things they want to work on, things they like to do. And I think sometimes well-meaning not-for-profit entities aren't focused enough on the economy as what's going to help really raise these boats."

"What makes a successful entrepreneur?"

"Passion. I mean, you gotta find the application of something that people will buy, obviously. But in the end, it's perseverance. More than anything else, it's perseverance. Most people fail as entrepreneurs because they can't stand the heat, you know? You have to become an evangelist and surround yourself with smart people who can help you succeed in getting the thing done that you've set out to do. And once you find that you've accomplished this, and you've got everybody, you know, coming around and eating the bread, well that's just an interim step, because it keeps going. You have a little bit of success, and then you have another plateau where you have a lull, and then a little more success. It's a long road. People ask me, you know, what about balance and everything. There's no balance in being an entrepreneur. You've gotta be all-in, always thinking about it in the shower or wherever you are, thinking of ways to constantly make it better. You've always got a competitor in the background trying to eat your lunch, so to speak. So it becomes all-encompassing, all-consuming. The true entrepreneur, who has nothing, goes for it. And those are usually the ones who make it."

"I've biked through lots and lots of places that used to churn out widgets nonstop, but now sit empty. What's going to replace manufacturing here?"

"Well, we still have a wonderful higher education system in the U.S., and so the ideas are being generated in our universities. All of the prototyping is done here. Things may not be manufactured large-scale in the U.S. but they'll be designed and tested here, and the parent companies can certainly be U.S. companies, and can farm out large-scale production to China or wherever.

That's why we have to try to get our kids to take math and science—not exclusively math and science, but we need to understand how technology works so that we can be good contributors to the economy that's coming."

"You've run businesses," I said, "hired people, all of that. What message would you have for any employee today about how to stay employable in an economy that is always changing?"

"My advice would be to change before you have to. What is great today is only good tomorrow. That's the market, pushing us. So you have to constantly retool, educate yourself, read, know what's going on in this world, because you're going to be left in the dust if you don't. The pace of change is accelerating. And it's hard to stay on it, hard for everybody. The older you get, the harder it is. But, as hard as it is, think about how cool it is! Our lives are getting so much easier. There are always new opportunities, but they might not be in the same place the old opportunities were."

"Last question," I said. "You've talked about how the U.S. is where the design and prototyping happens, this is where innovation takes place. Is there something unique about our country, our people, that gives rise to that?"

"Yep."

Chris didn't hesitate for a millisecond.

"It's the diversity in this country. There's no other country like the U.S. in terms of the diversity of the people. I spent a lot of time in Asia, and I saw how often it's just men making the decisions, and the rest just kowtow to the leader. Here, if you're the president of the company, maybe people give you a little respect, but you've got more people who are going to tell you like it is. We're more of the servant-leaders here, and you have a huge diversity of thought coming into the decision-making process that happens here. You get the best answers when you have the most diverse people solving problems. That's our secret weapon."

Day 38 and Route End
8/1916 miles
Rochester, NY → Houston, TX

ROUTE END

After breakfast with my hosts I pedaled south in the general direction of Park Avenue Bike Shop. The rig's empty shipping box had been waiting there since Brent Edstrom forwarded it from Duluth several weeks before. I wasn't really on tour anymore, and my flight didn't leave for hours, so I just sort of rolled around in lazy circles, first past three yellow buses unloading schoolchildren at the Rochester Museum & Science Center, then through the University of Rochester, then past the homeless camps hidden in the woods along the Leigh Valley Trail. I stopped by a college bookstore for no discernable reason—maybe just for the smell. Stacks of loose and boxed paperbacks lined the walls and filled the floors, leaving only a few distinct walkways between the door and cash register. I briefly wondered how much longer bookstores would be around.

Eventually I arrived at the bike shop, which charged me nothing for the trouble of storing the big, unwieldy bike case—a gesture of kindness and support I appreciated as much as any, even if it didn't surprise me. I could hardly count the number of times folks along the way had helped me get this far. After disassembling the rig and cramming it inside I affixed the shipping label and offered one of the employees $20 to drive me to the airport on his lunch break.

With so many people passing by at the airline gate, it felt odd not having my good pal the touring rig at hand to help jumpstart a chat. Until my next route—the American Southwest—I'd have to readjust to life without my rolling conversation-starter. Soon, I was just another traveler dozing in an airport chair. But below my clean ball cap, an overwhelmed mind worked to process new understandings and wipe away fractured misconceptions. Behind my drooping eyelids, dozens of faces and landscapes from the Great Lakes States scrolled past. Under the low music playing in my earbuds, voices ranging from worried to hopeful described the United States. And beneath my fresh t-shirt, a vindicated heart swelled with pride. *Conversations With US* was now entirely part of me, and would remain so throughout America's 50 states and beyond.

The boarding call stirred me awake. Glancing down at my fingers' odd new tan lines, I corrected my half-dreamt reflections on the past few weeks. Not *everything* from the tour would stay with me forever.

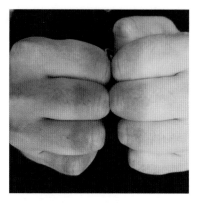

Appendix 1:
What Is Cyclotouring?

Whether you call it cyclotouring, bicycle touring, or just plain crazy, traveling by bike can be one of the best ways to experience a place. Here you will find a broad overview of how works. I'll cover most of these topics in more detail in later Appendixes.

Why a bike?

If you want to be challenged, get some exercise, suffer and enjoy the elements, see and smell and hear your surroundings, meet and chat with random people at every stop, eat anything and as much as you want, protect the environment, and save money on gas, your bottom belongs in the saddle of a touring bicycle.

What types of tours are available?

The spectrum of tour types runs from solo and self-supported (like *CWU*) to group luxury packages where vans haul your stuff, concierges make your reservations, and hot gourmet meals are waiting for you at each stop.

How fit do I have to be?

If you ever meet a person who is 100% in shape and ready to go before their tour begins, be sure to snap a photo—it's a rare sight indeed. Likewise uncommon are those who begin a tour with so little conditioning that their muscles completely fail on Day 2. Most folks fall somewhere in-between. Cyclotouring can be tough some days but overall is not a heavily athletic endeavor. Basically, if you develop a preparatory training program that takes into account your level of fitness and the profile of your tour, you start it soon enough, and you stick to it fairly well, you should be fine.

What gear do I need?

Most of us have to budget for a tour, which means allocating funds among gear, hotel stays, airfare, food, etc. Outfitting doesn't have to break the bank, but smart spending on the right gear can really bolster the quality of your ride.

Bike

Obviously, a good place to start is with a comfortable, reliable, well-tuned rig with good components that you know how to operate/adjust/repair. I undertook *CWU* on a Surly Long Haul Trucker 27-speed with 26" wheels. Many other companies manufacture superb touring bikes. Or, you can tour on just about any trustworthy bike capable of carrying a load.

Cargo

Touring requires at least a basic set of gear and equipment. Broadly speaking, you can hire someone to haul your stuff around for you, or you can carry it yourself by pulling a trailer or attaching racks to your bike for strapping things and toting panniers (aka saddlebags). I employed the rack and pannier setup.

Clothes

Cyclotourists should bring along clothes for expected and unexpected weather. I strongly recommend high-visibility clothing that also protects you from the sun. This doesn't have to be expensive, nor does it have to be spandex or cycle-specific. Carry something warm even in the summer and keep one clean set of off-bike clothes for special occasions.

Equipment

A basic cyclotouring kit would include tools that you know how to use, key spare parts, snacks, a rearview mirror, sunscreen, clothes, a toiletry kit, cash and a bag of coins (quarters in the U.S.), sunglasses, handlebar mount and spare battery for your smartphone (don't tell me you want to tour without a smartphone), appropriate map apps and/or paper maps, front and rear light, helmet and gloves, water bottles, basic first-aid supplies, and an air pump and patch kit (depending on your tire setup). From there it all depends on what kind of tour you have planned whether you include camping gear, filming equipment, a laptop, etc.

Is it dangerous?

The short, honest answer is that cyclotouring is not an extreme sport, but it does carry more risk than your average sightseeing vacation. Fortunately, many components of that risk are under your control: your level of competence on a bike in traffic, the extent to which you make yourself visible, your choice of cycling routes, your type of tour, your preparedness, the size of your touring group, and whether you're paying attention (Do you use a rearview mirror? Do you have earbuds crammed into both ears?). Every year cyclists die in automobile collisions and other accidents. Happily, many, many times more enjoy safe and memorable rides.

Where can I learn more?

CWU's Appendixes are good places to start, as is the Logistics section of the project website, *www.conversationswithus.com.* For other perspectives I recommend the following:

Adventure Cycling Association

The ACA is the preeminent North American nonprofit organization dedicated to inspiring and empowering people to travel by bicycle. I recommend beginning your research here. *www.adventurecycling.org*

Local bicycle advocacy organizations and bike shops

Many cities and larger towns have a nonprofit or informal group that promotes bicycling. These organizations are great for meeting folks who have done bike tours. Also, chances are that at least one of the mechanics at your local bike shop has done some touring. Lean up against the counter while your bike is being tuned and make a new friend.

Local bookstores

Or an online seller, of course. I found the Sierra Club's *Bicycle Touring* by Raymond Bridge to be very helpful when I first started planning the project. Many other great books exist on the subject.

Google

Everybody knows about Google! The internet is full of blogs and websites maintained by experienced cyclotourists who are happy to share what they've learned. *Crazy Guy On A Bike* is one of the classics. Many cyclotouring social media stars can likewise help point you in the right direction.

ACKNOWLEDGEMENTS

A New York publicist once referred to me as 'non-networked,' by which I think she meant I would have no big names or publishing houses listed in my Acknowledgements section. I undertook the entirety of *Conversations With US* on my own, from outfitting the touring rig and adjusting its gears to receiving those first boxes of printed books and trying to find a place in the living room to store them.

Of course, no one ever really accomplishes anything "on my own." I owe an enormous debt of gratitude to the hundreds of individuals, networked or not, who contributed to the success of the project.

The folks who gave of their time and entrusted me with their sometimes very personal stories and thoughts deserve the most recognition. Your willingness to share was the fuel that kept me going, mile after mile.

I would never have met my interviewees had it not been for the kindness and support offered by strangers while I trekked across the country solo. Too legion to list here, these people invited me to sleep in their homes or camp in their yards, helped me across dangerous bridges, aided with bike shipping or repair logistics, made phone calls to set up interviews for me, and covertly covered my check at bars and diners throughout the USA.

Transitioning from pedal to prose and then from prose to print was a journey unto itself, one culminating in the formation of my own publishing company: Spoke & Word Books. I am deeply thankful to several individuals and groups whose encouragement, editorial prowess, gentle criticism, and professional guidance helped turn a torrent of rambling words into the closest thing to a work of literature as I am able to achieve.

Thank you: Houston Writers Group at Rice Village and Charlottesville Writers Critique Circle (for the superb feedback and camaraderie); James River Writers, WriterHouse, Inprint, Houston Writers House, and the Independent Book Publishers Association (for offering collegial support and guild solidarity); Bike Houston and Peloton Station (for backing up the biking part of me); the numerous opposing counsel who scanned my every court-filed sentence, and Mark Maney (for forcing me to write right);

J. Fink, Brian Jackson, Kuralay Rivera, and Jain Lemos (for their creative and professional design assistance); and for specific help on this specific manuscript with edits, proofs, and suggestions: James Cole, Ed Barber, Broocks Willich, Richard Wise, Trudy Hale, Steven Smith, Elizabeth Howard, Libby McNamee, Cameron Baumgartner, Miguel Wagman, Stefan Bechtel, and my mom, Pat Tolar.

Finally, I want to acknowledge all of those who came before me—related by blood and not; living and not; directly part of my life and not—who gave of themselves to help make the United States of America a country where pursuing a dream is possible, and who helped put me in a position to do just that.

CREDITS

Photographs

All photos were taken by the author using a Samsung Galaxy smartphone, unless otherwise noted herein, or below.

Page iii: Kuralay Rivera of 1001 Angels Photography
Page 172: my host Mike snapped this photo of me and Jackie Mayer
Page 246: Steve Whitman
Back cover author portrait: Dave Cowley

Photograph Subjects

Page 94: Cloud Gate
Created by Sir Anish Kapoor; commissioned by the Millennium Park Foundation; dedicated in 2006.

Page 101: Chicago Mural
Created by the Greetings Tour (Victor Ving & Lisa Beggs); completed in 2015. www.greetingstour.com

Page 159: Spirit of Detroit
Created by Marshall Fredericks; commissioned by the Detroit-Wayne Joint Building Authority; dedicated in 1958.

Page 245: Mercury
Created by J. Guernsey Mitchell; commissioned by tobacco magnate William Kimball; dedicated in 1881.

Graphics

Several of the graphics herein were obtained from Wikimedia Commons, a nonprofit media file repository making available public domain and freely-licensed content.

Maps

Back cover; inside front cover; opposite Contents page; chapter headings: J. Fink
Opposite copyright page: amCharts

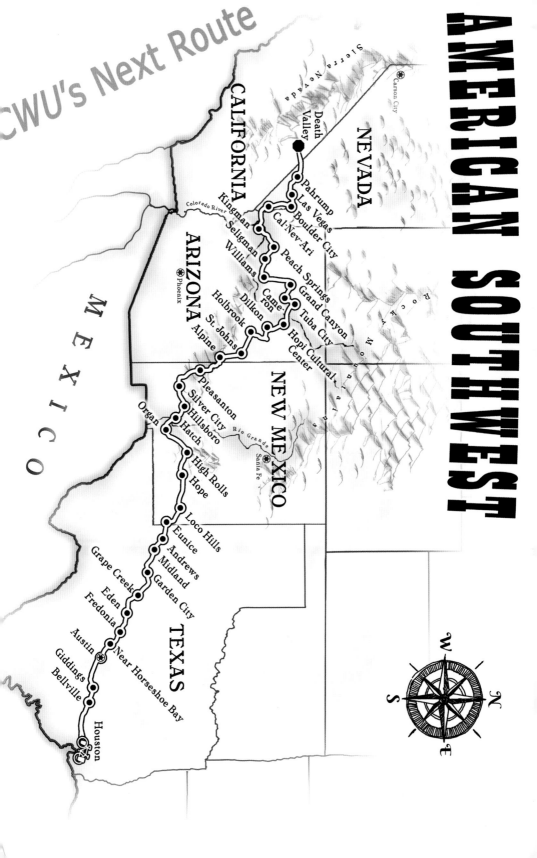

Your Author

Day 26—Sandusky, Ohio
near the local newspaper HQ

Chris Register completed his first long-distance bike ride at 14 years old, pedaling 40 miles to visit a motorcycle dealership one afternoon (it seemed like a good idea at the time). His dad had to come pick him up. His first extended period without showering came during a 23-day Outward Bound trek through New Mexico's Gila wilderness. Years later, combining these early feats naturally resulted in a cross-country bicycle tour.

After graduating with a degree in Environmental Studies from the University of North Carolina at Wilmington, Chris served two years as a Peace Corps Volunteer in El Salvador, then backpacked alone through Central and South America. He studied law at Georgetown University and litigated multiparty lawsuits in federal court before shifting focus to *Conversations With US*. He now lives and writes in Charlottesville, Virginia.

Chris's nationwide cycling odyssey has been featured in newspapers, local TV news segments, and public radio programs throughout the United States. *Conversations With US — Great Lakes States* is his first book.